AIR POWER
AND THE
ROYAL NAVY
1914-1945

a historical survey

ELEMENTARY.

Britannia (*in holiday mood*). "'WHAT ARE THE WILD WAVES SAYING?'"

Mr. Punch. "WELL, IF YOU ASK ME, MA'AM, THEY'RE SAYING THAT, IF YOU WANT TO GO ON RULING 'EM, YOU'VE GOT TO RULE THE AIR TOO."

AIR POWER AND THE ROYAL NAVY

1914-1945

a historical survey

Geoffrey Till

JANE'S PUBLISHING COMPANY
LONDON · SYDNEY

This book is dedicated to my parents

Copyright © 1979 Geoffrey Till

First published in Great Britain by
Jane's Publishing Company Limited
Macdonald and Jane's Publishers Limited
Paulton House, 8 Shepherdess Walk
London N1 7LW

ISBN 0 354 01204 5

Design: Judy Tuke

Photoset, printed and bound
in Great Britain by
REDWOOD BURN LIMITED
Trowbridge & Esher

CONTENTS

ABBREVIATIONS

AA Anti-aircraft
ABE Aircraft Bomb Experiments Committee (1937)
ACNS Assistant Chief of the Naval Staff
Admty Admiralty
AM Air Ministry
AP Armour-piercing (shells or bombs)
A/S Anti-submarine
BLE Bonar Law Enquiry (1921)
BuAer Bureau of Aeronautics, US Navy
Cab Cabinet
CAS Chief of the Air Staff
CCC Churchill College Cambridge
CID Committee of Imperial Defence
CIGS Chief of the Imperial General Staff
C-in-C Commander-in-Chief
Cmd Command Paper
COS Chiefs of Staff Committee
DCNS Deputy Chief of the Naval Staff
DNAD Director of the Naval Air Division
DNC Director of Naval Construction
DRC Defence Requirements Committee (1933–5)
FAA Fleet Air Arm

F/R Fighter-Reconnaissance
HA High-angle (AA guns)
HACS High Angle Control System
JTC Joint Technical Committee for Aviation Arrangements on HM Ships
LA Low-angle (guns)
MAP Ministry of Aircraft Production
Med Mediterranean
NAAGC Naval Anti-Aircraft Gunnery Committee (of 1921 and 1931)
NAD Naval Air Division
NAS Naval Air Section
NHB Naval Historical Branch
NMM National Maritime Museum
PRO Public Record Office
RAA Rear Admiral Aircraft Carriers
RNAS Royal Naval Air Service
RNVR Royal Naval Volunteer Reserve
S/R Spotter-reconnaissance (aircraft)
T/B Torpedo-bomber (aircraft)
TSR Torpedo-spotter-reconnaissance (aircraft)
VCS Vulnerability of Capital Ships Committee (1937–9)

PREFACE

On the morning of July 26, 1909, the *Daily Graphic* recorded the first flight across the Channel. "M Blériot," it said, "has guided an aeroplane in a given direction, and under not too favourable conditions, over the strip of water which makes England an island. There is no need to labour the point. The lesson is for all to read. What M Blériot can do in 1909, a hundred, nay a thousand aeroplanes may be able to do in five years' time. When Mr Farman flew a mile, it was possible to say that an ingenious toy had been invented. But a machine which can fly from Calais to Dover is not a toy, but an instrument of warfare of which soldiers and statesmen must take account." On the way, Blériot flew over the 26kt French destroyer *Escopette*, itself racing for England. The aeroplane flew "high over our heads," the captain said. "We cheered as it passed and in a very few minutes it was lost to sight, although we were steaming at our top speed the whole time." The implications of Blériot's flight for the future of sea power were bleaker than the cheering crew of the *Escopette* seemed to realise, and what follows is primarily an attempt to explore some of the problems it ultimately raised.

This book is about the impact of air power on the Royal Navy; it is not another operational history of the Fleet Air Arm. My concern is to show how Their Lordships and the Navy generally reacted to the aeroplane after their first daunting view that it "would not be of practical use to the Naval Service." To do this, I have sliced the whole subject into five main areas: people, ships, aircraft, organisation and battle doctrine. I have also looked at the operations of war, concentrating largely on the Norwegian campaign of the Second World War and on what followed it. Air power had a very substantial impact on the conduct of naval operations and I have tried to show both the Navy's expectations and the eventual outcome. My general proposition is that in its handling of this new development, the Navy did less badly than is often said to be the case.

I have had a more general theme in mind as well: how the advent of air power affected the role of the Navy in the defence of Britain. Strategic and institutional tensions between the Navy and the Air Force run through this book as a kind of leitmotif. Generally they made it more difficult for the Navy to conduct its business as efficiently as Their Lordships would have liked. I have tried to show, however, that this rivalry should not simply be put down to what one of the participants called the "psychological elements of pride of service, prestige and loyalty of conviction" of either the Navy or the Air Force. In its way, the competition between the two services reflected the basic dilemmas confronting the country's political and military leaders. The impact of air power on naval operations therefore provides an interesting and manageable microcosm of many of the fundamental issues of British defence in the twentieth century. For this reason alone, it seems to me, the subject is worth studying.

Much of the material for this book was derived from the collections of papers held at the Public Record Office, the National Maritime Museum, the Archive Centre at Churchill College Cambridge and the Fleet Air Arm Museum at Yeovilton. I have given more details at the end of the book, but would like now to acknowledge my debt of gratitude to the staff of those institutions for their help. I have also made use of the published literature and am particularly grateful for the efforts exerted on my behalf by Judithe Blacklaw, Olive Morris and their colleagues in the library of the Royal Naval College, Greenwich. I am also grateful for the assistance of J. D. Brown of the Naval Historical Branch.

One of the most enjoyable aspects of my research for this book has been meeting and corresponding with the past and present members of the Royal Navy and Royal Air Force whose names now follow. Many of them have granted me interviews and supplied me with their reminiscences, photographs and personal papers with a generosity and patience which I have found extraordinary. Many of them also have read parts of my manuscript and have saved me from countless errors of fact and interpretation, though responsibility for any inaccuracies which survive must of course remain mine. Nor do the views expressed in this book necessarily reflect official opinion in any way.

I am extremely grateful to the following for their help: Vice-Admiral Sir Conolly Abel-Smith; Vice-Admiral Sir Edward Anstice; Cdr P. M. T. Banyard; Capt G. F. M. Best; Wg Cdr M. J. Butler; Rear-Admiral D. R. F. Cambell; Lt Cdr J. Casson; A. Q. Cooper; Air Vice-Marshal P. Cracroft; Cdr D. J. Ellin; Capt R. M. Ellis; Air Marshal Sir Aubrey Ellwood; Capt G. A. French; Capt H. St J. Fancourt; Capt the Revd G. Gowlland; Rear-Admiral D. H. Hall-Thompson; Admiral Sir John Hamilton; Gp Capt E. G. Hopcraft; J. Howard Williams; Cdr C. A. Jenkins; Rear-Admiral Sir Rowland Jerram; Admiral of the Fleet Sir Caspar John; Capt C. N. Lentaigne; Cdr P. Leyton; Lt Cdr J. H. Malcolm; Vice-Admiral Sir Ian

McGeoch; the late Capt S. W. C. Pack; Admiral Sir Reginald Portal; Cdr C. F. B. Powell; Lt Cdr M. Raybold; Cdr R. H. S. Rodger; Lt Cdr F. C. Rice; Capt G. A. Rotherham; Admiral Sir Mathew Slattery; Rear-Admiral E. H. Shattock; Vice-Admiral Sir Richard Smeeton; Major J. G. Struthers; Rear-Admiral A. D. Torlesse; Lt Cdr A. H. Waite; Lt Cdr D. W. Waters; Gp Capt H. A. Williamson.

As far as other toilers in the vineyard of naval history are concerned, I am particularly indebted to Professor Bryan Ranft and Capt Stephen Roskill for the help they have offered my research at every turn along the way. I am also very grateful for the help I have received from Professor Peter Nailor, Dr Roger Knight, Alan Pearsall, Hugh Lyon, Dr John Gooch and Richard Hough. I am equally indebted to Kathy Mason for her help with the typing and to Ron Shaw and Andrew Smith for their help with the photographs.

I have adopted several conventions which may require some explanation. First, I have usually called all Flag Officers "Admiral" unless their precise title is relevant to the point being discussed. Secondly, I have also found it more convenient to refer to the Navy's aerial component either as the Royal Naval Air Service (RNAS) for the period up to 1918, or as the Fleet Air Arm (FAA) thereafter. In fact, the FAA only officially came into existence in 1924, and ended with the Admiralty's final assumption of full control over it in 1939. Other names followed until the FAA re-emerged as the officially accepted title in 1953. In practice the term FAA has had wide currency outside these periods, and I have followed suit.

Finally, I would like to record my gratitude to my wife, Cherry, for her continued encouragement, complete tolerance and enormous industry with the typewriter. Without her, quite literally, this book would not have been possible.

Geoffrey Till

CHAPTER ONE

NORWAY 1940

"This ramshackle campaign . . ."

WINSTON CHURCHILL

In the early hours of April 7, 1940, the German battlecruisers *Scharnhorst* and *Gneisenau*, flying the flag of Vice-Admiral Gunther Lütjens, slipped their moorings and steamed down the River Jade. They were soon joined by ten destroyers carrying 2,000 alpine troops bound for Narvik, and the heavy cruiser *Hipper* with a further four destroyers taking soldiers to Trondheim. Soon the whole force was steaming north across the Skaggerak, bound for Norway and the first major clash of arms between the British and the German navies of the Second World War. These were the first moves in a carefully orchestrated campaign, involving virtually the whole of the German Navy, to seize Norway in a sudden *coup de main* before the British had time to react. Grand Admiral Raeder, Commander-in-Chief of the German Navy, planned to launch simultaneous assaults on the Norwegian coast at six widely separated points, ranging from Narvik in the north, through Trondheim in the centre, to Oslo in the south.

"The operation in itself," admitted Raeder, "is contrary to all principles in the theory of naval warfare," as it would be carried out in the teeth of British naval supremacy.[1] Initial success, therefore, depended on the achievement of complete surprise. Raeder then hoped that any subsequent Allied reaction would be countered by the ability of German air power to cancel out British advantages in ships and geography. For this reason Operation *Weser* depended upon the closest co-operation between the German Navy and the Luftwaffe, and in particular with Generalleutnant Geissler's *Fliegerkorps X*. Geissler was to move forward from northern Germany into Norway and operate his aircraft mainly from airfields in the Stavanger and Trondheim areas. *Fliegerkorps X* alone would deploy about 330 bombers, 100 fighters and 570 auxiliary aircraft of various kinds.

The Norwegian campaign in the spring of 1940 was in fact the first sustained naval operation of the Second World War to be decisively affected by air

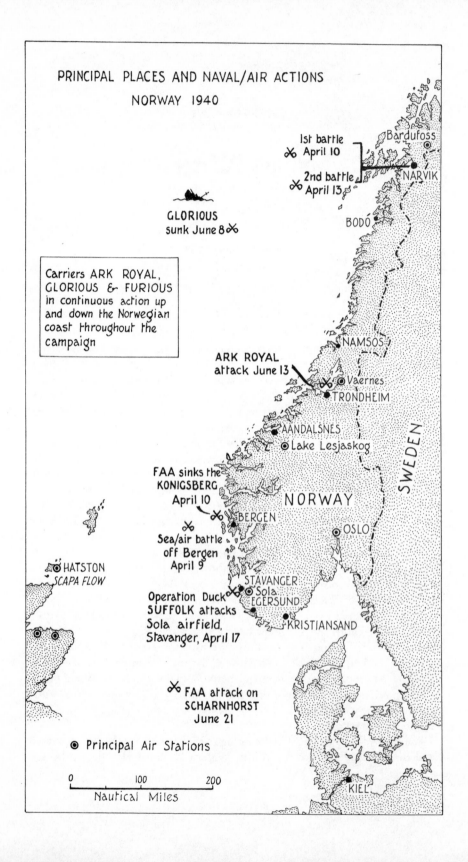

PRINCIPAL PLACES AND NAVAL/AIR ACTIONS
NORWAY 1940

1st battle
April 10

2nd battle
April 13

Bardufoss

NARVIK

BODØ

GLORIOUS
sunk June 8

Carriers ARK ROYAL,
GLORIOUS & FURIOUS
in continuous action up
and down the Norwegian
coast throughout the
campaign

NAMSOS

ARK ROYAL
attack June 13

Vaernes
TRONDHEIM

AANDALSNES
Lake Lesjaskog

FAA sinks the
KONIGSBERG
April 10

NORWAY

SWEDEN

Sea/air battle
off Bergen
April 9

BERGEN

OSLO

HATSTON
SCAPA FLOW

STAVANGER
Sola
EGERSUND

Operation Duck
SUFFOLK attacks
Sola airfield,
Stavanger, April 17

KRISTIANSAND

FAA attack on
SCHARNHORST
June 21

⊙ Principal Air Stations

0   100   200
Nautical Miles

KIEL

power. After two inter-war decades of theoretical controversy, air and sea power actually came together for the first time in varying patterns of mutual support and hostility. All the celebrated pre-war bomb-and-battleship theories were at last tried out in a real shooting war. For the first time, also, both the German and the British navies had to cope with the problems of exploiting their own air power efficiently and avoiding the attentions of the enemy's. Finally, the Norwegian campaign proved to be the first critical test of the Royal Navy's Fleet Air Arm (FAA). For all these reasons, a brief account of the naval/air operations of the Norwegian campaign would seem to be a good prologue to any study of the effects of air power on the Royal Navy.

Even before the departure of the *Scharnhorst* and *Gneisenau* on April 7, there had been indications of unusual German naval activity, though much of this only became clear in retrospect. A Hudson of Coastal Command reported a German cruiser and six destroyers steering north of the Horns Reef at 0848hr. There were other reports, too, but they were all ambiguous enough to be considered "of doubtful value and may well be only a further move in the war of nerves."[2] The first reliable report came when a force of 12 Blenheims from Bomber Command located and attacked the German squadron as it was heading north-west across the north of the Skaggerak at 1325 on April 7. The attack proved to be as ineffectual as most other air strikes on ships up to that point, and there were no hits. The strike leader did however send off a full sighting report which, unfortunately for the British, took four hours to reach Admiral Sir Charles Forbes, C-in-C of the Home Fleet.

These enigmatic movements and sightings could have signified almost anything. The German Navy could have been conducting routine operations in the North Sea, or perhaps making preparations for some foray against the trade routes of the North Atlantic. Part of Forbes' fleet was already at sea in support of the mining of Norwegian territorial waters, and it was not inconceivable that the German moves heralded some response to this. Whatever the case, something was obviously afoot, and so, soon after 1730 on April 7, Forbes ordered the rest of the Home Fleet to sea. Within three hours all but one of the major British warships in the area were at sea. As this confusing day drew to a close, the already rough weather began to deteriorate markedly.

The one major warship left behind was the aircraft carrier *Furious*, swinging restlessly at anchor in the Clyde. As there were no other carriers in the Home Fleet, it seemed likely that the only aircraft available to Forbes would be the handful of seaplanes carried on the cruisers and battleships then steaming across the North Sea. The best carriers in the Royal Navy were the *Glorious* and the *Ark Royal*, both of which were far away in the Eastern Mediterranean, doing training work essential for the rapid expansion of the FAA which was then taking place. Even so, their absence from the Navy's most likely scene of action at such a time was most unfortunate. The *Furious* herself was only partially combat-ready and had not operated very much with the rest of the Home Fleet so far. This doubtless explains why Forbes had not ordered her to sea; indeed, Admiral Forbes' dispatch shows that he did not regard the *Furious* as being part of the Home Fleet that Sunday. But her energetic commanding officer, Capt T. H. Troubridge, chafing at this inactivity, got up steam on his own initiative and requested permission to join the Home Fleet. At 1637 on April 8 the Admiralty accordingly ordered him to fly on his aircraft and to sail north in company with the battleship *Warspite* to rendezvous with Forbes two days later. On board were 18 Swordfish torpedo/spotter/reconnaissance aircraft – but no fighters. Her Blackburn Skua fighter/dive bombers were not at Campbeltown with the Swordfish but 100 miles away at Evanton and "therefore too far off to comply with what was obviously an urgent order."[3] Troubridge was consequently forced to sail without them. Thus it was that the Home Fleet steamed into its first historic encounter with the land-based air power of *Fliegerkorps X* completely bereft of fighter protection.

Early on April 8, meanwhile, the destroyer *Glowworm* was sunk off Trondheim by the heavy cruiser *Hipper*. By the close of that tempestuous day, Forbes, now concentrating his forces in the North Sea opposite central Norway, was sure that German invasion was imminent, although he still had not exactly located the forces preparing for it. The *Furious* arrived too late to organise an air search, and so two Coastal Command flying boats were sent out on reconnaissance and the battleship *Rodney* launched her Walrus flying boat to join them. By now Forbes was so sure of the situation that he told the pilot to make for land at the end of his flight and give himself up to the Norweigan authorities in the confident expectation of release the next day when the Germans finally landed. In fact, though, the main naval groups that the Home Fleet sought had already slipped past and were nearing their objectives of Narvik and Trondheim.

The Germans did land as Forbes expected, and went ashore at Narvik, Bergen, Trondheim, Egersund, Kristiansand and Oslo early the following morning, making the maximum use of *Fliegerkorps X*, especially in the south. In the far north the *Scharnhorst* and *Gneisenau* successfully diverted British attention away from the landings at Narvik and onto themselves. They were determinedly engaged by the stately old British battle cruiser *Renown* in a running fight through the snow squalls of a stormy day for an hour before fading away northwards into the murk. Admiral Lütjens wanted to report on his situation but dared not break radio silence. He therefore sent off a seaplane on a valiant and dangerous flight to Trondheim, where it arrived soon after the Germans had seized control.

Coastal Command discovered several German warships at anchor in Bergen, and so Vice-Admiral Geoffrey Layton was ordered to take the 18th Cruiser Squadron, supported by seven destroyers of the 4th and 6th flotillas, into Bergen to deal with them that night. This dangerous project was soon called off, but not before Layton's force had approached Bergen closely enough to provoke a strong reaction from *Fliegerkorps X*. As he withdrew, Layton deployed his destroyers round the cruisers *Southampton* and *Glasgow*, which were bound to be the main objectives of any air attack. For three hours that afternoon 47 Junkers Ju 88s and 41 Heinkel He 111s attacked the squadron with a mixture of shallow dive and high-level bombing in the first sustained sea/air battle in history. The Germans concentrated initially on Layton's force, especially his cruisers, and near-missed both.

Sea conditions were appalling, with waves breaking over the forward AA guns and spray cascading over the gun directors high up on the ships, especially the destroyers. One of these, the *Gurkha*, was commanded by Sir Anthony Buzzard, a noted gunnery officer. "After years of training," wrote Admiral Vian later, "presented at last with live targets, he was excessively annoyed by his inability to hit them and turned his ship away from wind and sea, to better the conditions for the control and fire of her guns."[4] This manoeuvre soon isolated the *Gurkha* from the mutual fire support afforded by the rest of the squadron. An easy target, she was quickly overwhelmed by German aircraft. Her crew were taken off by the cruiser *Aurora*, but *Gurkha* became the first significant warship to be sunk by aircraft in the Second World War. The air menace lessened as Layton rejoined the rest of the Fleet because the bombs had to be shared between more targets and the volume of defensive fire was much greater. Subsequent air attacks failed, except for the solitary aircraft that approached the flagship *Rodney* from the starboard bow after the main battle was over and hit her with a 1,100lb bomb. The bomb broke up against the *Rodney*'s armour, doing little damage, though 18 men were hurt and the captain was covered in foam from a defective fire extinguisher.

It is difficult to assess the implications of this first sea/air battle. The actual damage suffered by the Fleet was small. Though several other ships were slightly damaged, only the *Gurkha* had been sunk, and that was a result of obviously mistaken tactics. Although *Fliegerkorps X* was largely operating from airfields over 300 miles away, conditions were generally in its favour, for the British had no fighter protection and their AA gunnery was much impeded by the weather. Though some ships had used up over 40 per cent of the AA ammunition in this engagement, the Fleet had shot down only four aircraft. Admiral Forbes, for one, was shaken by the experience and decided that surface ships could not operate so far south in the absence of fighter protection. Other British naval officers merely concluded that there was more need for efficient AA gunnery and tactics, and for fighter protection, than had been foreseen before the war. This first encounter was therefore not conclusive.

Forbes decided to leave the area and see what British air power could do. There was some thought of sending the *Furious* in to attack the German warships at Bergen, but the afternoon's bombing persuaded him against returning to the area without fighter protection. That evening, 12 Wellingtons and 12 Hampdens from Bomber Command attacked Bergen instead, but without significant effect. The following morning the FAA went into action when the COs of Nos 800 and 803 Sqns, based at Hatston, decided that they could just about reach Bergen with their Skuas. As the trip was 560 miles or so there and back, the operation would be touch-and-go. Exact navigation and absolute surprise were therefore required, because the Skuas would have no margin for error or for evasive flying. This, however, was the kind of thing the FAA was trained for, and on April 10 a force of 15 Skuas, operating at extreme range and in difficult weather conditions all the way, made a precise landfall within 30 seconds of their estimated time of arrival.

German AA defences at Bergen had been instructed to assume that any single-engined aircraft in the area must be friendly and so were caught completely by surprise as the Skuas began their attack runs on the light cruiser *Königsberg*, moored alongside the quay. Diving at 60° from 8,000ft, the Skuas achieved some of the most accurate bombing of the war, with all 15 of the 500lb bombs either hits or near-misses. The cruiser caught fire, turned over and sank. It was a model attack in every way and was indeed the "spectacular success for naval aviation" that a subsequent Admiralty communiqué described it as. (The BBC evidently thought otherwise: "The RAF," they said that evening, "have done it again!") Either way, air power had claimed its greatest success so far, and one that was well noted by the world's air forces and navies.

Only one Skua was lost on the way home, a remarkably low casualty rate for so hazardous an enterprise. This was a feature of all the operations subsequently launched from Hatston throughout the Norwegian campaign. Although originally sent there to provide air cover for the Home Fleet based at Scapa Flow (a task evidently beyond the hard-pressed resources of RAF Fighter Command, though it was indisputably their responsibility), the Skua squadrons carried out many raids on the Norwegian coast, sinking enemy shipping, attacking German oil reserves and supporting Allied forces ashore, sometimes in conjunction with Bomber Command. All these operations were undertaken at the very limit of the Skua's endurance. The naval wives tended to gather in the Royal Hotel, across the bay from Hatston, to watch the aircraft going out and count them coming back. The remarkable extent to which the totals were the same was no small tribute to the expertise of the FAA in this kind of operation.

Meanwhile Forbes, driven north by German air power at Bergen, was concentrating his forces to contest the German hold on Trondheim and Narvik. On April 10 a force of ten large German destroyers was worsted by five small ones under Capt B. A. Warburton-Lee at Narvik, and Forbes gathered his forces to attack Trondheim the following day. He was already too late, however, for the heavy cruiser *Hipper* had left for Germany the previous evening, and the *Scharnhorst* and *Gneisenau* were already slipping south behind him, passing in fact within 40 miles of the Shetlands. On April 11 the *Furious* launched the world's first real torpedo strike, against German ships at Trondheim, in the hope of finding the *Hipper*. But it was all very disappointing: there were only a couple of destroyers for the Swordfish to attack and their torpedoes exploded prematurely in the shallow water. Forbes passed on to the north, but not before *Fleigerkorps X* had found and attacked the destroyer *Eclipse*, sending her back to Lerwick badly damaged. Even more ominous a portent for the future was the arrival of Ju 87 Stuka dive bombers at Vaernes near Trondheim. The influence of the Luftwaffe was spreading north with disconcerting speed.

The Home Fleet's target now was the group of German warships bottled up at Narvik further to the north, and first in were *Furious'* aircraft. The Admiralty suggested, after the disappointment with torpedoes at Trondheim, that dive bombers be used this time. Forbes passed this recommendation on, clearly expecting the FAA pilots to be able to sink everything they found. But this attack, carried out on April 12, was a failure too, and an entirely predictable one. Since the *Furious* had no Skuas, she had to use Swordfish as dive bombers. The unfortunate pilots had to fly a round trip of 300 miles in open cockpits, at least partly in atrocious weather described in one of their reports as "ceiling 100 feet, visibility 250 yards, very heavy snowstorms."[5] Moreover, a preliminary reconnaissance had not been possible and the observers' maps were only photographic copies of Admiralty charts. Lacking contours, they were not the most useful navigational aids for almost blind flying among mountains. The Germans were amazed when the first of the slow and vulnerable-looking Swordfish biplanes appeared out of the cloud to attack them. "They look," thought one at the time, "as though they're standing still in the sky."[6] The Swordfish which made it dropped their 200lb bombs, sank several small Norwegian "puffers" and caused some casualties, but inevitably failed to live up to the expectations of the C-in-C. Three aircraft were lost but their crews were recovered safely.

This failure made necessary another surface action at Narvik to finish off the German warships. Accordingly, the battleship *Warspite* and nine destroyers steamed up into the 40-mile-long Ofotfjord at 1230 the following morning, April 13. They were to locate and destroy all enemy ships and batteries ashore, supported by synchronised dive-bombing attacks from the *Furious*. Despite the apparent disparity of forces, the whole thing was a hazardous enterprise for the British as the fjord was full of narrow creeks and inlets where destroyers or submarines could lurk in ambush.

For this reason, much depended on the Swordfish seaplane carried on the *Warspite*. Piloted by Petty Officer Airman F. C. Rice and commanded by Lt Cdr W. L. M. Brown, this aircraft's role in the battle was possibly decisive. Launched before the battle began, the Swordfish flew up and down the long

fjord, locating the German ships and warning of the approach of their torpedoes. Typically, Brown spotted the destroyer *Erich Köllner* waiting in
ambush in the Herjangsfjord, poised to fire a sudden salvo of torpedoes when
the British squadron came unsuspectingly past. Being forewarned, however, the
British destroyers approached the spot with their guns and tubes already trained
to starboard and so were able to smother the *Erich Köllner* with torpedoes and
gunfire as they sped across the mouth of the fjord. Some of the aircraft's signals
did not get through and some of the ships were, very surprisingly, not listening
on the Air Reconnaissance frequency, although they were all equipped to do so.
Nevertheless, this four-hour flight was invaluable. The crew were also trained
to spot the fall of shot, but the close range at which this savage encounter took
place made this unnecessary. The destroyers fired with their guns virtually at the
horizontal. Behind them, but still usually well within visual range, came the
Warspite, in action for the first time since the Battle of Jutland in 1916. The thun-
der of her huge 15in guns brought avalanches of snow cascading down the
mountains towering all around. Every so often there were louder explosions still
as torpedoes, missing their targets, blew up on the rocks of the shoreline.

Amidst all this sound and fury, the *Warspite's* Swordfish watched and reported, performing exactly the ancillary battle tasks that British naval aircraft
were chiefly intended for. These functions, however, were always thought to
include the direct attack of enemy warships, and exactly on schedule, despite difficult weather en route, the *Furious'* Swordfish arrived to dive-bomb the
German destroyers as best they could. Although these stately aircraft had little
hope of hitting a manoeuvring destroyer with this kind of attack, and lost two of
their number in trying to do so, their action at least contributed to the ultimate
confusion of the *Hermann Künne* and *Bernd Arnim*. Bad weather also prevented
decisive intervention by a force of Heinkel 111 high-level bombers sent north
from Trondheim to attack the British ships. In fact, the main success in this area
was scored by the *Warspite's* indefatigable Swordfish seaplane. Flying at 1,000ft
at the head of the Herjangsfjord, the pilot spotted a German submarine on the
surface and dropped the two 100lb AS bombs he had brought along for just such
an eventuality. One of the bombs fell down the submarine's forward hatch, and
the Swordfish's crew looked back to see the hull of the U64 cocked up in the air
and members of her crew swimming for the shore through the icy waters of the
fjord. "I doubt," wrote Admiral Whitworth afterwards, "if a shipborne aircraft
has ever been used to such good purpose."[7]

Now that all the German warships at Narvik had been destroyed, the Navy
could turn its attention to operations further south. The British had decided to
challenge the German occupation not only of the north but of Trondheim and
central Norway as well. This was a much more dangerous proposition, calling
as it did for naval and military operations in the teeth of German air supremacy.
A reconnaissance in force by the cruisers *Glasgow* and *Sheffield*, with supporting

destroyers, in the Namsos, Aandalsnes and Molde area on April 12 had already been heavily attacked by *Fliegerkorps X* Ju 88 bombers operating from Stavanger. Shortly afterwards the large airfield at Vaernes near Trondheim was made fully operational. Allied forces landed at Namsos two days later but got off to an ominous start when the Sunderland flying boat carrying General Carton de Wiart, the expedition's commander, was badly shot up by a German fighter as it landed.

This rough welcome set the tone for the whole of the campaign in central Norway. Except for the few hours of darkness at this northerly latitude, German aircraft harried British ships all round the clock. At Namsos on April 15 a total of 60 bombs exploded in the vicinity of the destroyer *Somali* alone. Five days later there occurred the first of many heavy air raids on the three small ports of Namsos, Aandalsnes and Molde, which the Allies were using to support themselves in the area. Namsos, largely a wooden town, was practically razed to the ground in an attack that began at 1000 on April 20. By nightfall, reported one observer, "the whole place [was] a mass of flames from end to end and the glare on the snows of the surrounding mountains produced an unforgettable spectacle." The same treatment was meted out to Aandalsnes and Molde shortly afterwards. Whenever the German aircraft found ships in the harbours and fjords they always attacked them in preference to targets ashore, which at least partly explains the enthusiasm of the troops for the Navy's presence!

Ships were constantly harried but hit surprisingly rarely. In fact, the topography was difficult for both attacker and defender. Ships were at a particular disadvantage because the radar of the AA cruisers was blanked out by the towering walls of the surrounding mountains; aircraft then appeared over the fjords without warning and often at angles which the destroyers' guns could not reach. In the narrow fjords there was also little sea room for evasive manoeuvre and little cover for concealment; during air raids the ships therefore weaved about as best they could and with all their AA guns blazing away. The sloop *Black Swan*, for example, fired 2,000 four-inch shells and 4,000 pom-pom rounds in two days at Aandalsnes, but still left for Scapa with a three-foot bomb hole below the waterline.

Although ships usually survived such attacks, they found it difficult to do their job, and any ambitious undertaking in central Norway seemed dependent on the Allies' finding some way of disrupting *Fliegerkorps X*. A whole series of devices was tried. Bomber Command attacked German airfields repeatedly. On the night of April 22/23 a force of Whitleys flew 750 miles to attack the airfield of Vaernes and a subsidiary German airfield on the frozen Lake Jonsvand nearby. In this case they could not find the targets in the unfamiliar country, but more generally these attacks showed how very difficult it was to put airfields out of action by high-level bombing alone. Command of the air was best contested by aircraft in the area, and there was an obvious need to get modern

RAF fighters ashore. The trouble here was that Germany had already seized the existing airfields in the area, forcing the Allies to establish new ones in very unco-operative countryside and weather conditions. A temporary air station was es-tablished on the frozen Lake Lesjaskog on April 23 and 24, and obsolescent RAF Gladiators were flown in from the carrier *Glorious* to support Allied ground forces in the area. Conditions were appalling: equipment and stores were grossly inadequate, it was ferociously cold and the lake was subjected to constant air attack. Some of the RAF ground crew fled into the woods, leaving their officers and sergeants to refuel and rearm the aircraft and the naval contingent to fire the AA guns. In these circumstances it was no small achievement to get up 40 sorties. But whatever the individual skill and valour of the pilots, this attempt to chal-lenge German air supremacy was obviously doomed to failure. Within 48 hours Lake Lesjaskog had been abandoned,[8] and an attempt to maintain patrols with Blenheim fighters from Hatston also quickly proved impractical.

The RAF's failure left the Navy to take on *Fliegerkorps X*. One of their first attempts was the aptly named Operation Duck on April 17, when the cruiser *Suffolk* bombarded Sola airfield near Stavanger for 45 minutes with her eight-inch guns. Unfortunately for the British, atmospherics largely cut communi-cations between the *Suffolk* and her spotting Walrus amphibian, and many of her shells overshot, reducing the effectiveness of the bombardment. Although some damage was done to Sola, the *Suffolk* herself was in turn subjected to seven hours of counter-attack by German aircraft. Her long-suffering crew counted 33 separate attacks, twelve of them by Ju 88s acting as dive bombers, and used up practically all of her AA ammunition. There were numerous near-misses, "which made nutmeg-graters of our waterline," but only one direct hit. At 1037 a 1,000lb bomb from a Ju 88 penetrated the ship and exploded beneath X Turret, devastating the turret, killing its crew and doing great damage to the ship. The *Suffolk's* speed was cut to 18kt and she took in 1,500 tons of water. Even in this enfeebled state, she survived another 23 attacks and struggled home with her quarterdeck awash.[9]

Since this episode has been cited as evidence of the "Admiralty disdain of the air threat," it is worth looking at it more closely.[10] First of all, Operation Duck was not necessarily misconceived. After all, it was intended to *reduce* the air threat to naval operations in the Trondheim area by putting Sola airfield out of action. The *Suffolk* accordingly made her approach at night, bombarded at dawn and was originally intended to make off to the west at high speed, being protected from retaliation by a force of RAF Blenheim fighters. Although the effectiveness of an artillery bombardment as a means of putting an airfield out of action was over-estimated and it was undoubtedly a hazard-ous operation, it does not appear to have been impossibly so.

The trouble came virtually at the last minute. In his dispatch Admiral Forbes pointed out that "the operation was complicated by the introduction of a secondary object – a sweep up the Norwegian coast on completion of the bombardment."[11] This referred to a signal which had reached the *Suffolk* from the Admiralty at 2300 the previous evening. Instead of making off to the west, the *Suffolk* was ordered to turn *north* "to intercept enemy destroyers". Her captain was thus forced to loiter about for two hours off the enemy coast, knowing full well that a heavy air attack would probably follow. This, says the *Suffolk's* executive officer of the time, "cooked our goose,"[12] especially as the change in position made it more difficult for the RAF Blenheims to find her.

Operation Duck was wholly conceived in the Admiralty and the last-minute change in plan looks very like one of the "Midnight Follies," of which we shall hear more later. It was popularly believed in the Fleet that Churchill himself had intervened in the operation and had inspired the last-minute alteration of the original scheme. Admiral Forbes' dispatch makes *his* disapproval of the enterprise very clear: "I was at sea when this operation was ordered and carried out," he wrote. "I took it for granted that a very strong air escort would be provided, since the *Suffolk* would be within easy range of enemy airbases, including those in Germany; and I also took it for granted . . . that the vulnerability of these ships to even a 250kg bomb was fully appreciated." Forbes clearly did not believe that everyone at home, and especially those responsible for the turn north, had properly absorbed the new realities of naval warfare in the air age.[13]

This belief also lay behind the rather confused, and confusing, exchange between Forbes and the Admiralty about Operation Hammer, the plan for a naval assault on Trondheim itself. The Admiralty was keen on it, Forbes much less so. "It was only in the Fleet," he wrote later, "which had practical experience in the matter, that the scale of air attack which could develop on the Norwegian coast was properly appreciated."[14] The Admiralty planned to have 45 naval fighters covering the expedition from the carriers *Ark Royal* and *Glorious*, but Forbes doubted whether this would be enough in these narrow and difficult waters. In the end, caution prevailed and the operation was called off.

The presence of these two carriers in Norwegian waters for the last week of April allowed the Navy to make its most determined response to *Fliegerkorps X* so far. Both carriers launched heavy air attacks on Vaernes airfield on April 25, which were followed up by further strikes later. These attacks were moderately successful and the Germans had to draft in 800 civilians to repair the damage done. The carriers also sought to maintain small standing air patrols to protect Allied positions ashore, and generally harassed German forces as much as possible. The Navy was forced to operate under several distinct disadvantages, however. The main naval fighter was the Blackburn Skua, a two-seat fighter/dive bomber whose performance as a fighter left so much to be desired that it was actually slower than the bombers it was supposed to intercept. The most common German fighter in the area, the two-seat Me 110, had a speed advantage of no less than 125 mph, while the gulf between the Skua and the even more lethal Me 109 was such that it was a very good thing for the British that so few 109s had been deployed to Norway.

Although the FAA was in fact astonishingly successful on many occasions, in view of the low quantity and quality of its aircraft, it was soon made clear that German aerial supremacy could not be seriously challenged. The Navy found it difficult even to protect its own carriers. On April 18, for instance, a single high-level bomber located the *Furious* in a fjord off Tromso. It made one leisurely approach run and dropped two small bombs to mark the wind before circling round to make a second, more careful approach. The aircraft then dropped two large bombs, which landed close enough to damage the carrier's port turbines, reduce her speed to 20kt and contribute to the decision to withdraw her from Norwegian waters. Although the *Furious* had no fighters at all, this was still a most disdainful attack.[15]

Even the *Ark Royal* and *Glorious* were forced to operate at between 80 and 100 miles offshore, which put their aircraft at even more of a disadvantage. During the evacuation of the area Admiral L. V. Wells (an air enthusiast who had previously commanded the *Eagle*), in command of the *Glorious* and *Ark Royal*, had to retire because he was unable to ". . . maintain a position from which aircraft could give support to our forces in the Namsos and the Aandalsnes areas owing to continuous bombing."[16] This was in fact a tacit admission that the FAA had finally been honourably defeated by land-based air power in the shape of *Fliegerkorps X*.

This defeat, which had been foreseen for some time, made inevitable the evacuation of central Norway, an operation which occupied the Navy from April 29 to May 3. The campaign ended as it began: with the Allies constantly harried by the Luftwaffe. The evacuation was largely conducted under the fragile cover of fog or darkness. Some British destroyers, including the *Maori* and *Kelly*, attempted to approach Namsos under cover of mist on May 1. But the *Maori's* mastheads stuck up out of the low-lying mist, attracting bombing attacks which caused 23 casualties through near-misses. German units, operating from Vaernes airfield and making the maximum use of formations of Ju 87 Stuka dive bombers, pursued the evacuation convoys over 200 miles out into the North Sea on May 3. The British ships formed into rough line-astern, with the AA cruiser *Carlisle* bringing up the rear. It was perfect bombing weather. The third attack badly damaged the French destroyer *Bison* and a small group of British ships fell back to rescue her crew and passengers as the rest of the Fleet steamed on. German aircraft overhead, the sea on fire with burning oil, many dead and wounded, the British destroyers *Grenade* and *Afridi* tied up alongside transferring personnel, fire hoses playing on some of the *Bison's* burning depth charges – the whole scene was a grim warning of the vulnerability of small ships to aircraft. But despite further air attacks, the operation was successfully completed and the group, except for the doomed *Bison*, soon rejoined the rest of the force. Just when it seemed as though their ordeal was over, a last force of Ju 87s arrived and this time sank the *Afridi* with a loss of about 100 lives, including many unfortunates previously rescued from the *Bison*.

The Navy's fighters were still on the *Ark Royal* and *Glorious* to the north with the rest of the Fleet, which was also receiving its fair share of German air attacks. These strikes did not do any great damage, and "with gunfire as a deterrent and some fighter cover it was evident that an air attack might be less formidable than had lately been feared."[17] While one bomb did hit the sea a bare ten yards from the *Ark Royal*, and might completely have changed the complexion of the encounter had it been just a little closer, it was clear that even a few fighters made a significant difference to the ability of a naval force to withstand air attack. In fact, though, the evacuation of over 10,000 troops from central Norway was completed with surprisingly few casualties considering the conditions in which it was carried out.

While this was going on in the Trondheim area, the Royal Navy was also active in the north, where the Allies were seeking to recapture Narvik from the Germans. Allied forces landed at Harstad on April 15, and nine days later the *Warspite* appeared in the Ofotfjord once more to see whether a bombardment of Narvik would induce the German garrison there to surrender. When the shoot was going satisfactorily the *Warspite*'s Swordfish seaplane went off on a reconnaissance flight and landed in a small fjord to the north. Two of the crew went ashore to see if they could discover anything of the Germans in the area. In the course of their exploration one of the them sent a postcard to his wife from the small post office nearby. It eventually arrived at his home, franked Berlin and Madrid.

The German forces in the Narvik area were not in fact persuaded to surrender by this show of force. Instead they were reinforced and supplied by Ju 52s, and regularly operated a small fleet of seaplanes. They knew also that a relief column, well supported by *Fliegerkorps X*, was advancing north from Trondheim. This advance was greatly helped by German air supremacy. On May 10, for example, German troops were landed at Hemnes from a small commandeered Norwegian steamer and sustained by seaplanes. These troops came ashore behind the forward British outpost at Mosjoen, a good example, reported General Auchinleck afterwards, of the way in which "the possibility of the enemy carrying out such outflanking operations caused continuous dispersion of the troops trying to hold defensive positions . . . and prevented sufficient concentration to enable any of the positions selected to he held successfully."[18]

German aircraft also attacked Allied forces in just the same way as they had further south. The main bases at Harstad and Skaanland suffered 140 air raids in eight weeks. For the most part the German aircraft were operating from the Trondheim area 300 miles to the south, well beyond the range of the Ju 87s, which had proved particularly dangerous to ships there. The Ju 88 was the main menace, operating round the clock in the almost perpetual daylight and usually at 20,000ft. They were relatively safe from the Skuas and often practically invisible to their intended victims. "Owing to their speed and height," reported one officer, "they often released bombs before we saw them, and it is always disconcerting when the first thing one knows about enemy aircraft being in the vicinity is the bang and splash of a bomb exploding near one."[19] In such narrow and congested waters these attacks were bound to exact a steady toll of damaged and sunk warships. The cruiser *Penelope* and the destroyers *Vansittart* and *Kelly* were damaged at Harstad on May 10, the Polish transport *Chobry* was lost on May 14, the battleship *Resolution* was damaged off Tjeldsundet in the north on May 18, followed by the cruiser *Southampton* near Harstad a few days later. The radar-equipped AA cruiser *Curlew* was the most serious loss on May 26, towards the end of the campaign, and there were other less serious casualties.

The FAA was also deeply involved in the Narvik campaign. In the early days Swordfish from the carrier *Furious* performed a multitude of roles in support of Allied troops ashore, and a Walrus squadron operating from Harstad did useful work. When the *Ark Royal* appeared in the area her Skuas mounted fighter patrols and her Swordfish attacked the iron-ore railways. The value of close support from carrierborne aircraft was perhaps best demonstrated when the French Foreign Legion landed at Bjerkvik on May 13. The *Ark Royal's* aircraft reconnoitred for the troops, strafed enemy positions, carried out tactical bombing and provided fighter protection – all the comforts supplied by *Fliegerkorps X* to German troops further south. In the course of these operations the crew of the *Ark Royal* learned how very demanding of men and material such operations were. The problems were exacerbated by the far-northerly latitude and a flying programme which often went on for 20 hours out of the 24.

Nevertheless, there was still a clear need to establish air stations ashore. Airfields were set up with some difficulty at Bardufoss and, much less successfully, at Skaanland, and the carriers ferried in some RAF Gladiators and, at last, a number of Hawker Hurricanes. There was jubilation amongst the troops when modern fighters roared over the rooftops of Harstad for the first time. It seemed as though German air superiority was on the point of being seriously contested at last. Indeed, in a few days the RAF notched up 638 sorties in the Narvik area, engaged in 95 air combats and shot down 27 enemy aircraft for the loss of seven.[20] The activities of the RAF did much to justify Lord Cork's contention that operations against German strongpoints in the Narvik area would only be possible under air cover. The attack on Narvik town began on the night of May 27/28. As it happened, British aircraft were grounded by fog the following morning. German bombers were thus able to disrupt the naval side of this operation, though not enough to prevent it from being a success.

All the same, the situation elsewhere was fast deteriorating. The Germans had invaded France and the Low Countries on May 10 and their progress across France posed more immediate threats than a Norwegian campaign ever could.

Accordingly, the British decided finally to abandon Norway to its fate. It is an indication of the improved situation in the air that, in the three or four days after June 4, the Royal Navy successfully embarked nearly 25,000 men and carried them home without significant interference from *Fliegerkorps X*. The most serious threat to the evacuation was in fact posed by the *Scharnhorst* and *Gneisenau*, which had once again evaded British aerial reconnaissance and arrived in northern waters to do what damage they could.

In the late afternoon of June 8 a lookout on the *Scharnhorst* spotted smoke on the starboard bow and the German battlecruiser went to investigate. There soon came into view a masthead which proved to belong to the carrier *Glorious*, sailing along quite alone save for two destroyers, the *Acasta* and *Ardent*. Admiral Marschall went to action stations and took his ships to windward so that the carrier would have to turn towards him to fly off her aircraft. Instead, the *Glorious* made off, for a while shielded from her powerful adversaries by a smokescreen laid by the *Acasta* and *Ardent*. But once the battlecruisers had the range with their 11in guns, the *Glorious* was doomed. Heavy shells smashed into her flight deck and hangars, destroyed the bridge and set the carrier afire. Soon the *Glorious* lost way, developed a heavy list to starboard – which sent her aircraft sliding down the flight deck and into the icy sea – and sank with the eventual loss of over 1,500 officers and men. The *Ardent* was destroyed too, and then the *Acasta*, though not before she had put a torpedo into the *Scharnhorst*, forcing Marschall to turn back to Trondheim and so helping to save British evacuation convoys further to the north. Curiously enough, Grand Admiral Raeder was not impressed by the *Glorious* affair, which he called "mere target practice and so hardly to be termed a momentous victory," in evident disappointment at Marschall's failure to disrupt the British evacuation. Nonetheless, this was a tragedy of the first order for the FAA.[21]

In retrospect it is easy to see that serious mistakes were made in this encounter. The *Glorious* should not have been authorised to proceed to base independently in such dangerous waters. Various factors seemed to have been at play. Although acquainted with naval flying, her captain, G. D'Oyly Hughes, was not an aviator and had a personal preference for independent action. He was in dispute with his Commander (Flying), whom he had placed under arrest and left at Scapa Flow. D'Oyly Hughes was evidently anxious to return to base in order to end what must have been a highly uncomfortable situation as soon as possible. It would seem that for this reason the *Glorious* signalled the *Ark Royal* in the early hours of June 8, requesting permission to proceed ahead to Scapa Flow "for the purpose of making preparations for impending courts martial."[22] Accordingly, the *Glorious* and her two destroyers parted company with the *Ark Royal* and the rest of the fleet at 0350 – a detachment which we can see in retrospect should neither have been requested nor granted. The point was however that the British simply did not expect to find hostile warships in waters which they had once more got used to considering theirs to command and use. The *Scharnhorst* and *Gneisenau* were not after all even known to be at sea. The British forces, moreover, were committed to several operations at once and were in such a state of disarray that Coastal Command was not even informed that an evacuation was in progress and that special vigilance was necessary.

There were some reports too that the *Glorious* was short of fuel and so needed to take the quickest route home. Since she had topped up before she left Scapa this seems very unlikely. But it might explain the captain's otherwise rather mystifying order to reduce speed to 17kt at 0700, unless, of course, it was the destroyers which were in difficulty. An alleged shortage of fuel may also partly account for the failure to maintain an air patrol which led to her being surprised by two surface warships. More fuel would certainly have been consumed if the *Glorious* had tried to operate aircraft, especially as the wind direction meant that she would have had to steam back towards Norway to do it.

Shortly after she had left Norwegian waters, the *Glorious* had flown on a number of RAF Hurricanes which their pilots, led by Sqn Ldr K. Cross (one of the few survivors), were determined not to abandon. This very gallant act by pilots quite untrained in the skills of deck-landing in aircraft unfitted for it demonstrated once and for all that carriers could operate high-performance fighters. In the meantime, they had greatly complicated the accommodation arrangements on the hangar decks. Also, after so much strenuous activity, the crew of the *Glorious* were exhausted and their captain may well have wished to spare them the probably unnecessary rigours of a search patrol. But neither of these possibilities would seem really to have justified the lack of an air patrol which might have alerted the *Glorious* to the danger she was in.

Once the *Scharnhorst* and *Gneisenau* were in contact, the *Glorious* had little chance. She had only three Swordfish fitted to carry torpedoes, and even though one of these aircraft and a section of Gladiators were supposed to be at ten minutes' notice, it apparently proved impossible to range and fly off aircraft in the 40 minutes or so between the sighting of the German ships and the arrival of the first fatal shell. This penetrated the flight deck, exploded in the upper hangar and wrecked all the aircraft inside. In point of fact, though, it would probably have made little difference to the outcome. As the Naval Staff observed afterwards, the air striking force would have been very small. "A stronger surface escort," said the Director of the Naval Air Division, "would appear to have been desirable."[23] Whatever the explanation, it was a sad ending for a ship whose exploits matched her name.

The Norwegian campaign ended with two FAA attempts to avenge the *Glorious* by attacking the *Scharnhorst*. The first was a dive-bombing attack at Trondheim on June 13. Two days before, the RAF had bombed German warships at Trondheim and claimed to have scored three hits with 250lb bombs, one on an eight-inch cruiser and two on a smaller vessel. The Admiralty then "suggested that Skuas should be used to finish off the enemy ships."[24] In fact no less a ship than the *Scharnhorst*, recovering from the damage inflicted on her by the *Acasta*, awaited the attentions of the FAA at Trondheim.

It was a very tough proposition, as Me 109 and Me 110 fighters were known to be nearby at Vaernes airfield and the whole fjord was well defended with AA guns. The target was also at the landward end of the fjord, 30 miles from the sea, allowing coast-watchers to give up to 20 minutes' warning of the approach of the Skuas, a task made all the easier by the almost perpetual daylight then prevailing. The Admiralty sought to reduce these risks by enlisting the aid of the RAF, which agreed to arrange for a force of Blenheims to provide fighter cover while Beaufort bombers attacked Vaernes airfield itself. It was decided that the *Ark Royal* should use her Skuas rather than her Swordfish, presumably in the belief that there might not be room in the fjord for a torpedo attack.

The attack confirmed all the worst fears of the Naval Air Division at the Admiralty about the use of Skuas in such circumstances. The weather was clear and there was no surprise. The RAF fighter escort failed to materialise and the Beauforts' attack on Vaernes merely alerted the Germans to the fact that something significant was about to happen. The 15 Skuas made their 170-mile flight and went into the attack, led by Lt Cdr J. Casson. All except the last section of the Skuas worked their way round the *Scharnhorst* in order to attack her from bow to stern, and were heavily engaged by AA fire as they did so. They dived from 3,000ft and, since they had no dive-bomb sights, the pilots released their 500lb semi-armour-piercing bombs when the ship disappeared beneath a mark on the engine – as though they were dropping apples into a bucket from the back of a galloping horse. There was only one hit, and that bounced off the *Scharnhorst's* armour and failed to explode. As the Skuas recovered from the dives, they were pounced on by the much faster German fighers and all but one of the survivors escaped only by resorting to low-flying evasion in the sea-mist. Lt Cdr Casson himself crashed into the fjord at 120 mph and was very lucky to survive. Only seven of the Skuas returned to the *Ark Royal*.

The Naval Air Division plainly did not think the possible benefits worth the possible cost. The Skuas, unless they achieved surprise, had an estimated "right to expect" only one hit and a 25 per cent chance of a second, but would probably lose a third of their number to AA gunfire and up to another third to hostile fighters. In short, the chances of this attack proving to be a success were so poor as to raise grave doubt about whether it should have been carried out at all.[25]

A week later, when on June 21 the *Scharnhorst* was reported to be at sea and heading for home, the FAA units at Hatston managed to lay on a rapidly improvised torpedo attack. Six Swordfish torpedo aircraft, hitherto employed mainly on anti-submarine patrol duties, took off and located the *Scharnhorst* after a 240-mile flight, itself no mean achievement, and attacked in the face of heavy AA fire. Fortunately for the German battlecruiser, the airmen's inexperience showed. They immediately dived to attack without manoeuvring for a favourable position and with little attempt to co-ordinate the direction and timing of their approach. They all missed and two Swordfish were shot down. "This attack," said a Naval Staff report afterwards, "the first of its type against a capital ship in history, can only be described as a gallant failure with an inadequate force."[26]

The escape of the *Scharnhorst* was the last flicker of the Norwegian campaign of 1940. For the Royal Navy in general and the FAA in particular there had been both defeats and victories in these last two feverish months. Reasons for the one or the other are mainly to be found not so much in the hot moments of war but in the policies and decisions of the previous 20 years of peace. The performance of the Royal Navy and the FAA in the Norwegian campaign was directly and almost inevitably determined by what had gone before.

CHAPTER TWO

PERSONNEL AND POLITICS

"Their honour and courage remained throughout as dazzling as the snow-covered mountains over which they so triumphantly flew."

CAPT T. H. TROUBRIDGE
Commander of the *Furious*, off Norway, April 1940

In February 1911 a Mr Francis McClean offered to instruct Royal Navy officers in flying, using his own aircraft from Eastchurch on the Isle of Sheppey. The Admiralty accepted the offer and 200 officers volunteered, of whom four were accepted for a training programme which started the following month. In this quiet way began the Navy's association with air power. Fostered by the energetic First Lord, Winston Churchill, and for a while by Admiral Jellicoe, the Second Sea Lord, progress in naval aviation was rapid. The Fleet Review of July 31, 1914, was enlivened by the appearance of 16 seaplanes which flew over the Royal Yacht in line-ahead to salute the King and, perhaps, to remind the Fleet that a new dimension in warfare had come into existence. The First World War began for Britain four days later and by the end of it the Royal Naval Air Service (RNAS) mustered some 55,000 officers and men. Its expansion had been extremely rapid, but was mainly based on the incorporation of 874 RNVR officers and some 50,000 officers and men who enlisted "for hostilities only," many of them entering the Navy through the great recruiting and training centre at Crystal Palace, London. Some of this work was later done at the Royal Naval College, Greenwich, where the new entrants appear to have made an unexpected impression. "There is no doubt," wrote the Admiral President, "that these young and growing officers have large healthy appetites and consume more food than the average class of naval officers under instruction."[1]

There were those, however, who thought this expansion unwise and overdone. Even had the RNAS not been incorporated into the RAF in April 1918, it would not have been easy to transform it into a peacetime service: of this enormous force, only 397 officers, 217 ratings and 604 boys were on the permanent list.² The RNAS also seemed to some to be in danger of outgrowing its capacity for steadiness and self-regulation. It grew too autonomous and some senior officers detected an almost adolescent indiscipline and insouciance about this new branch of the service. Some of its young flight commanders even had the temerity to drop the "flight" in their titles and go about London in an aura of assumed seniority. This situation was to be corrected, but not before some permanent damage had been done to the name of flying in the Navy, at least in the eyes of its more orthodox senior officers. "The RNAS was also unsatisfactory," it was argued after the war, "because the officers and men belonged to a semi-independent service. It really failed because it was too rapidly expanded. This resulted in it growing much larger than was necessary for naval needs and consequently it overlapped the RFC in much of the work it undertook."³ The RNAS had entered areas – like strategic bombing – where the Admiralty felt it had no business, to the detriment of the development of naval aviation proper. This also meant that a large number of the real pioneers of the RNAS had too little sea experience for them to be sure of reasonable promotion in the post-war Navy, one reason why virtually all of them left the Navy when the time came.

Although in the short term the immediate exigencies of war meant that it made little difference to naval operations, the creation of the Royal Air Force on April 1, 1918, resulted in the transfer of virtually all the Navy's air personnel, and the accumulated experience they represented, into a new and separate service. The loss of 55,000 officers and men aroused belated and ultimately justified apprehensions about the extent to which the Navy's air needs would be met in the future. Worse still, with the disappearance of so many air-minded senior officers, would the Navy of the future be able to decide wisely what its air needs actually were?

When the First World War ended, though, there were more immediate troubles and confusions. The exhilaration of apparent victory soon yielded to grave anxieties about the social, political and economic state of the country. There were riots and strikes, demonstrating soldiers in Whitehall, tanks on the streets of Glasgow and windy extravaganzas in the press about the imminent perils of anarchy and Bolshevism⁴. The problems of adjusting to the uncertain conditions of peace were difficult for all the services, particularly the fledgling Air Force. For the RAF demobilisation amounted practically to disintegration, and this of course affected Air Force personnel serving with the Navy. Their equipment was sparse and their morale occasionally poor. In the spring of 1919 pilots in the *Argus* were described as grossly inefficient and "practically passive resisters". This however was certainly an extreme view and within a few weeks the same officer, Admiral R. F. Phillimore, was describing the same pilots in very different terms: "Without the incentive of war and with no certainty of being ever selected for a permanent commission," he wrote, "the wonder is that so many . . . of these gallant young fellows . . . take the risks they do."⁵ The real trouble, thought Phillimore, was that the present system meant that the Navy could not assume responsibility for the well-being of the pilots who flew for it. Urging the Admiralty Board to fight to get the Naval Air Service back, he fired some of the first shots in a bitter campaign that was to last the next 20 years.

Both sides in this rancorous controversy were animated by high principle. "The Admiralty do not complain against the present RAF officers concerned in naval air work, nor do they complain of their work," Admiral Fuller told the Balfour Committee of 1923, "but they do complain against the principle of being entirely in the hands of officers of a service other than the Navy."[6] The Admiralty considered itself the authority responsible for the conduct of war at sea and wished to supply, administer and direct all the forces engaged in it. Whether they operated in the air, in surface ships or in submarines, all personnel needed to develop a "sea sense" and a thorough understanding of the principles, tactics and strategy of naval warfare. Warfare at sea, of whatever kind, should be conducted by men who thought of themselves primarily as seafarers and who were consciously "all of one company". Had not the Spanish failed, argued Admiral Oliver, because of the dissensions between soldiers and sailors in their ships? "We have," he added, "after centuries of experience, deliberately adopted the system which led to the downfall of Spanish sea power."[7] How, the Admiralty asked, would the Air Ministry have reacted had the Government decided that the Army should provide all the RAF's air gunners? Unity of purpose, they argued, clearly demanded unity of personnel, materiel and direction. The authority responsible for the conduct of warfare at sea should have jurisdiction over all the forces whose primary function was to wage it – and this of course included the FAA[8].

Unfortunately, the Air Ministry had its unities too, and believed as passionately in the indivisibility of air power. "The science of the employment of aircraft," claimed Trenchard, "is in its broad principles the same over sea as over land and experience in the past has proved that those whose sole duty it is to study aerial problems developed such employment faster and to a higher pitch than it could be developed by any individual service (such as the Navy in the war) which had many other grave problems to consider."[9] The air was the air wherever it was and took on no special quality when it was over the sea. The essential thing was to provide a force that was well equipped and manned by those experienced in the science of air warfare. Naval flying held no special mysteries and its particular requirements could be learned by trained airmen without undue difficulty. The idea was to produce a force of generalist, rather than specialist, airmen who would provide the best foundation for the huge expansion expected to take place in war.

The men of the FAA should therefore be flyers first and seafarers second, and their service should be directed by the Air Ministry – the fount of British air power, especially as the Admiralty could not be relied upon to develop air power properly. "It is unsound," argued Trenchard, "that the development of air power in relation to the functions of battleships and other naval units should be controlled by a department whose interest and concern is with sea power and not with air power. Unless the Navy turns itself into a full air service, it can only follow that the possibility of the use of air power as a substitution for naval power will be stifled and that any experimental work tending to reduce the value of the battleship as a unit will be paralysed . . ."[10]

The dispute between the two services over the control of the FAA ranged, therefore, from operational matters to the niceties of high philosophy, the allocation of economic resources and, as will be shown later, the design and supply of materiel. But the central issue of the whole 20-year conflict was the supply, training, administration and direction of the Navy's flying personnel. Here the struggle was at its fiercest and most sustained.

The issue surfaced early. In December 1918 the Secretary of State for Air produced a comprehensive plan designed to make the Air Ministry and the Royal Air Force permanent by establishing the case for a centralised authority and service responsible for all military operations in the air. The First Sea Lord at this time was Admiral Sir Rosslyn Wemyss, "an absolute gentleman" in the eyes of the King, and he gave these aspirations his blessing.[11] In November 1919 he was relieved by the glittering Admiral Sir David Beatty, C-in-C of the Grand Fleet, who also soon proved to be generally indulgent of the ambitions of airmen, as was only to be expected after his early support for the establishment of an independent air service.[12]

But while senior management was thus being sweetly reasonable in trying to give the new service a fair start, there was a rising chorus of protest from the Fleet about the degree of training, number and general attitude of the RAF contingents serving afloat. Dissatisfaction with the results of the present policy was voiced most loudly by Admirals Sir Richard Phillimore, the Admiral Commanding Aircraft, and Sir John de Robeck, one of the most prestigious of contemporary Flag Officers, both of whom thought there was more to the present difficulties than the deficiencies of a demobilising air force. The Air and Naval Staffs were soon involved in complex discussion over the conditions of service of RAF officers aboard HM Ships and of those naval officers who would have to join the RAF in order to fly with the FAA. Both sides wished to maintain the fullest authority over their own personnel and to gain as much as possible over officers and men serving with them only temporarily. Correspondence between the two sides during 1919 accordingly showed growing difficulties in agreeing such things as the length of time one side's officers would serve with the other, the uniform they would wear and their general status. The Air Ministry began to suspect that these objections merely masked a Navy desire to re-establish the RNAS by showing that the present system could not work, and might even suggest a preference for the dissolution of the RAF as a whole. The Admiralty, for its part, began to entertain the gravest doubts about the Air Ministry's readiness to provide the Navy with the kind of air service which it thought it needed.

Since the growing hostility of the Navy was dangerous for the Air Force in its present vulnerable state, Trenchard decided to go and see the other service chiefs at the Admiralty in November 1919. He outlined to them his theory of the indivisibility of airpower, promised them that their short-term aerial needs would be met as soon as possible, stressed the Air Force's present difficulties and suggested that the small part of the RAF "specially trained for work with the Navy [would probably become] in future an arm of the older service." In return for this he asked for a year of truce and tranquillity to allow the Air Force to sort itself out. Trenchard sought to relieve his usual majestic incoherence by pacing up and down the room and, as Beatty shortly joined him, the two contestants were soon passing and re-passing each other like medieval knights, while Sir Henry Wilson, the Chief of the Imperial Gereral Staff, leaned sardonically against the mantlepiece.[13]

In the event, a truce was arranged on the following terms. The Charter of the RAF, presented to Parliament a few days later, apparently contained a provision for the ultimate return of the FAA to the Navy. Some courtly and gracious letters were exchanged between the two departments, their Lordships emphasising how averse they were to "taking any steps which, in the opinion of the Air Ministry, would retard the development of the Air Force." Admiral Phillimore, trying vigorously to use the Postwar Questions Committee as a means of destroying the present arrangement with the Air Ministry, had already been told to stop these activities.[14]

But this truce did not lead either department to make any appreciable changes in its policy on personnel. When in January 1920 the Air Staff sought to show how the future naval air service envisaged by Trenchard would still actually be a part of the Air Force, an exasperated Capt Barry Domvile of the Plans Division complained that "no useful purpose will be served by continuing this correspondence with the Air Ministry. The two Departments differ on points of principle to such an extent as to hold out no hope of obtaining an agreement."[15] Feelings like this prompted many members of the Naval Staff to urge that the matter be officially taken up with the Government, but the civilian members of the Admiralty Board were against this, knowing that the Admiralty's past intransigence on the matter of a separate air force, to be described later, would probably lead to their case being rejected out of hand. "I am quite certain that we should be courting disaster," said the First Lord, Walter Long," if we were to approach the Cabinet at this stage. . . . The Cabinet is not an impartial tribunal. Some members are committed to the view that the Air Ministry should be given a fair trial; others have no knowledge of the case."[16]

Matters remained in this unsatisfactory state for some time. The new Assistant Chief of the Naval Staff (ACNS) was Admiral Sir Ernle Chatfield, who took over the running of the Admiralty's air campaign from his arrival in March 1920. In July he extracted an official apology from the Air Staff for a letter of theirs which he regarded as offensive in tone, but finally produced an agreed scheme for the secondment of naval officers to the RAF for training and subsequent service in the FAA. The resulting Fleet Order was cool in tone, attracted only nine volunteers – of whom two were unfit and a further three retired under the "Geddes Axe" – and inspired not entirely unjustified suspicions in the Air Staff that the Admiralty had deliberately sabotaged the new scheme. Early in the new year the arrangement, which had clearly failed, was allowed to lapse, and there the issue stood for the next few months.[17] To some extent it was overtaken in early 1921 by more far-reaching arguments about the relative strategic importance of the three services in the defence of Britain. These debates, to be described later, worsened inter-service relations, made negotiation over personnel issues more difficult, and seem to have inspired the Admiralty to abandon the pursuit of compromise and seek some final solution, with the Army as an ally.

Field Marshal Sir Henry Wilson, the CIGS, then intervened, launching a vigorous attack in September 1921 on Lord Balfour's argument for an independent air force. He sought to show that the older service were perfectly aware of the possibilities of air warfare but denied that they demanded a separate air force. On the contrary, "if grafted onto the well established and well proven stocks of the older services, the young shoots of the Air Force would draw increasing strength and nourishment from them. Their growth will thus obtain far greater proportions and bear infinitely more fruit than if compelled to struggle for existence in the weed-choked soil of a redundant bureaucracy."[18] But how should the Admiralty react to this unrestrained War Office assault on the Air Ministry?

The balance was probably tipped by the arrival at the Admiralty of another trenchant letter from Admiral de Robeck, stressing the ill-effects of the present arrangements on naval efficiency. Admirals Chatfield and Oliver (the Second Sea Lord), who both had a deep preference for an annihilating victory rather than a negotiated settlement in the matter, used this evidence to persuade Beatty to fight to the finish. Reluctantly, Beatty agreed that it would be a dereliction of duty to accept the present situation and so lent his support to an official campaign for repossession of the Naval Air Service. "I cannot believe," he told the First Lord, "that the Government will attribute the earnest and reasoned representations of the naval and military authorities to mere prejudice or conservatism; if, indeed, this is the belief it is clear that they no longer possess the confidence of the Government."[19]

The Admiralty decided, however, to hitch its star to the outcome of the War Office's attack on the very existence of the Air Ministry, and in particular to Sir Henry Wilson's tactic of challenging the whole economic justification for a separate air force before the Geddes Committee of National Expenditure. The

War Office argued, and so the Admiralty had to agree, that the older services could develop air power at least as effectively as could the Air Ministry, but at less cost. "We have at last," wrote Chatfield in October 1921. "started to officially attack the Air Ministry, but only indirectly at present through the Geddes Committee."[20]

This was soon to prove a dangerous strategy, but in the meantime hopes were high at the Admiralty and the Naval Staff started calculating the number of personnel they would need to run their own air service. The First Lord (Lord Lee), Beatty, Chatfield and other senior members of the Naval Staff had soon to go to Washington for the Disarmament Conference, leaving the running of the campaign in the hands of the heroic but somewhat intemperate Admiral Sir Roger Keyes of Zeebrugge fame. Excitement ran high towards the end of the month when the Geddes Committee asked what the older services would do if there was no Air Ministry. The Deputy CIGS (Field Marshal P. W. Chetwode) wrote an "'informal and unofficial letter" saying: "This is our best chance and we should make it a joint endeavour." Meetings between the two departments were arranged and signals were sent across the Atlantic about the necessity of having proposals ready "so that advantage may be taken of favourable attitude of Geddes Committee towards abolition of present Air Force." In anticipation, a high-level Admiralty meeting on November 14, 1921, put some of the finishing touches to a scheme for running the Naval Air Service.[21]

The Admiralty soon proved to be rather premature in thus arranging the obsequies of the RAF. Contrary to expectation, Trenchard was able to convince the Geddes Committee that the present arrangement was in fact the most economical, and the Committee so reported in December 1921.[22] However, the fact that the Geddes Committee recommended that the Air Estimates be cut proportionately more than either of those of the other two services should perhaps temper the admiration that Trenchard's biographer heaps upon his subject for his skill in handling this committee. The Air Ministry was not out of the wood yet.

For the next two months, addressing Churchill's committee of adjudication, Beatty personally handled the Admiralty's assault on the whole of the Geddes Report's treatment of the Naval Estimates with a skill that won the chairman's admiration.[23] Both the older services persisted in their joint and separate campaigns for an end to the present system, and the political and military atmosphere was thick with intrigue and rumour. The matter was temporarily resolved on March 16, 1922, when Navy and Air Force officers crowded into the Distinguished Strangers' Gallery of the House of Commons and heard the Lord Privy Seal, Austen Chamberlain, reject a motion calling for the Navy to have its own air service and pledging the Government to the continued existence of an independent Air Force. As it happened, Capt Barry Domvile was sitting next to Trenchard during the debate. "Austen Chamberlain," he wrote in his diary afterwards, "made a monotonous reply which I could see was dictated by the Air Ministry and was most misleading ... Trenchard has been more artful amongst the politicians than we have."[24] Domvile was right to the extent that Churchill had drafted most of Chamberlain's speech and had made use of Trenchard in the process. However, the fact that the Admiralty had lost the support of such past friends and admirers as Lord Balfour and Winston Churchill over the previous year seems to indicate that they had made the worst of a good case over the FAA by lending their support to the War Office campaign against the RAF. This was especially true in that it was not necessarily in the Navy's interest for the War Office to win. After all, noted Chatfield, "We have got to take great care that we do not get 'out of the frying pan, etc,' i.e. to put ourselves in any way under War Office control in air matters."[25]

Chamberlain's speech did however contain some provision for improving co-operation between the Air Force and the Navy, and Churchill insisted that "it will be a great mistake for the Air Ministry not to put the Admiralty at their ease in this matter."[26] This was the basis for the mediation attempt between the two services which Churchill started the day after Chamberlain's speech and which continued sporadically until the summer. The issue now was simply the relative responsibility of the Admiralty and the Air Ministry for the personnel and materiel of the FAA, but recent events had so soured relations that progress was slight and the effort petered out.[27]

It only did so, however, after the Admiralty had formed another committee, on "Procedure for transfer of the Naval Air Unit from Air Ministry to Admiralty Control," in July 1922. This action seems to justify Trenchard's darkest suspicions about the purity of the Navy's intentions at this time and also suggests that the Admiralty had not reconciled itself to the idea that the FAA should remain part of the RAF. In these circumstances, agreement between the two services was unlikely.[28] But the Navy recognised that it was being optimistic, and a few weeks later the Admiralty told Admiral Madden (who had just laid down command of the Atlantic Fleet): "So far as can be seen at present it is improbable that the Admiralty view in regard to naval air requirements being formulated by the Naval Staff and met out of Admiralty votes, also the Admiralty view in regard to design and supply, will be acceded to. The point of difference will be narrowed down to the vital question of the personnel of the Naval Air Unit and the responsibility for the control of that personnel."[29]

Larger events now began to affect the issue. The Chanak crisis in the autumn led to the famous meeting at the Carlton Club and the collapse of the Coalition Government under Lloyd George. In the election which followed, the Conservatives under Bonar Law swept to complete power for the first time in 17 years, and Sir Samuel Hoare became the new Secretary of State for Air. Suddenly, "the whole future of the Air Force and the Air Ministry was in imminent danger," wrote Hoare later. The mood of the new Government seemed to favour the abolition of the RAF for reasons of economy and Hoare consequently attended his first Committee of Imperial Defence (CID) meeting in a state of "nervous dejection". He nevertheless put in an anxious plea for a full inquiry before any such step was taken. Unexpectedly, he got what he asked for, thereby winning at least a stay of execution.[30]

Though the controversy over the shape of British air power simmered through Christmas and into the New Year, it gradually became clear that a full and further inquiry was inevitable because the Admiralty was not prepared to let the matter rest where it was, as Beatty effectively told Prime Minister Bonar Law in February 1923. The last week of that month saw veiled threats of resignation, extensive lobbying, argument and controversy in which the irreconcilable nature of the positions of the two services' uniformed chiefs became unmistakable. The Navy wanted its own air service, but this was quite unacceptable to Trenchard and the Air Staff. Belatedly, Beatty had restricted his claims to the return of the FAA. But this was a distinction without a difference in the eyes of the Air Staff, who doubted whether the RAF would survive such a loss. The upshot of all this was the establishment in March 1923 of a committee under Lord Salisbury to consider, amongst other things, the place of air power in national defence. The Salisbury Committee soon spawned a subcommittee under Lord Balfour to report on the specific problem of the FAA.

Both sides were optimistic about their chances. The RAF had beaten the Navy at rugby for the first time at Twickenham a fortnight before. Perhaps taking this as a favourable omen, Trenchard was quietly confident of the results. Three days after the formation of the Salisbury Committee was announced, he wrote to a friend: "Another inquiry has been ordered, which will decide once again in favour of the Air Force."[31] The Navy also set to work with a will, hopeful of the outcome of their labours. Beatty told his wife: "We cannot afford to be beaten over it. It takes a vast amount of preparation, and that alone occupies most of my time, and we stand or fall by the result."[32] In both departments the staff worked into the small hours night after night to prepare their case, the groundwork for the Admiralty being done by Capts Tom Calvert and Dudley Pound of the Plans Division and Cdr Bell Davies of the Naval Air Section. A comprehensive review of the arguments is not possible here, but the Navy aimed generally for the "solution of principle," the so-called "clean cut" whereby they would get everything except possibly the design and supply of aircraft. Trenchard would have resigned over such a solution. While the Air Staff refused to yield on the principle, they were prepared to make practical concessions on various issues, particularly the conditions affecting the personnel of the FAA.

The Balfour Subcommittee comprised Lord Balfour himself and Lords Weir and Peel, of whom only the last was completely uncommitted. Lord Weir, an ex-Air Minister, engineer and industrialist, was an air enthusiast whose presence, thought Air Secretary Hoare, would "really make all the difference to the impartiality of the inquiry and to the value of its recommendations, and it would indeed be a calamity if you could not take part in it."[33] Balfour, a former First Lord, was familiar with the problem and sympathetic to the naval view but showed in his inter-service adjudication an inclination towards great independence of mind. Unfortunately for the Admiralty, while he was not as he feared "a clog upon the proceedings," he was elderly and beset with bad colds and phlebitis, and had to retire for long periods to Norfolk, missing many of the meetings. Sir Maurice Hankey, the influential secretary of the CID, kept him posted of developments in what he called "an uncommonly good and interesting inquiry". Hankey reported to him on the course of the meeting, saying that Beatty was "impressive with a touch of petulance that on the whole did not detract from his presentation of the case." "Sam Hoare," reported Hankey towards the end of the inquiry, "was very cut up about the possibility of losing this inquiry [and made] a sort of personal appeal to me to see if there was any way in which the facade of a single Air Force could be preserved."[34]

Perhaps not surprisingly in view of their past associations, Balfour produced a first draft calling essentially for a clean cut, while Weir came down just as heavily on the Air Force side. The dénouement was a tense session in the invalid's bedroom in the Grand Hotel, Sheringham, where Weir unavailingly tried to persuade Balfour to change his mind. Hankey broke the impasse by suggesting a visit to the carriers *Argus* and *Eagle* at Portsmouth, stepping in for Balfour, who could not go. All three men were impressed by the good personal relations they found on board and Balfour allowed himself to be persuaded out of his advocacy of a clean cut by these unexpected findings. The Committee was then able to submit an agreed report by July.

The subcommittee's findings and the records of its deliberations indicate that Trenchard and his colleagues were neither as persuasive nor as victorious as his biographer suggests. The Army campaign against the Air Force was certainly deflated fairly easily in the main Salisbury Committee since, according to Hankey, "there was not much sting behind the attack"[35] and the Air Staff had staved off the clean cut that Beatty sought. But the concessions made went a long way towards satisfying the Navy. It is hard to see, for instance, how the fact that the Admiralty was to pay for the FAA, that it was to be given what it wanted by the Air Ministry, and that all the observers and 70 per cent of the pilots were to be naval (the latter attached to the Air Force but in naval uniform) can reasonably be described as "administrative trimmings". The later description of the Balfour Report as a "narrow defeat on points" for the Admiralty seems to be nearer the mark[36], though it has to be admitted that the Admiralty did not see it in this light initially.

A draft of the Report was issued on July 21, 1923. The first Bell Davies heard of it was when he walked into the Plans Division to find "Pound sitting at his desk studying the report with a scowl on his face; Tom Calvert was walking about swearing."[37] Later the atmosphere became less gloomy once the report had been more fully digested. Nevertheless, the Sea Lords insisted on further concessions, requiring particularly that naval officers be "attached" rather than "seconded" to the RAF. On July 23 Amery, the First Lord, wrote anxiously: "I am afraid that I shall be faced with general resignations, and I doubt very much if any other senior Admirals would take on the vacant posts." He explained the sticking points to Lord Salisbury the following afternoon, and the latter realised that "without these . . . amendments the Sea Lords would resign!! We must talk to the Prime Minister about this."[38] Admiral Keyes was the moving spirit in all this and urged his colleagues to resign en masse. Beatty was more prepared to compromise and "took the line that 'we are in for a long period of peace and can afford to try the experiment,'" however distasteful it was and provided that the Navy could win certain significant concessions in the meantime.

There was a great deal of activity over the next week, with two special Admiralty Board meetings and much general coming and going. The Prime Minister, Stanley Baldwin, was in an unenviable position. The Sea Lords were resolute that the Report as it stood should be rejected, while Hoare and Trenchard were equally determined that it should not. On July 31 the Cabinet spent most of the day discussing the matter and eventually decided to accept the Balfour Committee's recommendations. This was announced by Baldwin in the House on August 2. The terms of his speech showed however that the Sea Lords had won a very significant concession: they had all along insisted that the scheme be regarded as experimental. "It is impossible," said Baldwin accordingly, "without experience to pronounce a final judgement on these arrangements."[39]

The Admiralty's conduct of this campaign had on occasion left much to be desired. The Sea Lords had a certain tendency to play to the gallery, and the atmosphere in which the inquiry was conducted was heavy with rumours of resignation and inspired press leaks, some of which had some substance.[40] Moreover, in June Admiral Fuller, the Third Sea Lord, attacked the Air Ministry's possession of the FAA on financial grounds before the parliamentary Select Committee on Estimates in a way which was as irregular as it was ill-judged. Most of all, perhaps, the Navy's past association with the War Office attack on the notion of an independent Air Force seems in retrospect to have done the Admiralty case more harm than good.

The Sea Lords did not yield to partial defeat gracefully. For the next few months they attempted to gain further adjustments in their favour which would get them nearer to their object of an FAA in which "the personnel . . . both officers and men, should . . . be naval and form an integral part of the personnel of the Fleet, under the sole authority of the Admiralty."[41] The First Lord had to persuade his naval colleagues to be more circumspect lest the Cabinet think they were trying to reopen the whole question of principle again. The normal procedures of inter-departmental negotiation were clearly reaching their limits by January 1924, and the arrival on the scene of new political chiefs for the Admiralty and the Air Ministry, following the formation of the first Labour Government under Ramsay MacDonald, seemed to make little difference. Eventually the Government asked Lord Haldane to mediate between the two contestants over how exactly the Balfour Report should be implemented. Haldane held a series of meetings with Trenchard and Keyes, who were actually brothers-in-law, which culminated in the Trenchard-Keyes Agreement. Forwarded to the Cabinet on July 4, 1924, this effectively laid the foundations of the Dual Control system, under which responsibility for the FAA was shared between the Air Ministry and the Admiralty for the next 14 years.

In the event, though, the armistice lasted for only just over a year. In August 1925 the Government set up a new committee under Lord Colwyn to investigate the possibility of further reductions in defence expenditure. In the following November Prime Minister Baldwin once more announced that the continued existence of the Air Ministry as a separate institution would be one of the matters considered. Both the War Office and the Admiralty resurrected their claims for their own separate air wings, the Board evidently deciding to reopen the issue in August. Assistant Chief of the Naval Staff Admiral Sir Frederick Dreyer did most of the staff work this time and tried to make it clear that the Navy neither sought the abolition of the RAF nor control of the design and supply of aircraft. The Navy did however want to take over the RAF's shore-based maritime aircraft as well as the FAA proper, arguing that this would save the country £100,000 a year.[42]

The Air Ministry's reaction to all this can easily be imagined. "For Heaven's sake, let there be no more committees," said Trenchard to Churchill, who was now Chancellor of the Exchequer, "to waste their time and ours on issues which have been tried and retried a dozen times during the last few years." A few days later he put the same argument to Baldwin: "How can [the older services] settle down to work with us in harmonious co-operation," he asked, "when senior officers are perpetually lecturing and talking about how the air service is going to be broken up and given back to them in a year or two?"[43] As it happened, the Air Ministry gained full support from the Colwyn Committee, whose eventual report savaged the Admiralty in terms which suggested that its members were thoroughly exasperated with the Sea Lords for reopening the issue yet again. As a symbol of their displeasure, and as a measure of their belief that air power could substitute for sea power, they reversed the 70:30 ratio of "attached naval" and RAF pilot officers in the FAA to 40:60 in the Air Ministry's favour, although this was actually something of a compromise on the Air Staff's original vengeful claim of 20:80. The renewed antagonism between the two departments was clearly exhausting the patience of politicians then grappling with the far more important matter of the General Strike, but the Prime Minister was eventually forced to arbitrate between the two on July 2, 1926. While the Admiralty was allowed to keep its 70:30 ratio, it was to accept the Air Ministry's share in responsibility for the FAA and was not to attempt to extend its influence to connected establishments ashore, or to Coastal Area Command.[44]

The whole affair severely damaged relations between the two services, inflaming some of the main actors in the drama. Sir Christopher Bullock, the combative Secretary of the Air Ministry, wrote a few days after the Baldwin arbitration: "I should like to see how much we should get out of the Admiralty if we started making a series of concrete demands designed to reduce the present level of navalisation of the FAA and get back even a part of the many concessions we have made during the past few years."[45] Soured by the experience of recent years, the Air Staff took a hard line on the various minor personnel issues which surfaced over the next few years, sometimes discerning subversion where it was not apparently present. This was the case in the dispute over whether the Navy could have rating pilots (the Trenchard-Keyes Agreement only applied to officers) and on several more details of the process of attachment of naval officers, all of which was referred to Lord Salisbury for a decision in March 1928. Salisbury found for the Air Ministry in the first case and for the Admiralty in the second, but in the course of his adjudication observed that ultimately "the FAA may cut loose from the remainder of the air service and become in all respects a special branch of the Fleet like any other."[46] Clearly there was at least a measure of support in Government circles for the Admiralty's contention that the present situation could not be regarded as final. Further encounters in this prolonged campaign thus seemed likely, but for the moment at least there was a truce between the two departments.

It might be imagined that this high-level antagonism between the Admiralty and the Air Ministry would have percolated down to the RAF and Naval officers serving in the FAA, but this was not so. Inter-service hostility was almost exclusively confined to the directing headquarters rather than the fighting forces themselves. The Balfour Committee had been agreeably surprised by the good spirit found in the *Eagle* and *Argus*, and for the rest of the period carriers continued usually to be happy ships; some, like the *Glorious* under Capt C. E. Kennedy-Purvis, were outstandingly so.

This alone would seem to challenge the assertion that "the Air Ministry supplied . . . many low-quality officers to Coastal Command and the FAA."[47] But there are several other reasons for doubting the truth of this proposition, and of the connected view that naval airmen were not valued once they had been reabsorbed into the mainstream of RAF life. For example, one of the pioneers of naval aviation, Marshal of the Royal Air Force Sir William Dickson, in fact eventually became Chief of the Air Staff. More significantly, the Admiralty never complained about the quality of the personnel it was receiving from the RAF, except briefly in the very early post-war days, though it would have gained great political advantage from so doing if such complaints could have been substantiated.

On the contrary, carrier captains were prepared to admit that there was not always "after two years in a carrier . . . much to choose between a RAF pilot and [his] RN [colleagues] . . ."[48] Some RAF officers actually specialised in naval air work, accumulating so much experience in the process that they were acknowledged to be particularly well fitted for positions of command in the FAA. The Admiralty's complaint was in fact that there were not enough RAF officers of this type because their time in the FAA was generally too short. By the mid-1930s they usually served only two years of the intended four with the Navy, tending to reduce the number of RAF officers with the experience necessary to make good wing commanders and squadron leaders in carriers later on. The RAF was entitled to half of these appointments but found it increasingly difficult to fill them to the Navy's satisfaction. More generally, the Navy felt that however enthusiastic and able the RAF officers were, they normally had insufficient time to acquire and then develop the specialised skills needed, for example, in night operations from carriers. Too much time was taken up with initial carrier training and too little with more advanced work because of the fast turnover of RAF officers in the FAA. Just as they were reaching the peak of their performance, complained the Admiralty, they left. It is thus hardly surprising that nearly all the innovations and bright ideas came from naval officers in the FAA.

The services also disagreed significantly on the proportion between Navy and RAF officers in the FAA but this had finally been fixed at a ratio of 70:30 in the former's favour. The Air Staff were very irritated at the speed with which the Admiralty had worked to meet this proportion, whose achievement they had understood was only to be expected after ten years or so. Using a temporary surplus of young officers in the mid-1920s, the Admiralty had however acted much faster than this. "The excessive navalisation of the FAA," complained Hoare, "makes it a continued focus of unrest . . . swamped by naval officer pilots and observers . . . this festering sore in the relations of the Air Force and the Navy carries its infection elsewhere."[49] Although some of them were essentially political, the reasons for the Admiralty's determination to reach and maintain its full ratio partly reflected strictly professional concerns. The Naval Staff, for example, had always held that the Air Ministry's refusal to allow the RAF establishment in carriers to carry out ship's duties meant that these vessels would need a higher-than-normal complement. The provision of accommodation for ships' companies thus inflated by Dual Control would obviously make it more difficult to design efficient carriers.

RAF personnel were unevenly distributed around the Fleet, their main concentrations being in the carriers rather than the small FAA detachments serving in those cruisers and battleships which operated aircraft. As a typical example of their density, the 1,100-strong complement of the *Glorious* of 1932 included a

FAA component of 70 officers and 280 men. In round numbers, 20 of the former were naval observers, a further 30 were naval officers temporarily attached to the RAF as pilots, and the last 20 or so were RAF officers. The 280 or so men in the *Glorious's* FAA unit were largely RAF maintenance crews and ground staff, but included some naval ratings who flew in the larger aircraft as Telegraphist/Air Gunners(TAGs), operating the gun and handling communications. The RAF contingents wore different uniforms and had different service customs. Their officers naturally disliked the fact that service in carriers entailed the loss of such privileges as their marriage allowance, found some naval customs irksome and restrictive, and had not after all joined the RAF to go to sea. Opportunities for friction were legion, but in fact they produced it only very rarely.

Their immediate naval shipmates came in two varieties: observers and pilots. Naval Observers had been established unilaterally by the Admiralty in 1921 after some wrangling with the Air Ministry. The Air Staff had generally maintained that since these officers had to be skilled in the science of aerial warfare and could learn the necessary naval skills relatively easily, they had better provide them. The Admiralty completely reversed the emphasis, insisting that oversea navigation and gunfire spotting required a naval specialisation of a high order. Eventually, and at Trenchard's own suggestion, a test was arranged. The Air Staff selected an RAF officer with long experience in spotting for the Army during the war to try his hand in a naval test firing. Afterwards, "the selected officer insisted that specialist observers were a necessity, [and] the Naval Observer Branch came into existence."[50]

The RAF had a share in the training of observers, mainly at Lee-on-Solent and concentrating on such things as airmanship, signals and wireless telegraphy, but they remained naval officers throughout. As such they participated in ship's duties like any other naval specialist officer, taking their turns at watchkeeping and so forth. When the carriers were in harbour the pilots left with their squadrons to live "a lordly life of dalliance" ashore, while the observers stayed behind, usually cleaning, painting or storing ship. They were ostentatiously naval and affected a natural superiority to the "drivers and chauffeurs" they flew with and later sometimes commanded in the air. "The brains of the FAA," went the common tag, "are in the observer's seat". Possibly because of this and their early start, the observers played a decisive part in shaping the development of British naval aviation, particularly when they came to plan and direct operations.

Their problem was that as naval officers pure and simple they had insufficient status within the FAA itself. In view of their contribution to naval flying, this was plainly anomalous and probably played a part in inspiring the Danby FAA Committee of 1934–5 to urge the combining of the pilot and observer roles into a single flying speciality. The idea had been raised in the Fleet some years earlier, partly as a possible means of reducing the FAA's disproportionate appetite for officers. But nothing was done about it, for two reasons: it was generally thought that the abolition of Dual Control was a better solution and, later, that it would delay the expansion programme of the mid to late 1930s. The whole issue provoked controversy in flying circles, the opponents of the scheme claiming that it would produce people who were overqualified for operational tasks. Later experience was to show that this view was largely correct. Unusually, the Controller of the Navy, Admiral Henderson, appealed for a decision to the First Lord, who compromised by promising to introduce the scheme – but not yet.[51]

Matters were even more complicated for the naval officers who served in the FAA as pilots. For the first few years of the inter-war period there were very few naval pilots in the FAA, much delaying their achievement of command positions. It was not until 1927 that Lt Conolly Abel Smith became the first naval officer to command an FAA flight, when he took over 403's Flycatchers in the *Hermes*. The situation improved after the Trenchard-Keyes agreement of 1924, when naval officers began to join the FAA in large numbers. All manner of men then volunteered to go into naval flying. Some of them, anxious to avoid the humdrum life of ship's duties and watchkeeping in a peacetime navy, went in search of adventure. Some were attracted by the 30 shillings a week extra flying pay. The more thoughtful ones joined because they thought the air the "coming thing" in the naval war of the future.

Orthodox criticism tended to focus on the shortcomings of the pilots rather than of the observers. "It is true," noted the Naval Assistant to the Second Sea Lord in April 1937, "that the volunteers are generally inferior in regard to brainpower," as indicated by their level of attainment in previous courses. Pilots, he claimed, had the lowest level of attainment of any other specialist branch.[52] It was generally agreed, however, that this was largely a result of the deplorable effects that Dual Control was having on recruitment by this time. Nevertheless, suspicions like this tended to reinforce the prejudices of the surface-bound. Such activities as Lt Cathcart-Jones' dive-bombing of the bridge of the Mediterranean Fleet flagship with "roundhouse paper" in 1928 tended to reinforce the ambivalence of senior officers about what seemed to be a peculiarly lighthearted breed of naval officer.[53]

But this apparent irresponsibility was more than counterbalanced by a particularly high level of professional dedication to the development of air power at sea. Perhaps partly because they were sometimes misunderstood and underrated, the personnel of the FAA were especially concerned to show how valuable their work could be. They developed a strong *esprit de corps*, produced a constant stream of new ideas and did much to convert the sceptical by the weight of their collective enthusiasm. There was a certain tendency for the more junior members of the FAA to regard themselves as something of a service within a service, but their seniors were anxious to nip any such signs of separatism in the bud. The FAA was and should remain an integral part of the Navy. For this reason, pilots were occasionally allowed to do ship's duties to keep their hand in while they were attached to the FAA, and after four years or so did two years' general naval service before coming back to the FAA. Wherever possible, pilots were treated in just the same way as any other naval specialists.

British and American practice diverged a little on this. In the US Navy an officer could remain attached to naval aviation almost throughout his career. In June 1927 it had been decided that only aviators could command carriers and naval air stations, and so captains and Flag officers had to "qualify" at such advanced ages as 47, for Capt E. J. King in 1928, or 52, for Admiral Halsey in 1934. The British, however, made no such special provision for aviators. In the Admiralty's view the handling of such difficult vessels as carriers required seamanship of a high order. Since some of the best carrier captains and general air enthusiasts were in fact not qualified aviators, there is something to be said for this view. More to the point, the transfer of the Navy's first generation of flyers into the RAF meant that there were hardly any aviators senior enough to command the big carriers. Whereas by 1926 the US Navy had one vice-admiral, three rear-admirals, two captains and 63 commanders who received flying pay, the Royal Navy had only one rear-admiral and a few commanders and junior captains by the start of the Second World War.[54] Although opposed in principle to the idea of specialist command, the Royal Navy might in fact have followed the US practice had the necessary officers been available.

Despite all this, however, naval officers attached to the FAA under the conditions of Dual Control were in an anomalous position. Usually they volunteered for the FAA after about five years in the Navy and stayed in it for about 14 years, including training, with a two-year general service break in the middle. They usually began their FAA careers at Netheravon before going on to the RAF's very successful Flying Training School at Leuchars, Fife. Throughout they were regarded as "attached" to the RAF, wearing naval uniform with a small distinguishing badge on board ship but coming under RAF discipline and control for the very extensive time they spent ashore in air training. They held two ranks – Navy and RAF – which were frequently not strictly parallel, resulting in difficult situations in which who commanded whom depended on the exact circumstances of their service at the time. Where two departments shared responsibility for the careers of FAA personnel, administrative problems and injustices were bound to occur, especially when the details could be considered by the suspicious to impinge on the matter of principle.

The Navy particularly disliked the way in which FAA personnel ashore disappeared into the maw of the RAF when the carriers came into harbour. Chatfield, the First Sea Lord, drew a heartrending picture of the situation: "When one was C-in-C, one used to find the captains of the aircraft carriers were the most enthusiastic captains [but, when in harbour] there is his ship, empty. All the people he commanded are gone, they are out of the ship. . . . I used to find the captain of the carrier walking about disconsolately with nothing to do." This discontinuity of service split the ship's company and so it was "jump and slump all the way along."[55] This criticism, though, was not well made. Squadrons had to be disembarked when the carriers were in harbour so that air-crew could carry out flying training, bombing practice and so forth. When the Admiralty campaigned to have some air stations of its own later on, its argument about such disembarkations was quite different.

But if these were irritating inconveniences, there was a developing crisis in recruitment which worried the Admiralty far more. A temporary surplus of young officers in the 1920s had got the manning of the FAA off to a good start, but thereafter demand began to exceed supply, especially during the expansion of the 1930s occasioned by worries about the growth of Japanese air strength. Whereas the Air Ministry had annually trained about 24 naval officers as pilots up to 1934, the Admiralty wanted to increase this to 144 a year by 1941. But vol-unteers were simply not available in this number and, according to the office of the Second Sea Lord, had practically ceased coming forward by April 1937.[56] As far as FAA reserves were concerned the situation was no better. Attempts to build these resources up from RNR and RNVR sources in the 1920s had failed in the face of Air Ministry ambivalence and Treasury hostility, and little progress had been made subsequently. As a result, there was only a 20 per cent officer reserve for the FAA by 1935.[57] The Air Ministry tended to say that it could be safely entrusted with the responsibility for providing adequate reserves for the FAA, but a share of the blame for the lamentable situation that had arisen by the late 1930s has to go to the Admiralty itself. The Navy tended to argue that "the loss of pilots would be comparatively small apart from some major engagement which might not take place for a long time after the outbreak of war." The Navy worked out its reserve requirements largely on the basis of the final fleet action and "the subsidiary operations we can carry out with FAA before this action must be dependent on our first-line pilots being available for this Fleet Action . . . ."[58] While the Air Ministry recognised an ideal target of a 450 per cent RAF reserve, was willing to compromise on 300 per cent and recommended a 200 per cent reserve for the FAA, the Admiralty, unimpressed by Air Staff representations and woefully underestimating the air losses of the first year of a European war, were content to aim for 100 per cent, which it in any case failed to achieve.[59] The requirements of the Norwegian campaign caught the Admir-alty completely by surprise. The Admiralty's failure to foresee the extent to which it would be occupied and stretched by such "subordinate operations" as this was to prove to be a significant source of future weakness.

But while special factors affected the question of reserves, what was the reason for the continuing shortfall in general FAA recruitment? To a certain extent there was a manning problem affecting the Navy as a whole. "Calcu-lations showed," wrote Bell Davies, "that the requirements of the specialist branches, including destroyers and the FAA, would eventually absorb the whole of the Lieutenants' and Lieutenant-Commanders' Lists without leaving any for 'salthorse' (i.e. non-specialist) duties.'[60] The US Navy had the same problems too and found the number of pilots lagging behind that of aircraft to a worrying extent. The advent of a new and demanding specialisation at a time of falling manpower levels made life difficult for personnel managers in both navies. But having said all this, the FAA was still reckoned to be "the least popular form of specialisation" by the summer of 1937.[61]

One of the reasons for this was certainly the dark suspicions of junior officers about the attitude of their seniors to naval flying and the people who volunteered for it. "We had always been brought up to believe," wrote one such officer," that the intrusion of the RAF was to be discouraged with the utmost vigour, and those of us who might have had inclinations to fly carefully suppressed their feelings in order not to appear disloyal to their service . . ." The memoirs and reminiscences of FAA pilots and observers are full of stories of their seniors discouraging them from volunteering for the FAA. Typical of such experiences was that of one aspirant who was told by his captain that the air was "poppycock" and that flying would "ruin his career". The fact that the captain's name was Tom Phillips, who commanded the ill-fated *Repulse* and *Prince of Wales* ten years later, makes this example particularly significant.[62] These discouragements were especially common in the early interwar period and must have served to divert young officers into safer branches of the naval profession.

It is difficult to be precise about the influence that a specialisation in naval flying had on subsequent careers, not least because by the time the first wave of young FAA officers entered the promotion zone for high command in the late 1930s, the imminence of war and the Navy's re-possession of the FAA had transformed the situation. Generally, though, the later careers of the naval airmen of the 1920s offer little evidence to suggest that they suffered as a result of their choice of specialisation. If anything it was the reverse, with one of the first batch of naval pilots eventually becoming First Sea Lord.[63] Nevertheless, fears of what *might* happen were more important in affecting choice of careers than was experience of what actually *did* happen. In any case, the whole process was something of a self-fulfilling prophecy.

Although some would-be FAA officers were undoubtedly put off by the apparent prejudice of their seniors, fears about the possible effects of the Dual Control system on their careers was a much more important source of discouragement in the early days. A survey of officers in the Mediterranean Fleet was held in 1926 to find out why they had decided against a career in naval flying. The objections were very varied. "In some cases, objection is made to the general type of officer, socially, in the RAF." Others were worried that while observers were staff officers and so had good prospects, the pilot was only an engine driver, ". . . a necessary job to have filled but not requiring very high mental attainments . . . [a specialisation producing] technical knowledge of little use in the higher ranks of the service . . . Many state that they joined the Navy to become naval officers and they do not intend to waste the four most receptive and valuable years of their service in a job where they had little or no opportunity of handling and dealing with men, learning command and gaining sea sense." But above all there was anxiety about "who will be the pilot's friend?" Who would look after them, the Air Ministry or the Admiralty, in order to ensure that their interests were safeguarded, so they did not suffer as had other specialist branches in the past?[64] Far from furthering a person's career, Dual Control could actually damage it. If the Air Ministry, for its own peculiar reasons, decided against promoting a man in his RAF rank, this could have serious results on his subsequent naval career. The 1932 agreement that naval officers should be entitled to half the squadron leader and wing commander posts in the FAA provided only slight relief[65], and did little to calm the fears which so diminished the flow of volunteers.

The Admiralty tried many expedients to improve the situation. In early 1932 they introduced a compulsory flying acquaintance course of the kind operated by the US Navy, but this made little difference.[66] From November 1926 the Admiralty had wanted to follow the American lead in another direction, expanding the pool of possible volunteers by extending it to ratings, or "aircraft coxswains" as they were rather quaintly called. The Air Ministry steadfastly refused to countenance any such scheme[67] and the matter was put to Lord Salisbury for a decision in 1928. He concluded that one of the original objectives of having naval officers in the FAA was to permeate the higher ranks of the Navy with knowledge of the air. Since this could not possibly justify the inclusion of ratings within the Navy's 70 per cent FAA personnel ratio, the Air Ministry objections must be upheld. Encouraged, however, by the success of the Air Ministry's own small airman-pilot scheme and by the performance of its own recently introduced rating observers, and ever more desperate to increase the number of volunteers for the FAA, the Admiralty reopened the issue in 1934. Initially the Air Ministry stonewalled this proposal as it had six years before, finally yielding under great pressure to the extent of offering to train a dozen or so naval ratings as an experiment.[68] But by now this was too late. Deeply concerned by the general crisis in manning and exasperated by its institutional inability to solve it, the Admiralty had already decided to reopen the campaign to regain control of the FAA.

After the Salisbury arbitration of 1928 the dust of battle settled for something like six years until growing anxieties about FAA personnel led the Admiralty to set up the Danby Fleet Air Arm Committee in October 1934 to examine the working and organisation of the FAA. Its chairman, Admiral C. F. S. Danby, had commanded the *Furious* and his committee was dominated by experienced naval aviators. Its final report of April 12, 1935, was a detailed and exhaustive denunciation of the deficiencies of the present system, focusing particularly on personnel difficulties. "The Committee find," it stated, "that the majority of the FAA's difficulties are traceable ultimately to the existing policy of 'dual control' . . . "[69]

Two weeks later, Chatfield, now First Sea Lord, called a special meeting of the Sea Lords and other key Staff officers to discuss the problems outlined by the report and the Air Ministry's refusal to train rating pilots. A paper on this was written for the First Lord, and on May 9, 1935, the full Board of Admiralty decided to reopen the campaign to regain control of the FAA.[70]

Initially the Admiralty would concentrate on particular grievances. But this was merely a tactical consideration: the Admiralty wanted victory, not accommodation. Although the Air Ministry was distracted by its own expansion programme and the situation in the Mediterranean was clearly deteriorating, it was a good time to choose. The Navy now had as First Sea Lord the capable Sir Bolton Eyres-Monsell (later Viscount Monsell) and the First Sea Lord was Admiral Sir Ernle Chatfield, "the finest officer the Royal Navy produced between the wars."[71] Under Chatfield the Navy now had its best leadership since the days of Beatty and so would be much more formidable in its dealings with the Government and the other services.

As a first step, Monsell wrote to Prime Minister Ramsay MacDonald on May 20, 1935, asking for permission to bring the matter to the attention of the Cabinet. The Secretary of State for Air, the Marquis of Londonderry, protested and so MacDonald promised to deal with the problem himself. MacDonald's political powers were fading by this time, however, and he was replaced as Prime Minister by Stanley Baldwin three weeks later, having made no move in this direction. Monsell let the dust settle for a month and contacted MacDonald again. On July 29 the latter took the problem to Baldwin, who said that while he was "wholly opposed" to the reopening of the controversy, some way of improving co-operation between the two departments over naval aviation ought to be found.[72] The reluctance of politicians to seize the nettle of interservice discord and the urgent distractions of the Abyssinian crisis combined to produce a brief lull in the Admiralty campaign until the autumn, when the assiduous Hankey attempted to mediate between the disputants by chairing two high-level meetings at No 2 Whitehall Gardens.

At the first of these Chatfield made the totality of the Navy's objective perfectly clear. "Broadly speaking," he said, "the Admiralty wishes to control entirely the FAA and experience has now proved conclusively that this is necessary."[73] "It is no exaggeration to say," he added later, "that the FAA is well on the way to being ruined and as it is one of our vital weapons that is something which I as First Sea Lord cannot allow to happen."[74] The Navy was encouraged in its determination to go the whole hog by rumours that Air Ministry opposition was less solid than it appeared. "I hear very confidentially," one naval officer reported to Hankey, "that there is a distinct school of thought in the Air Ministry that the FAA had better go over to the Navy – so far as personnel is concerned." The reason was thought to lie in the RAF's increasing difficulty in providing officers to fill the FAA's senior posts. "We should not force the Air Ministry into a corner," he added.[75]

Nevertheless, the Secretary of State for Air, Sir Phillip Cunliffe-Lister (later the Earl of Swinton), refused to allow the reopening of the question of principle – he correctly argued that it had been the Prime Minister's intention to keep it closed – and was only prepared to discuss detailed matters of personnel and procedure. Since one side was clearly not interested in producing it, compromise was impossible. After a second meeting in November, Hankey was forced to admit that his mediation effort had failed and that progress required further instructions.[76] He was, he added, very disturbed at the general lack of co-ordination between the two services.

Early in 1936 the Admiralty began pressing for some kind of inquiry. In January Monsell suggested that Sir Warren Fisher (the Permanent Secretary of the Treasury) might conduct an impartial investigation into the workings of the Balfour system. This was inevitably turned down by the Air Ministry, which considered that it would infringe on the matter of principle. Monsell, who was about to give up his post, urged his naval colleagues to be cautious. He argued that it would be unwise to press for a general inquiry, something which would probably be rejected anyway. Would it not be better to wait for a more auspicious time later and work merely for tactical gains at the moment?[77] However, in the following month Sir Thomas Inskip was appointed to act as Minister for the Co-ordination of Defence. Knowing how restive the Sea Lords were, Monsell wrote to him in April. "The Admiralty," he said, "are very gravely concerned about the efficiency of the FAA; indeed this is giving the Naval Staff, and myself, far more anxiety than any other matter affecting naval defence. . . . We have not got sufficient pilots or observers and we have not got adequate reserves of personnel." Generally, he concluded, the issue was ". . . a most pressing subject."[78]

The Secretary of State for Air, now the Earl of Swinton, was plainly infuriated by the Navy's persistence in this matter. He called Monsell's letter "a really amazing document" in view of the Prime Minister's decision against the reopening of the matter of principle. When he got wind of the idea of an inquiry, Lord Weir (who was acting as the Government's unofficial adviser on air matters) also objected strongly, saying that ". . . today the case for adhering to these arrangements is a hundred times stronger than it was in 1923." Foreshadowing his future threatened resignation over the issue, he added: "You will remember that I have a heavy responsibility on all this as I was responsible for causing Lord Balfour to change his mind and thus secured the unanimous report of 1923 . . ."[79] Baldwin eventually authorised Inskip to proceed but restricted him to an inquiry on personnel issues only.[80]

On June 6, 1936, Monsell was replaced as First Lord by Sir Samuel Hoare, who soon showed himself to be less enthusiastic for the FAA campaign than his predecessor had been. To a certain extent, though, the initial detachment that he showed probably reflected little more than the natural embarassment of a man now having to demolish a system which he had been active in creating 13 years previously. It is not easy, after all, for a poacher to turn gamekeeper. Later on Hoare became a more obviously enthusiastic campaigner, and his contention that the situation had changed – with the RAF now able to stand the loss so much better – undoubtedly had much effect, at least on the uncommitted. For the moment, though, he advised his new naval colleagues to trust in Inskip, to put their case grievance by grievance, and not to pursue their ultimate goal too crudely, lest their vigour prove counter-productive.[81]

Inskip held four meetings through the last two weeks of July, during which various members of the Naval and Air Staffs exhaustively discussed many matters of detail. It soon became clear, however, that it was the question of principle that really divided the contestants. At the first meeting Inskip said that the existing system was not to be extensively disturbed, and the point was made more forcibly by Swinton during the third. "The fundamental thing is [that] the FAA is an integral part and branch of the Air Force," he said, "and . . . I cannot sit here and listen to a discussion of a proposal which proposed to make the FAA something quite different."[82]

The Sea Lords soon had to consider how they would react to the report when it came. Would their ultimate purpose of gaining complete control of the FAA be best served by acceptance or rejection of the various compromise proposals that Inskip was bound to produce before long? One of the most articulate proponents of the "grand slam" was the ACNS, Admiral C. E. Kennedy-Purvis, who argued that if the Navy did accept a compromise it would presumably be expected to give the new arrangements another fair trial of twelve years or so. "Anything," he said, "which is not said during the opportunity now presented can, and possibly will, be considered by the Government to be comparatively unimportant." Chatfield was evidently not quite sure of the wisdom of so proceeding and pointed out that Inskip, the Cabinet and indeed the First Lord would have to be convinced if the Admiralty was to be successful. He also seemed quite pleased with the results of the Inskip Inquiry so far.[83]

Inskip eventually reported on November 3, 1936, recommending that RAF officers be attached to the FAA for four years, that ratings be trained as pilots as an experiment, and that a 100 per cent FAA reserve be assured for the Admiralty. Two days later he wrote a somewhat ambivalent letter to the Prime Minister. On the one hand, Inskip said that it would be difficult to hive the FAA off from the RAF and "I should myself be most reluctant to see a change now." On the other, he admitted that the present situation was not satisfactory and that his present recommendations were not likely to make it so. "The absence of common ground between the services is very disquieting," he said, and suggested the possible necessity of some further form of inquiry.[84]

Reactions to the report were mixed. Chatfield had evidently been persuaded that acceptance of the Dual Control system, even if now modified, was out of the question. "The Navy feels it has been let down badly," he wrote, and "has not attained the efficiency it should have. . . . Consequently, in the interests of the Navy . . . it is essential that this disastrous experiment should be terminated and the system changed." He went further than this, even hinting at resignation, in the letter he wrote to the First Lord on the day Inskip's report came out: "As a member of the Board who alone has had continuous knowledge of the serious unpreparedness of the FAA," Chatfield said, "I hold more responsibility than my colleagues and I feel continuous concern for my position and how I should act."[85] Hoare transmitted these opinions to Baldwin, making his own sympathy with them quite apparent.

While the Navy's leaders were thus ostentatiously nailing their colours to the masthead, the Air Ministry was much dismayed by the increased prospect of further controversy. Inskip's references to another, wider inquiry alarmed Swinton very much. "I must say," he wrote, "your letter is a great discouragement. I think you will agree that I have done all I possibly can, not only to make constructive suggestions myself, but to bring my people along. The latter has not been easy, not because they are unreasonable, but because they feel very strongly that every criticism they make is used as a lever to force the big change."[86] About this time, too, there was renewed controversy in the press and a resurgence of agitation in the Commons. Many of the great figures of the past, notably Keyes and Trenchard, returned to the controversy with gusto and the engagement became general and violent. Past antagonists, like Churchill, Capt F. Guest (one-time Secretary of State for Air) and even Air Cdre J. A. Chamier (of the Air League), were coming over to the Admiralty's side on this issue.[87] But having had its fingers badly burnt in its backstairs intriguing of the 1920s, the Admiralty was now determined to keep everything above-board. "I do not favour outside propaganda and never have," wrote Chatfield. "It is my duty and my preference to act constitutionally and to trust to that."[88] Circumstances were, in any case, so much more favourable for the Admiralty now than they had been before that their dangerous tactics of the past were clearly unnecessary.

By the end of November 1936 the need for an inquiry into the principle behind the control of the FAA was increasingly accepted, although several key actors in the drama, such as Hankey, thought it might do more harm than good.[89] By the middle of December 1936 Inskip was investigating the possibility of an inquiry, perhaps involving Lord Halifax and the President of the Board of Trade, Walter Runciman (shortly to be replaced by Oliver Stanley).

Even so, it took another six months of detailed negotiation before the actual terms and personnel of the inquiry were finally settled, and this rather than the principle of control became the major subject of dispute between all the interested parties. Throughout, it was the Admiralty which maintained the pressure. On February 11, 1937, Chatfield went to see Baldwin to tell him that since the Navy expected its grievance to be investigated, ". . . they cannot understand my personal failure in this matter and that I still remain in my post. . . .My position as First Sea Lord has become intolerable and unless an immediate inquiry is held I should lose the confidence of the service. . . ."[90] Towards the end of the month terms of reference had been agreed and various papers on the subject produced by the Naval Staff were sent over to Inskip.

Then came a check in the proceedings. Lord Weir threatened to resign if a full inquiry was held, and Hankey and Sir Horace Wilson, acting as the Prime Minister's agents, sought to persuade Chatfield to accept that the matter be referred to the Chiefs of Staff for examination at Staff level. Describing Weir's actions as most unpatriotic, Chatfield not surprisingly rejected this "fantastic proposal" out of hand. At lunchtime on March 11, 1937, with a statement having to be made in the Commons at three o'clock, he agreed, however, that Inskip should "thrash out the problem in all its aspects with the Chiefs of Staff" and then at an appropriate moment he would bring in Halifax and Stanley "to help him come to conclusions."[91] Three such meetings with the Chiefs of Staff were held, one in April and two in May, but predictably they proved to be little more than a rehearsal of previous positions and made no material contribution to a solution.

At the end of May Duff Cooper took over as First Lord. A week later, Chatfield, now thoroughly exasperated, complained that progress was unacceptably slow and that Inskip was not moving as fast as he had promised towards the final inquiry with Halifax and Stanley.[92] Hoare, now at the Home Office, also did his best to keep the pressure on. At last Inskip settled on three days in early July for the final inquiry. Then, for no very clear reason, an urgent phone call on June 25 cancelled these arrangements. Shortly afterwards, Chatfield, clearly furious, made it clear that "unless this inquiry can be immediately held and completed before the House rises it is no longer justifiable for me to continue as First Sea Lord."[93] It was quickly agreed that Inskip would carry on his inquiry alone. Apparently content to go ahead on the basis already supplied to him by the main disputants, Inskip laboured on the matter for the next three weeks, occasionally spurred on by Chatfield, and produced his report for the Prime Minister on July 21.[94]

The Admiralty had begun to act as though the mere holding of an inquiry was tantamount to its recovery of the FAA, and Inskip's verdict showed this confidence to be well placed. While denying the Naval claim to Coastal Command, he recommended that responsibility for the FAA should be entirely returned to the Admiralty. The unexpectedly sudden termination of the inquiry and its unwelcome main conclusion aroused a storm of protest in the Air Ministry. "How can I or the Air Staff be expected to accept a decision on an issue on which we have not been heard?" asked Swinton angrily, claiming that his Department's views on the organisational and administrative side of the case had not been considered. "I thought we had all agreed that the great issues of strategic and co-operational self-sufficiency must be decided first; and that the services must have their orders on these first.'"[95] Inskip was swayed from his conclusion neither by this nor by a protest visit by the Chief of the Air Staff and two of his colleagues a few days later, and his findings were considered by the Cabinet on July 29. Although Swinton objected to them once more, he was evidently resigned to their being accepted. Hoare argued that the RAF could now stand the loss and commented that "when he went to the Admiralty, he had tried to quieten down this [controversy] but had found it impossible." Inevitably, the Cabinet accepted Inskip's findings, which were duly announced in the Commons the following day.[96]

This speech by the Prime Minister, Neville Chamberlain, was the eagerly awaited culmination of a 16-year-long campaign by the Admiralty. The Navy had never really accepted the Dual Control system and this alone made it ultimately unworkable. Nevertheless, there were so many encumbrances in the system that it is hard to see how the FAA could have kept pace with its foreign counterparts, even had both departments co-operated with the best will in the world. But if the energy displayed and consumed in the fight for repossession had been devoted to the fullest tactical and strategic development of naval aviation, the Royal Navy would have been much better prepared for the trials of war in 1939.

In the course of his speech Chamberlain requested individuals "to refrain from firing shots" in the national interest,but the end of the affair nevertheless left a distinct aftertaste. Retired officers were particularly disappointed at the Navy's not getting Coastal Command as well, and their grumblings made the well known columnist C. G. Grey urge the Government to "take strong action to stop this service agitation, which, viewed psychologically and intellectually, is definitely Bolshevism.'"[97] In the more discreet corridors of power, too, there was further friction. There was, for instance, some dispute over who was to be responsible for the intermediate training of FAA pilots – the Air Ministry or the Admiralty – and over the disposition of various airfields. The Navy clearly believed that these issues were more important than they appeared on the surface. "For years," wrote Admiral Henderson, " – ever since I have had anything to do with the FAA – we have been struggling hard to make real use of shore bases for operational training." Without them, he argued, the Navy would have to devote too much carrier time to elementary training and too little to really important advanced work.[98] After all, the operational efficiency of the

Navy rested on such minor points, perhaps accounting for the heat which some of these remaining issues generated. Inskip was suspected of taking away with his left hand what he was giving with his right. "It seems," said Chatfield, "that some hidden pressure is being applied to the Minister for Co-ordination of Defence to retain Air Ministry control over what has been handed over to the Navy."[99] So strongly in fact did the Admiralty feel about such things that it went over Inskip's head to appeal directly to the Prime Minister, but with little success.[100] The obvious imminence of war, and the equally obvious need for the fullest co-operation between the services, was making intransigence of this kind increasingly inappropriate, and compromises were eventually reached. The Admiralty formally assumed full administrative responsibility for the FAA on May 24, 1939 – three months before the start of the Second World War.

The last vestiges of controversy were soon swallowed up in the interservice co-operation required for active preparation for war. Taking over the FAA and its attendant shore stations and providing the personnel for 50 squadrons posed enormous problems for the Admiralty. The Navy did not have the numbers of trained airmen these tasks required, as was shown in the Munich crisis, when it proved impossible to complement the carrier *Furious* without stopping the training of new pilots.[101] The Air Ministry, which had itself embarked on a huge expansion programme, had nothing to spare but did its best to meet the Navy's more immediate needs. A few RAF officers volunteered to go over into the FAA, but the Admiralty's idea of compelling others to do so was soon found to be impracticable. The problem of providing enough maintenance crews was even more difficult and was the main reason why the Navy's full assumption of control was several times delayed. Eventually the Air Ministry agreed to lend the Navy 1,460 maintenance personnel and several hundred officers, most of whom were still in the FAA in December 1940. In fact the Admiralty assumed that a degree of dependence on the RAF would continue until 1944.

The problem was aggravated at every turn by the fact that the Admiralty was not not only assuming the burden of running its own air wing but was also planning more than to double its size. New sources of manpower would obviously have to be tapped as a matter of urgency, and the Admiralty soon found it necessary to abandon the particularly restricting personnel requirements that it had usually insisted on before. In 1935–6 the Admiralty had introduced rating observers – quaintly known as Observers' Mates and Boatswains[102] – largely from the ranks of the more experienced TAGs. Encouraged by the obvious success of this scheme, and released from the restrictions of Dual Control, the Navy moved on to the provision of rating pilots. The first 20-strong batch arrived at Leuchars Flying Training School in May 1938. Early the following year one of them landed for the first time on the *Courageous*, demonstrating thereby the arrival of a new and valuable source of naval flyers. Although it was at first believed that ratings could not take tactical decisions and so should not be put into positions where they might have to do so, the FAA easily accomodated this new sort of naval flyer. There were also few social problems in a branch of the Navy that was more egalitarian than most and where air seniority and expertise was the main source of a man's repute.[103]

While these new arrivals came from the lower deck, they at least had years of naval experience behind them. This could certainly not be said of many of the short-service commissioned officers who began to flood into the FAA from February 1938. In the past the Admiralty had resisted the introduction of such an idea, arguing that extensive sea experience was a prerequisite for efficient naval airmen. However, the manpower targets of the expanding air arm could only be met if this requirement were largely waived. New entrants under the scheme were between 17½ and 22 years old and were expected to complete an extendable period of at least seven years in the FAA. They wore a miniature "A" in the executive curl of their gold stripes, and were paid at a starting rate of 5/- per day, with an extra 4/- flying pay. They were flyers first and foremost, and were not expected to do ship's duties. By entering the Air (A) Branch they sacrificed many naval privileges and possible commands, but were able to concentrate on the business of flying to the exclusion of all else. They were steadied by a number of older officers, some of whom joined the A Branch because they saw it as a second chance to enjoy a successful naval career, having been passed over for promotion earlier. A number of RAF officers also took this opportunity to transfer into the Navy, some of them forming part of the Navy's first batch of Air Engineer Officers.

Not surprisingly, there were some apprehensions about this new breed of naval airmen. One of their course officers stood on the quarterdeck of the *Furious* in February 1938 waiting for the first batch of Air Branch officers, not knowing what to expect "but prepared for any eventuality from a Dartmoor convict to a Senior Wrangler."[104] In fact, he and the Navy were very pleased with the results of the scheme. Air Branch officers in general were immensely enthusiastic, either because, by flying with the minimum of distraction, they were doing precisely what they had joined for, or because they saw it as an opportunity for a new career. Although some of them actually did do ship's duties of one kind or another, they were inevitably less "naval" than the old hands of the inter-war FAA, especially when their number was vastly inflated by the great influx of RNVR (A) officers which began shortly afterwards.

The management of this flood of new entrants inevitably affected the efficiency of the FAA before and during the early part of the war. Many of its most experienced men and units were engaged in training the new entry. Thus, when the Norwegian campaign began, the *Ark Royal* and *Glorious* were away training in the Mediterranean and the *Furious* was only partly operational, with many of her aircraft and aircrew ashore. The high standards of the squadrons of the inter-war period were necessarily watered down by the arrival of large numbers of newly trained flyers whose expertise obviously could not always match their enthusiasm. When the *Furious* attacked Trondheim on April 11, 1940, all of her aviators were firing their first shots in anger and many of the pilots made their first night landings when they came back. Inexperience was even more evident in the disappointing performance of the Hatston Swordfish against the *Scharnhorst* on June 21.

Generally, though, the flying personnel of the FAA demonstrated a high level of expertise and resource, as shown by the *Warspite's* Swordfish at Narvik. In fact, since this aircraft was flown by a petty officer but commanded by a lieutenant-commander (O), this flight is as good an example of the Navy's pre-war personnel policy in operation as it is of its expectations about the tactical uses of naval air power. The FAA established a degree of moral ascendancy over its adversaries which its numbers and materiel quality certainly did not warrant and which is a considerable tribute both to the training and valour of its men. The exploits of Midshipman (A) L. H. Gallagher, a Skua pilot from the *Ark Royal*, illustrate the initiative so often displayed in this campaign. Failing to find his carrier after a raid and with his fuel running low, Gallagher returned to land and brought his aircraft down on Lake Lesjaskog, where he found a crashed RAF Gladiator. He refuelled the Skua with petrol from the Gladiator's tanks but could not start his own aircraft as he had no cartridge for the impulse starter. Borrowing a rifle, he went off with the Army until he came across a crashed Skua three days later. In the wreckage he found one cartridge and took it back to Lake Lesjaskog. His engine started and with the aid of a school atlas Gallagher navigated himself 350 miles back across the North Sea to Hatston, where he eventually rejoined his carrier.

Gallagher was one of those subsequently lost to the FAA as a result of the *Ark Royal's* later attack on the *Scharnhorst*. During the course of this campaign the steady attrition of operations in very difficult conditions, aggravated by the occasional disaster such as the *Scharnhorst* attack or the sinking of the *Glorious*, combined to produce a loss of about 100 aircraft and 125 aircrew – something approaching one third of the FAA's flying strength. Few officers of the inter-war period could have conceived of such a loss rate, or the need for large reserves and the enormous personnel expansion which it so clearly implied.

Despite the high casualty rate of the first few years, when "all the real cream were expended,"[105] the FAA had expanded eightfold by the end of the war, when it totalled some 84,000 officers and men and had doubled its share of the Navy's total complement. By 1943 the FAA had something like ten times its 1939 total of pilots.[106] This huge expansion tended to break up the patterns of skill and experience established before the war, and imposed a tremendous training task on the Navy, even though much of it was carried out in the United States and Canada. The great majority of the new recruits were men of the RNVR, which had formed an Air Branch in 1938. When war broke out the first group of RNVR (A) Officers were at Hyères in the South of France, doing deck-landing training on the old *Argus*, and by the end of 1939 about 130 of them had been absorbed into the Navy. They participated extensively in the Norwegian campaign and before long accounted for about 97 per cent of the FAA's flying personnel. In 1939 the names of RNVR (A) officers covered four pages in the Navy List, compared with a peak of 79 in double columns by 1944.[107]

Even so, it was still difficult for the Navy to get the numbers it required, especially in its preparations for the Pacific campaign. This was partly because the RAF was more in the public eye and so attracted the lion's share of new recruits. So unpublicised, in fact, were the FAA's activities that Churchill was able to write, in April 1943: "I cannot recall any important offensive operation that the FAA has performed since Taranto in 1941." As will be shown later, the FAA particularly prided itself on this famous attack, and the Prime Minister's misdating it caused much offence in the Naval Staff at the time. But his note was part of a more generalised assault on the FAA's personnel expansion programme. "I think," wrote Churchill later, "that it is rather a pregnant fact that of 45,000 officers and ratings . . . only 30 should have been killed, missing or prisoners during the three months ended April 30 [1943]. . . . The whole question of the scale of the FAA is raised by this clear proof of how very rarely it is brought into contact with the enemy."[108] In fact losses fluctuated greatly over the war but were usually much higher than this. Between May 1944 and January 1945, for example, 333 aircrew were lost out of the 7,000 or so in the FAA – a five per cent loss rate in a period not distinguished by any particularly hazardous operations.

Although this passage partly reflects a lack of understanding of what the FAA was actually doing at this time, it is probably better seen as a symbol of the growing unease there was in Britain in 1943–4 about the whole question of the war effort and manpower levels. Gradually the nation's leaders realised that, work as hard and as efficiently as they could, the British did not have the industrial and manpower resources to keep pace with their major foes and allies. This realisation made the Prime Minister querulous about the suspected misuse of scarce resources. The Naval Air Service came under his hostile scrutiny for this on several occasions, in startling contrast to his boyish enthusiasm for it during the First World War.

In fact, though, the FAA was obliged to keep to very rigorous manning levels, especially when compared to the contemporary prodigality of the US Navy. The Americans not only carried a complement that was higher than the British figure as a simple total but also larger relative to the number of carriers it operated. The US Navy operated twice as many carriers, but with five times as many men. This disparity in numbers showed itself in many different ways. While, for example, US escort carriers of early 1944 had a flight-deck crew of 80 specially trained men, their British equivalents had to make do with about 20 impressed seamen, stokers and Marines to do the same work. By the end of the war, also, the US Navy was able to organise its carrier personnel into Air Groups, two per carrier, with one on operational duty and the other reco-vering.[109]

The Royal Navy, on the other hand, remained short of men throughout, but particularly in the early part of the war. "The shortage of personnel," wrote Admiral Cunningham from the Mediterranean in November 1940," is seriously affecting operations and my ability to exploit to the full the great mobility and striking power which carrier-borne aircraft give us in the Mediterranean. I do not know what pilots and observers are on their way, but I request that every en-deavour be made to hurry out as many as can be spared . . ."[110] The problem was aggravated by the FAA's increasing appetite for men. The carrier *Indomitable*, for example, had in 1938 a designed complement of 136 officers and 1,256 men; by 1946 this had risen to 215 and 1,731 respectively. For this and similar reasons, there was continued shortage despite a huge increase in numbers. In its way, this increasing disparity between the US and Royal navies symbolised the extent to which Britain's general war-fighting resources had been surpassed by those of the United States by the end of the war.

CHAPTER THREE

THE SHIPS

*"We are equally proud of the honour of demonstrating
the value of the much maligned aircraft carrier . . ."*

CAPT T. H. TROUBRIDGE
Commander of the *Furious*, off Norway, May 1, 1940

The Royal Navy emerged from the First World War in a very strong position as far as its carrier strength was concerned. Although the composition of the Fleet at this time was subject to constant change – a fact which presumably accounts for the disparities in the published literature about the number of carriers the Navy actually had[1] – the Admiralty in December 1918 planned to retain and equip a "Flying Squadron" of six seaplane or aircraft carriers: *Furious, Vindictive, Argus, Pegasus, Nairana* and *Vindex*. By the end of 1919 two more were expected to materialise, *Eagle* and *Hermes* (the latter being the world's first purpose-built aircraft carrier), and discussions were also under way about the possible conversion of the *Glorious* and *Courageous*. Thus at a time when no other naval power had a single aircraft or seaplane carrier, the Royal Navy was planning the eventual disposition of no less than 10 of these revolutionary vessels.[2]

The Flying Squadron was the fruit of a great deal of technical and operational experimentation during the First World War. Experience before the war showed quite clearly that aircraft would be valuable in the conduct of naval operations, but the problem was to get them to the right place at the right time. In theory, obviously, it would be best if aircraft could be operated by the Fleet directly, rather than from shore stations, and this meant that ship designers and operators had ultimately to deal with the problem of launching and recovering aircraft at sea.

Initially, aircraft had to be launched by hoisting them out of the ship to take off from the surface of the sea and, ideally, gathering them in again afterwards. The disadvantages of this procedure became increasingly obvious, however. Carriers operating in this time-consuming way would tend to lose contact with the Fleet, making co-operation even more difficult than it was already and rendering them vulnerable to ambush by enemy forces. Also, with exasperating regularity, weather conditions in the North Sea were too bad for the seaplanes to take off successfully. Estimates inevitably vary, but one post-war study showed that only 35 of the 66 seaplanes launched operationally in the North Sea succeeded in taking off, and this takes no account of the many operations that were abandoned altogether, because of the weather, before such attempts were made.[3] As a case in point, the *Vindex* and *Engadine* attempted to launch 11 Sopwith Baby seaplanes to attack the German airship sheds at Tondern on May 4, 1916. Eight of these aircraft bent their propellers or flooded their magnetos trying to take off and had to be hoisted in again. One of the successful seaplanes immediately crashed into the mast of the accompanying destroyer *Goshawk* and another had to return with engine trouble. The sole survivor found his target in the mist and dropped two 65lb bombs, only to miss.

The theoretical desirability of being able to launch aircraft directly from the ship led to early seaplane carriers such as the *Ark Royal, Empress* and *Ben-My-Chree* being fitted with flying-off decks. But they were rarely used, generally proving too short – particularly in conjunction with a low ship-speed – even for light single-seater seaplanes, let alone the heavier machines required later for reconnaissance or torpedo duties. In August 1915, however, the *Campania* launched a single-seat seaplane, followed by a two-seater in June 1916, after her flying-off deck had been increased in length from 120 to 200ft. Seaplanes were used because they could land on the sea after their flight, but it was found that they could only be launched with some kind of disposable wheeled undercarriage.

Wheeled aircraft (or landplanes) were not only easier to launch, but were of much greater potential value in dealing with Zeppelins or for dropping torpedoes because their performance was not reduced by the weight and drag of the floats. Experiments in launching landplanes were conducted in the carrier *Vindex*, followed shortly by more in the *Manxman, Nairana* and *Pegasus*, all of which also carried two-seater seaplanes. The construction of the last two was especially significant in that they embodied, in rudimentary form, an aircraft lift, an important feature of the modern aircraft carrier. Another result of the same policy was the appearance of the carrier *Furious* in the first and most extraordinary of its many guises, with a huge 18in gun in the stern and a flying-off deck in the bows.

The seductive possibility of carrying aircraft with the Fleet without the need for cumbersome and vulnerable vessels built specifically for this task led at the same time to much effort being diverted away from carrier development and towards the launching of landplanes directly from fighting ships. This was done from the *Yarmouth* in June 1917 and by the end of the war 22 other cruisers had been equipped with similar small launching platforms. A pioneering flight from the *Repulse* on October 1, 1917, showed that platforms could be mounted on gun turrets capable of being trained into the wind, and many battleships were so fitted afterwards.

The problem with all these expedients, however, was that the aircraft could not be recovered by their ships. Unless they could reach land, the pilots were therefore forced to land in the sea in the hope of being picked up later. This hazardous procedure was expensive in aeroplanes, which were usually wrecked, and tactically very restricting in that commanders were reluctant to launch their one-shot aircraft until they were quite certain that no better opportunity would present itself later. This sometimes meant that they were launched too late or not at all. It was also recognised that the need to rescue stranded aircrew might prove embarrassing in the midst of a naval action.

Interest in carriers fitted with a special landing-on deck was stimulated by Sqn Cdr E. H. Dunning's brave but ultimately lethal feat of landing on the flying-off deck of the *Furious* in a Sopwith Pup on August 2, 1917. As a result of this, the new *Vindictive* was fitted with a 195ft flight deck suitable for flying off and landing on, and the *Furious* herself had her rear gun replaced by a landing-on deck at the stern. Neither of these moves completely solved the problem of recovery, however, and the *Furious* remained effectively a one-shot carrier as the air turbulence created by her bridge structure made landing on her deck almost as hazardous as ditching in the sea. In the justly famous Tondern raid of July 19, 1918, for instance, the *Furious* flew off seven Sopwith Camels, which successfully flew 80 miles to find, bomb and destroy the Zeppelins L54 and L60 in their sheds. Most of these aircraft were forced to fly on to neutral Denmark and the two aircraft which returned to the ship chose to ditch alongside rather than attempt to land back on the carrier.

The obvious answer to these difficulties seemed to be a vessel with a large and completely unencumbered flight deck offering the maximum in space and the minimum in air turbulence. One of the first attempts to grapple with this problem was made in 1915 by the extraordinarily inventive Flt Cdr H. A. Williamson, who roughed out a model of a vessel which included all the essential features of the modern carrier, such as an island and arrester wires. Such proposals caused much interest and industry, and the result was the *Argus*. This ship joined the Fleet two weeks before the Armistice and had a completely clear flight deck measuring 550ft × 68ft. The modern all-weather aircraft carrier had finally arrived.

A vast number of problems in carrier design remained to be solved, but the Royal Navy's accumulated expertise in such areas of carrier-associated technology as lift and arrester-gear design, flight decks and folding-wing aircraft put it in the best of positions to do so. Moreover, starting as early as the annual Fleet Manoeuvres of 1913 – in which the first seaplane carrier, *Hermes*, had participated – the Royal Navy had built up a store of experience in the operation of carriers with the Fleet. Much thought, for example, had gone into the question of the best position such vessels should take up as the Fleet deployed for battle, and the Battle Instructions had been rewritten several times to accommodate the latest technical and tactical thinking on the matter.

Much debate had also centred on the larger issue of how air power was best deployed at sea, for the carrier was certainly not the only means to this end. Airships, seaplanes, flying boats and aircraft launched from fighting ships all had advantages and advocates. But by and large the Royal Navy's research had focused on carriers, whereas the German Navy had concentrated on airships and the Americans had scattered their somewhat spasmodic efforts more evenly over the whole range of possibilities, especially the seaplane alternative.[4] For all these reasons, therefore, the Royal Navy seemed to have an almost unassailable lead in carrier design and operation as the inter-war period began.

Foreign navies certainly recognised the superiority of British experience in this field, and some officers of the US Navy in particular had kept a close eye on Royal Navy carrier progress during the war. After the American entry into the conflict, a stream of US officers came over to study British methods and carrier design philosophy. "So many of our ideas of naval (air) policy have been gained from the British," wrote one, "that any discussion of the subject must consider their methods."[5] Reports on the value and potential of British carriers like the *Furious* and *Vindictive* stimulated the normally cautious US Navy General Board into concluding in June 1919 that "to ensure air supremacy, to enable the United States to meet on at least equal terms any possible enemy, and to put the United States in its proper place as a naval power, fleet aviation must be developed to the fullest extent. . . ."[6] A fervent desire not to be behind the Royal Navy in anything reinforced US aspirations to exploit the potential of air power at sea for its own sake, and so American naval officers committed their country to what they called a "stern chase" of the British. For this and for other reasons, the co-operation of the war was followed by a decade of intense rivalry and some antagonism. The Royal Navy, anxious not to assist in its own eclipse, now restricted its old ally's access to British carriers, thereby causing great resentment. The US Navy had clearly to make its own way from now on, and the debut of the *Langley* in 1922 marked the American service's entry into the carrier race. In October of that year a US Navy pilot landed on the *Langley*, the first such landing on an American ship of any kind for over ten years. Despite their great achievements before the war, the Americans had clearly much leeway to make up.

Less concerned about their future rivalry, the British were more forthcoming to lesser naval powers such as Greece and France. Plans of the *Eagle*, for example, were passed over to the French to help in the somewhat leisurely construction of their first carrier, the *Bearn*. It was the Japanese, however, who profited most from British philanthropy in this particular field. The Japanese had decided to build up a naval air wing and, having long regarded the Royal Navy as their special mentors, asked for British assistance in 1920. The Admiralty was bitterly opposed to the idea that this request should be met, being suspicious of the purity of Japan's ultimate intentions. "The naval expansion of Japan," wrote the First Sea Lord, Admiral Beatty, "might become a considerable menace in the Far East. . . ."[7] This was the background for the suggestion by J. H. Narbeth (one of the most able carrier constructors of the period) for an elaborate deception of the Japanese officers currently roaming around British shipyards, notebooks in hand. Since it was then expected that flush-deck carriers were the way of the future, why not be very casual about the top-secret *Furious*, and attract their attention instead to the island-carriers *Eagle* and *Hermes* by a policy of ostentatious but deliberately careless secrecy? Ironically, it was the avenue down which Narbeth hoped to lure the Japanese, and which they perversely ignored, that turned out to be the right one.[8]

The objections of the Naval Staff to helping the Japanese were soon overborne by the Air Ministry and the Foreign Office, and a strong team of 30 ex-RNAS aviators was sent to Japan under the Master of Sempill. They laid the foundations of the Japanese naval air service in every area, from drawing up an air-training syllabus for naval cadets to providing assistance in the construction of the first Japanese carrier, *Hosho*. Alongside this, design teams from Sopwith and Shorts did much to launch the Mitsubishi Company on its successful career of aircraft construction. This all obviously saved the Japanese much time and effort, but they may have derived even more eventual benefit from the reinforcement this mission gave to the widespread and wholly mistaken Western notion that they were incapable of substantial technological progress on their own. "The Japanese are completely ignorant where the technical problems of naval aircraft are concerned," wrote the British Air Attache, "and the rate of progression depends entirely with the British Mission. . . . The ignorance of senior officers will be an effective brake for some time to come."[9] The holding of this view for longer than was actually justified was to prove very costly to the Royal Navy in the future.

But for the moment at least the British lead seemed assured. In March 1919 the Board of Admiralty assumed that the Royal Navy would very soon have a carrier force of eight vessels totalling 88,000 tons and deploying 118 aircraft in addition to the 161 carried by warships. Four of these ships were the essentially old-style seaplane carriers *Vindex*, *Nairaira*, *Pegasus* and *Vindictive*, totalling some 17,000 tons; the other four were true aircraft carriers, the *Argus*, *Furious*, *Eagle* and *Hermes*, with a total displacement of rather more than 71,000 tons.[10]

Early plans showed that senior officers were not content to let the Royal Navy rest on its laurels. Admiral Sir Charles Madden, C-in-C of the Atlantic Fleet, urged a vigorous carrier programme leading to the eventual creation of a war fleet of at least a dozen specialised carriers of various kinds. "It is necessary," he said, "to look well ahead. . . ."[11] Early in the following year the Deputy Chief of the Naval Staff, Admiral Brock, stressed that "the need for

One of the first naval flights. Lt C. R. Samson flying a Short Hydroplane off the *Hibernia*, anchored in Weymouth Bay, 1912. (Admiral Jerram)

Admiral Sir Murray Sueter. A difficult man but a brilliant pioneer of air power at sea. (FAA Museum)

When Winston Churchill became First Lord in October 1911 the RNAS gained a powerful ally – as this *Punch* cartoon of May 25, 1914, shows.

Opposite top The seaplane tender was the earliest form of aircraft carrier. HMS *Empress* with a short Type 184 seaplane aboard at Port Said, Egypt, 1916. (J. Howard Williams)

Opposite bottom A Sopwith Schneider single-seat seaplane just released by the *Empress* off Port Said, 1916. (J. Howard Williams)

A friend in high places. Admiral Sir John Jellicoe, C-in-C Grand Fleet and First Sea Lord. (Lady Latham)

Opposite top A Sopwith 1½-Strutter, piloted by Cdr Richard Bell Davies VC, takes off for the first time from the *Argus*, October 1918. Note the wind-direction flare. (Capt Fancourt)

Opposite bottom In August 1917 Sqn Cdr E. H. Dunning performed the very difficult feat of landing on the *Furious*. He was killed shortly afterwards while trying to repeat his success. (FAA Museum)

Some early forms of arrester gear. **Above** Bell Davies about to land in the "trap" on the flight deck of the *Argus*. The hooks on the axle of his 1½-Strutter were designed to catch the trap's longitudinal arrester wires. (Capt Fancourt) **Below** A Sopwith Pup on skids has overshot and run into the crash barrier on the *Furious*. (FAA Museum)

Some of the *Argus* deck-landing trials party. Rear-Admiral Sir Richard Phillimore (RAA) and, on the left, the first CO of the *Argus,* Capt H. H. Smith. (Capt Fancourt)

The world's first real aircraft carrier was the *Argus,* a flush-decker with a small charthouse which could be lowered or raised, as here, for navigational purposes. (FAA Museum)

An alternative way of taking air power to sea in 1918: a Sopwith Camel is lowered onto a platform built on X Turret of the battleship *Barham*. (Cdr Powell)

Wind speed and direction are tested. (Cdr Powell)

A Sopwith 1½-Strutter leaves the *Barham's* B Turret. (Cdr Powell)

A Fairey Flycatcher fighter takes off from the lower deck of the *Furious*. (Capt Fancourt)

Admiral Sir David Beatty photographed before the First World War wearing his famous "monkey jacket". He was later C-in-C Grand Fleet and First Sea Lord (1919–1927). Much of his energies in the 1920s went into the Admiralty's fight to regain control of the FAA.

Opposite top A Fairey Flycatcher flies past the *Eagle*. The 1924–5 Mediterranean cruise of this carrier greatly advanced the Royal Navy's development of air power at sea. (FAA Museum)

Opposite bottom The large and ungainly Blackburn Blackburn spotter-reconnaissance aircraft symbolised the importance which the Royal Navy attached to these demanding roles. Note the large portholes. (Admiral Torlesse)

Seaplanes were often used in amphibious operations. **Above** The *Argus* lowers a Fairey IIID into the Whangpao River, Shanghai, 1927. **Below** A detached flight of IIIDs operating near Wei Hai Wai. The FAA was involved in several such campaigns between the wars. (Capt Fancourt)

Admiral Sir Charles Madden (First Sea Lord 1927–30), who impressed the Air Staff with his early enthusiasm for the air. (Fox Photos)

Admiral Sir Reginald Henderson, shown here on the War Course at RNC Greenwich, 1931. Although not an aviator, Henderson gave the FAA its inspiration and its armoured carriers in the 1930s. He died of overwork in 1939.

A Fairey IIIF spotter-reconnaissance aircraft about to go over the side of the *Glorious*, with the crew jumping for safety. (Capt French)

The *Hermes*, the world's first purpose-designed carrier, seen over the tail of a Fairey IIIF. (A. Till)

A Hawker Nimrod fighter crashing into the sea from the *Glorious*, 1932. (Capt French)

A striking force of Blackburn Ripon torpedo bombers is marshalled on the *Glorious*, 1932. Note the attendant destroyer astern. (Capt French)

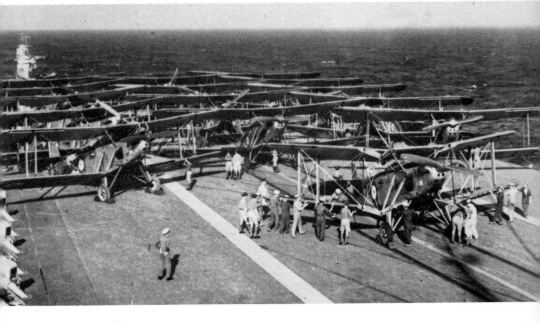

A Ripon drops its torpedo. The torpedo bomber was the Navy's standard attack aircraft. The swastika, seen here decorating the Ripon's wheel hub, had yet to acquire its present sinister connotation. (Capt French)

This Fairey IIIF has just landed on the *Hermes*. Illustrating the inter-service character of carrier aviation at this time, the picture shows Navy and RAF ground crew preparing to secure the aircraft. (A. Till)

aircraft carriers is urgent and other things being equal they should take priority." Accordingly, the carriers *Eagle, Furious* and *Hermes* were moved to the head of the queue in Portsmouth, Rosyth and Devonport dockyards respectively. Shortly afterwards it was decided to proceed with the conversion of the *Glorious* and *Courageous*.[12]

Longer-term plans had very much to be borne in mind at the Washington naval disarmament negotiations of 1921, and at this time the Naval Staff aimed at an ultimate peacetime fleet of 125,000 carrier tons, possibly allocated between five carriers of 25,000 tons each.[13] This would allow two carriers for both Main Fleets and one spare to cope with accidents and refits. At Washington, however, the US Navy vigorously fought for and eventually gained a total allowance of 135,000 carrier tons. This of course obliged the British to rethink, and by the spring of 1924 the Naval Staff had come up with a programme of construction which they hoped would cover the next ten years. Briefly, they assumed that – with the eventual scrapping of the *Argus, Hermes* and *Eagle*, and the completion of the *Furious, Glorious* and *Courageous* – the Royal Navy was entitled to another 68,000 carrier tons. This could possibly be allocated between two big carriers (as the US Navy was doing) or perhaps four smaller ships. In the end, they recommended that the construction of four new 30kt, 17,000-ton carriers should start in 1926, 1929, 1932 and 1935 respectively. The first should be complete three years after it was laid down, the remainder in four. By 1939 the carrier fleet would therefore comprise the *Furious, Glorious, Courageous* and the four new carriers, deploying some 242 carrier-borne aircraft between them.[14] This policy was formally adopted as a "Tentative Ten Year Programme" in early 1925. Although in retrospect the decision to opt for the smaller carriers was probably unwise, the programme as a whole provided for steady expansion at reasonable cost.

But even as the plan was being put forward, factors were at work which were beginning to undermine both its assumptions and its provisions. As planned, the four older (seaplane) carriers retired into the reserves, but the arrival of their replacements was much slower than had been originally anticipated in the autumn of 1920. The *Eagle* completed 18 months behind schedule in September 1923. The *Hermes* and *Furious* were both two years late (February 1924 and September 1925 respectively) and the *Courageous* five (February 1928). The delay to the *Hermes*, incidentally, meant that the ship was not the world's first purpose-built carrier, as is sometimes claimed: the Japanese *Hosho* actually commissioned first in December 1922, so revealing the vulnerability of the British lead.[15]

The construction of the four new carriers fared even worse than this. In May 1925 the laying down of the first was put back from 1926 to 1928, and the second was cut out of the programme altogether.[16] Almost imperceptibly, the laying down of the first slid back a further year to 1929, and then in the spring of 1928 the Plans Division suggested that US and Japanese construction did not make the new carrier an urgent necessity. The ACNS at this time was Admiral Dudley Pound (a future First Sea Lord). As we shall see later, Pound proposed first a reduction in the number of aircraft planned. Then he suggested that the new carrier be postponed until 1932–33 and the old *Argus, Eagle* and *Hermes* kept a little longer. This, after some discussion, was adopted by the First Sea Lord (Madden) in November 1928.[17] Although accepted by the Cabinet in 1925, the Admiralty's carrier construction programme had in effect completely collapsed within a space of three years. Shortly afterwards, moreover, the new carrier was deferred yet again to 1936 "unless foreign programmes rendered its earlier completion necessary."[18]

Since it had very serious consequences for the future of British naval aviation, it is important to identify the reasons for the collapse of this programme. The economic situation certainly contributed; gross trade and budget deficits and pre-Keynesian theory dictated savage economies in all fields of Government expenditure in the early 1920s if the country was to be restored to economic health. The Admiralty felt the now chill wind blowing from the Treasury just as much as all other departments of state, and the Navy's carrier programme was an early casualty.

A reluctance both to lose the possible rewards of past expenditure and to take up new and heavy commitments played an important part in the decision first to complete and then to retain all three of the older carriers, *Argus, Eagle* and *Hermes*. This had a number of unfortunate general results. For example, it strengthened the hand of those who sought to head off any large programme of new construction. The Chancellor of the Exchequer, Winston Churchill, used the Royal Navy's numerical supremacy in carriers to argue that Britain had "an unquestioned lead" and therefore little need for large new efforts.[19] Later, the First Sea Lord reconciled himself to the long postponement of the 1929 new carrier with the observation that the Royal Navy would have seven carriers to the US Navy's three "and numbers are of great importance."[20]

The economic situation also had important indirect effects on carrier construction. It played a part in the severe shortage of FAA manpower that so troubled the Board of Admiralty at the time and contributed to programme delays by reducing the Admiralty's design and constructional staff. In November 1923, for example, the Controller demanded an enquiry into the reasons for the delay to the *Hermes, Eagle* and *Furious*. In reply, the Director of Naval Construction pointed to shortages of staff and "the present abnormal pressure of work in the Department [with] so much design and construction in progress."[21]

The Government's reluctance to countenance heavy defence expenditure was reinforced by its general expectations of naval disarmament and international tranquillity in the era which started with the Washington Naval Treaty of 1921–2. The terms of the treaty itself were not particularly restrictive: Britain, being allowed an adequate carrier tonnage of 135,000 tons, had the option of replacing her earlier carriers with large and modern construction. Its effects, however, proved to be much more of a restraint than the terms suggest, because the anticipations produced by the treaty combined with the call for economic restraint to bring about the celebrated Ten Years Rule, under which the services were directed that they need not contemplate a major war for the next ten years. In 1925 this directive was applied to the Navy's preparations for a possible war against Japan, an act of self-restraint which played a significant part in the decision to postpone the 1926 new carrier to 1929. Its subsequent further deferral also reflected the hope that there would soon be further international reductions in carrier tonnage limits which would make its completion unnecessary.[22]

Other professional and technical anxieties manifested themselves in the repeated postponements of the 1926 carrier. Almost certainly, the greatest single cause of delay in the programme was not the need for economic restraint but the inhibiting effect of the very large number of technical uncertainties about carrier construction that still remained. Many questions were as yet unanswered. Should carriers have flush decks or islands, for example? After all, the time was not long past when plans could seriously talk of "an island . . . on each side of the ship, with a navigating bridge across [the] top . . . and a large yielding net . . . to be spread over [the] space thus enclosed in [the] middle of the ship in order to trap aeroplanes."[23] The ideal arrangement was still a matter for debate in the early 1920s, and the Royal Navy was in fact the first to settle on the correct solution.[24]

The British were much less surefooted on the question of the carrier's armament. Did carriers need to be able to take on enemy cruisers in an artillery duel and to what extent should they rely on AA guns for protection against air attack? The policy on the provision of guns for carriers was subject to constant change and caused much delayed construction of the *Hermes*, *Glorious* and *Courageous* — just as it did the US Navy's *Lexington* and *Saratoga*, in fact.[25] Both navies were also intrigued by the idea of the "Flying-deck Cruiser" and the "Battleship-carrier," hybrid warships capable of operating a reasonable number of aircraft and mounting a heavy gun armament as well.

Views on the ideal tonnage of Fleet carriers were also particularly subject to change. Given a definite ceiling on carrier tonnage, it was by no means easy to decide which was better: many small carriers or fewer large ones. Involved in this choice were complicated questions like the balance to be drawn between the higher aircraft/tonnage ratios of the larger carriers against the greater number of flight decks offered by the smaller ones. Once again, the Royal Navy came to the probably correct conclusion, that 20–23,000 tons was the ideal range, rather earlier than its competitors. It also pioneered the alternative idea of producing this size of carrier with two flying-off decks, as in the *Glorious* and *Courageous*.

Given such technical uncertainties, a certain flexibility of mind was no bad thing, though there were signs that during the 1920s this flexibility degenerated into indecision and a fainthearted readiness to let other navies take the risks. There was certainly a most noticeable "gradualism" in the British carrier construction programme, with every move depending upon the outcome of a previous one. Rather like a row of falling dominoes, the *Argus* trials affected the *Eagle*, the *Eagle* trials affected the *Hermes* and *Furious*, and these in turn helped determine policy on the 1926 New Carrier.[26] A delay in one part of such a process would inevitably mean that everything following it would be delayed too. Moreover, realising perhaps that in its legacy of old carriers it was already paying a heavy price for early pioneering work, the Royal Navy cautiously investigated everything to make sure it was right before building a ship that it might have to operate for the next 20 years. The Japanese and US navies, on the other hand, were more willing to make bold departures: both resolutely followed their first carriers with others that were three times as large, for example.[27]

In fact, the British sometimes consciously adopted a policy of "wait and see". Among the later reasons put forward for the second postponement of the 1926 New Carrier was, typically, a desire to see how the *Glorious, Courageous* and, above all, the new USS *Ranger* performed in practice.[28] The Royal Navy seems deliberately to have abandoned the initiative in this respect. "Our policy should be to maintain our freedom of action as far as possible," the Naval Staff argued, "so that we can meet at any time the building of new carriers by the USA."[29] While this policy may have been a good one as far as ultimate carrier design policy was concerned (after all, it did result eventually in the very efficient *Ark Royal*), it certainly imposed a penalty on immediate, modern carrier construction and all that went with it.

The Air Staff, of course, were well aware of these uncertainties, which served to confirm their own scepticism about the whole idea of the aircraft carrier. "I thoroughly agree with your view," wrote the Chief of the Air Staff in 1935, "about the policy of building large aircraft carriers. I am sure it is the wrong policy by reason of their vulnerability . . . the Admiralty do not seem to realise the extent to which ships are likely to be exposed to attack by shore-based aircraft." Carriers were so vulnerable to air attack, in fact, that they could not usefully be used within range of shore-based aircraft. Moreover, "there is a growing volume of opinion," the Air Staff reported, "that aircraft carriers do not constitute the best method of providing the air co-operation required by the Fleet." Aircraft carriers were "death traps," and many of their functions could be carried out by shore-based aircraft. By expressing such views the Air Staff offered much aid and comfort to the Treasury in its attempts to limit the Admiralty's carrier construction programme.[30]

Many naval officers also entertained doubts about the future value of carriers. They were undeniably awkward vessels to deal with. Flying operations required carriers to manoeuvre in perverse ways which much complicated Fleet handling. Their towering sides, flat tops, low standards of protection and poor gun armament made them so vulnerable to air and surface attack that valuable ships had to be detached to guard them. There were many outstanding design problems. For instance, because it was widely – and at the time quite reasonably – assumed that their aircraft could not be relied upon to stop an attack by enemy surface ships, carriers would have to be high-speed vessels. "It was generally agreed," at a conference in April 1931, "that if an aircraft carrier was to be able to act independently of cruiser protection and not be a hindrance and anxiety to the C-in-C, her speed should be sufficient to avoid action with more powerfully armed ships, and 32kt in the deep condition would be necessary."[31] These views reflected the fact that carriers were "sunk" with monotonous regularity in both American and British exercises of the period. Nevertheless, it was by no means easy to reconcile the need for speed with that for armour, guns and aircraft, and the apparent need to do so certainly imposed delays.

The coolness of some naval officers towards carriers was rooted in the belief that there were other and better ways of supplying the Fleet with its air component. In the USA Admiral Moffett had great hopes of airships and devoted much energy to their development.[32] The Royal Navy, on the other hand, moved from indifference to hostility towards airships and was clearly justified in so doing. Both navies were intrigued, however, by the possibilities offered by flying boats. The British Naval Staff expressed much interest in the concept of "an aircraft which would normally use the surface of the sea but could take to the air when necessary."[33] But it soon became clear that the flying boat's preferred habitat would actually be the air, and naval interest accordingly cooled. Occasional discussions of the possibility of replacing carriers with flying boats usually ended, as Chatfield noted, with a decision to continue with carriers "based on the improbability of any great advance in the capabilities of the flying boat in the near future making it fit to take the place in the Fleet of carrier-borne aircraft." In any case, British flying boats were the responsibility of the Air Ministry, and the Admiralty had little or no say in the policy governing them.[34]

Finally, there remained the option of using seaplanes carried in cruisers and battleships, a method which provided surface warships on detached operations with a measure of aerial self-sufficiency. The disadvantages, pointed out particularly by the Air Staff, were that this method of operation reduced the aeronautical performance and consequent value of the aircraft involved. There could thus be little doubt that for anything but reconnaissance or spotting such aircraft could only complement rather than replace carrierborne aircraft. The very extensive discussions held in the Fleet and by Naval Staff in the 1930s on the balance to be struck between ship and carrierborne aircraft solely concerned the issue of how aircraft might best be distributed. The primacy of carrierborne aircraft was not in question. Within these limits, however, the Royal Navy put great effort into the development of seaplanes, especially in the 1930s, and achieved a high level of skill. The best British cruisers could operate their seaplanes at night, guiding them back with blue lights, and in surprisingly rough seas, by turning their sterns to provide a temporary slick for the seaplanes to land on. All this, though, required a level of training not likely to be available in wartime.

The US Navy took an early lead in the operation of aircraft from orthodox warships, mainly because of its early development of the catapult. "Compared with the US," the Director of Naval Construction (DNC) noted in the summer of 1925, "our efforts [in developing the catapult] have been spasmodic," not least because of the way in which responsibility was divided between the Air Ministry and the Admiralty.[35] This was also partly a matter of deliberate design: "The Staff policy to go slow with catapults was adopted in 1922," Chatfield noted afterwards. "At that time we had very heavy commitments for aircraft carriers and it seemed better to spend available money in that way and to watch foreign catapult development rather than to try and develop both simultaneously."[36] The ability of the US Navy to pursue both lines of development at the same time must raise doubts, however, as to whether this policy of deliberate abstention was either necessary or wise. Nevertheless, the carrier still remained the best and principal means of bringing air power to the Fleet.

It is possible to feel, however, that delays in the carrier programme were imposed or accepted by senior officers, not so much because they felt there might be better ways of getting air power to sea, but because they were not totally convinced that this was an urgent necessity anyway. Looking back on Naval Staff deliberations at the time of the Washington Treaty, Admiral Backhouse wrote: " . . . it was also agreed at the time that it might be in our interest to keep down the numbers of aircraft carriers, especially with a reduced Fleet. It was felt that aircraft carriers were an extra and that they were of less importance to us than other classes of ships, besides being an expensive type to build."[37] Such observations indicate that a surviving scepticism about the potential of air power at sea was also a very likely cause of delays to its expansion. We have already seen, for instance, that discussions over the armament of carriers impeded their rapid completion, and a part may well have been played in this by convictions that the ability to fire guns was the distinguishing feature of the fighting ship. In one rather revealing passage the Naval Staff remarked: "It must be realised that when the ship is actually engaged with an enemy, it is impracticable for aircraft to be dispatched from or landed on the ship and therefore at such times [RAF personnel] should be capable of taking an active part in fighting the ship."[38]

Although general scepticism of the worth of air power at sea may certainly have played a part in the British carrier's loss of momentum in the 1920s, this kind of explanation should not be pressed too far. After all, while it was certainly true that as ACNS Dudley Pound much retarded air development in

1927 and 1928, it is also true that as Director of the Plans Division he had helped formulate the original 1925 Tentative Ten Year Programme in the first place. Equally, while Admiral Madden, as First Sea Lord, may have agreed to the second postponement of the New Carrier in 1928, he had as C-in-C Atlantic Fleet impressed the Air Staff as "extremely keen on all air problems,"[39] and had been responsible for formulating the requirement for a 12-strong carrier fleet. Thus there are no simple explanations of the causes of delay in the carrier construction programme.

It is however much easier to identify the generally very serious consequences of this delay. The first and most significant was the overlong retention of the *Eagle, Argus* and *Hermes*, ships aptly described by the First Lord as "... in the nature of gropings ... experimental and obsolete."[40] From the start, all three were considered too slow for Fleet operations and, since they collectively could operate only 48 aircraft while taking up one third of Britain's carrier tonnage entitlement, they were plainly very expensive to retain. For this reason there had from the start been a good deal of discussion as to whether these ships should all be completed. It seems reasonable to suppose that had the Naval Staff foreseen that the *Eagle* and the *Hermes* would still be operational 20 years later, they would not have supported their completion and retention in the first place. Having done so, however, they saddled their successors with a legacy which much reduced the carrying capacity of the Fleet.

This was a serious weakness, since the effectiveness of air power at sea was largely a function of number. The British would soon be at a further disadvantage, the result of their continued preference for large torpedo/spotter/reconnaissance (TSR) aircraft and for carriers with high standards of internal protection, both factors which limited carrying capacity. Moreover, the US Navy gained much advantage through its early mastery of athwartships arrester wires, which the British had investigated extensively in earlier days, when the problem had been different. The performance of the first naval aircraft was such that the difficulty lay not in stopping them after they had landed, but in preventing them from bouncing when their wheels first touched the deck. This frequently led to the wind getting under one wing and blowing the aircraft over the side. The need was therefore to hold the aircraft down, rather than to stop it, by making the flight deck "as adherent to an aeroplane as a flypaper is to a fly."[41] Accordingly, the British concentrated their early efforts on fore-and-aft wires and, when these eventually proved to be impracticable, abandoned arrester systems altogether in 1927.[42] This policy was enthusiastically supported by the airmen themselves, who thought landing was easier and safer without them. For the next five years the British did without, while the Americans forged ahead with their own athwartship wires. The Royal Navy eventually adopted athwartship wires[43] after experiments in the *Courageous* in 1931, but only after grave damage had been done to the British lead in carrier operations.

The absence of arrester wires reduced the Fleet's aircraft-carrying capacity in three quite distinct ways. First, as their performance increased, it grew more difficult to stop aircraft by wind pressure alone; carriers were forced to do a good deal of high-speed steaming into the wind, which wore out boilers (especially in the older ships), increased the need for refits and reduced carrier time on station. Second, the British needed the whole deck to recover their aircraft and so were not able to adopt the American practice of keeping large numbers of aircraft permanently on deck, in addition to those struck below.[44] British aircraft capacity figures therefore referred only to aircraft that could be stowed in the hangars. Third, the aircraft operating capacity of a carrier depended also on the endurance of the aircraft and the time taken to land it. One study, in 1925, showed that with a "landing interval" of five minutes per aircraft it was physically impossible for the *Furious* to put up all her 36 aircraft and recover them without some of them having to ditch into the sea after running out of fuel.[45] This relationship was recognised and British deck-handling parties evolved a routine that naval flyers of those days remember with admiration.[46] But since they had to stow their aircraft below in hangars while their USN counterparts had merely to roll them forward into the deck park, they were clearly operating under a severe disadvantage. In practice, this reduced the number of aircraft a British carrier could operate at any one time and so tended to reduce complement. Their experience in this area also had the unfortunate effect of persuading the British to take an excessively sceptical view of the aircraft complements of US and Japanese carriers.

For all these reasons, the decision to abandon arrester wires was clearly a retrograde step, leading the Royal Navy into a technological cul-de-sac and doing considerable damage to the development of British air power at sea. But this too was a story without a villain. It was a decision taken for the best of apparent reasons by the technical experts, wholly supported by the Air Staff (who believed that any form of mechanical retardation would damage performance and preferred airbrakes and oleo undercarriages) and the flying men themselves.[47]

The last great disadvantage suffered by the Royal Navy as a result of the failure of its carrier replacement programme was the fact that the diversity in age, speed and aircraft complement of British carriers made it more difficult to wield them as a tactical unit. The desirability of so doing was recognised from the start, and the early preference for carriers specialising in different Fleet functions (which simplified aircraft operation) clearly demanded that all the carriers be in roughly the same place at the same time.[48] The retention of the older carriers, with their increasing need for refits, and the existence of several fleets which all required their own carriers, made all this very difficult to arrange.

The indecisions, delays and financial stringencies of the late 1920s had therefore left the FAA with only moderate plans for expansion. Current think-ing envisaged the production of 241 aircraft by 1939, and the New Carrier, originally envisaged for 1926, had been deferred for ten years. British naval avi-ation was towed out of these doldrums by, of all things, the impending General Disarmament Conference at Geneva. Not for the first time, it took the imminent possibility of international limitations on arms to persuade the military that they needed a larger stockpile of weapons than they already had.

The ball seems to have been set in motion by the Controller, Admiral Sir Roger Backhouse, and the Director of the Naval Air Division, Capt C. E. Turle, who sent a proposal around the various naval staff divisions for a substantial increase in the projected aircraft strength of the Royal Navy. As a re-sult of the subsequent discussion, the Admiralty set aside the current figure of 241 aircraft by 1939 and discovered that it had an absolute minimum tactical require-ment for 405 aircraft and a legal entitlement under the Washington treaty to a total strength in excess of 500.[49] At the same time, Backhouse set up a conference to produce a design for the New Carrier, so as to prepare the British position for the naval disarmament talks to be held in Geneva in the following year. The conference decided that the New Carrier should be in the neighbourhood of 22,000 tons displacement, should carry 60 aircraft and be able to steam at 30kt at least. These parameters were explored in three alternative designs by the De-partment of Naval Construction by the end of 1931.[50]

Early in 1932, accordingly, the Admiralty proposed to the Foreign Office that Britain's negotiating stance at the forthcoming conference should reflect a formal national requirement for a naval air service comprising five such carriers and 400 aircraft. Despite strenuous objections from the Air Staff, this was the vision of the future that Britain's naval negotiators took with them to Geneva.[51]

Although this conference seemed likely to achieve little from very early on in its proceedings, it would obviously have been inexpedient for the Admiralty to have laid proposals for substantial expansion of the Fleet Air Arm before the MacDonald Government while the talks were still going on, especially as the Prime Minister himself was personally committed to the idea of arms limitation as a cure for the world's ills. For this reason, it was not until December 1933 that the First Lord, Monsell, put the Admiralty's proposals before the Cabinet. He asked for the *Ark Royal*, a 22,000-ton carrier with an aircraft complement of 72, to be included in the 1934 construction programme, pointing out that three of the six carriers currently in service with the Royal Navy were experimental and deficient in speed and complement. The US Navy, on the other hand, would have six modern carriers by 1935 and the Japanese had five, built or building.[52]

The Air Ministry objected to this proposal on five separate counts, and there were some pointed exchanges between the two departments over the next few weeks. The Air Staff argued that this was an unacceptably large increase in Fleet Air Arm strength, and one that was not justified by strategic necessity. The

Royal Navy, they claimed, had a "considerable superiority" over the Japanese, and acceptance of a small US Navy lead in deployed carrier tonnage (131,000 tons compared with 115,000) for the next few years "would not involve any appreciable risk." Moreover, they said, there were many technical uncertainties remaining in carrier construction and there was "surely much to be said for gaining experience, if possible, by the expenditure of other countries." They also thought that large carriers like the *Ark Royal* would be too vulnerable to air attack and doubted whether the ship could operate 72 aircraft, generally believing that 50 was about the maximum that could reasonably be hoped for. There was something to be said for this last point, as the *Ark Royal's* normal complement was in fact about 60, given adequate workshop capacity and storage. The rest of the Air Ministry's technical objections proved however to have been particularly ill-founded.

Although these Air Staff opinions were genuinely held, there is little doubt that their expression was coloured by departmental pique at not having been consulted in the preparation of the Admiralty's programme. Alluding to the vexed question of who actually "owned" the FAA, the Chief of the Air Staff noted: "The risking of so large a part of the RAF as six squadrons of the Fleet Air Arm in so vulnerable a type of ship is a matter on which we can definitely claim to be heard."[53] Although the Admiralty won this particular battle with the Air Ministry relatively easily, the significant thing is that it had to be fought at all.

The *Ark Royal* was eventually completed in 1938, having been delayed for some six years by this combination of naval faintheartedness and design uncertainty, Air Ministry opposition, economic restraints and the anticipation of naval disarmament. Fortunately for the future of the Naval Air Service, the *Ark Royal* proved to be a most impressive ship, incorporating many new design features such as the first British safety barrier and carrier-mounted "accelerators" (or, more familiarly, catapults), together with a good standard of protection. Its success shows that the Royal Navy certainly had not fallen significantly behind in carrier design by this time.

If the Naval Staff had little need for concern about the quality of British carrier construction, they were understandably anxious about its extent. During the course of their campaign for the *Ark Royal* they showed that while Britain, Japan and the USA would all have six carriers built or being built in 1934, the Royal Navy would lag badly behind the other two in numbers of carrierborne aircraft.[54] The need for further construction of modern carriers was reinforced by the impasse at Geneva and Germany's obvious intention to rearm. Accordingly, a new construction programme was put forward by the Defence Requirements Committee (DRC), which envisaged the building of 12 battleships (seven in 1937–9) and four carriers in 1936–42. Although the balance between these two classes of ship might be criticised for emphasising the old at the expense of the new, it was all needed if Britain was to have parity with Germany and Japan in 1942. The four new carriers were expected to replace the *Argus, Eagle, Hermes* and *Furious* as Fleet carriers and to serve alongside the existing *Glorious* and *Courageous* and the completing *Ark Royal*.

The DRC programme was put before the Cabinet on February 25, 1936, and the Admiralty was duly authorised to proceed. Accordingly, the 23,000-ton *Illustrious* and *Victorious* were laid down in 1937, with the *Formidable* and *Indomitable* following in 1938. Additionally, the Admiralty ordered the interesting *Unicorn*, an "FAA supply and repair ship" which was intended to support the operations of the *Illustrious* class. Throughout this period the Admiralty was aiming at an eventual "New Standard Fleet" for 1946, with an air component of 577 first-line aircraft and 14 carriers, of which eight would be new construction.[55] The *Ark Royal* and the *Illustrious* class represented the first five of these vessels, and the question of the next three was considered in the autumn of 1938.

The Admiralty's "Air Requirements in War Committee" of that year wanted another six new carriers to be laid down at a rate of one per year beginning in 1939. All this would eventually produce 11 new Fleet carriers, plus the *Unicorn* and two or three old carriers in reserve for use on such subsidiary tasks as trade protection. In October 1938 it was decided that three of the six should be authorised for the years 1939–41 but that the remaining three should be deferred for the time being for reasons of economy. The construction of the first two of these, the *Indefatigable* and *Implacable*, was in hand by the time the war began, but they were subject to constant delay and the third in fact never materialised. The carrier fleet, thus envisaged, comprised three Fleet carriers in home waters, two in the Mediterranean and two for the West or East Indies, with the last of the new carriers remaining at home for training purposes. There would also be the *Argus* for gunnery co-operation duties, the *Unicorn* FAA depot ship, and two or three carriers in reserve for trade defence.[56]

By the time the Second World War began, therefore, the Royal Navy had 14 carriers built or being built, compared with the US Navy's eight and Japan's 11. But the position was not as favourable to the British as these figures might suggest, for only half the Royal Navy's carrier fleet was operational in September 1939, and this included the three old first-generation carriers, the *Argus, Eagle* and *Hermes*. These old ships did not carry as many aircraft as their newer foreign counterparts; nor, for that matter, did the modern British carriers.

The main reason for this was the British insistence on very high standards of protection. The Royal Navy's ship designers had always tended to treat the hangar in a carrier as though it were a magazine requiring much protection. Even the "unarmoured" *Ark Royal* was in fact very well protected by foreign standards. The *Illustrious* class of armoured carriers merely went one step further when, in July 1936, it was decided to give these ships a three-inch armoured flight deck and 4½-inch side armour. Since it was desired to keep these ships to a displacement of roughly 23,000 tons, these high standards of protection reduced aircraft complement. The *Illustrious* displaced 1,000 tons more than the *Ark Royal* but carried only half the number of aircraft. The disparity seemed even greater when the *Illustrious* was contrasted with foreign carriers of the time. The Japanese carriers could all carry a much higher number of aircraft per ton of displacement, but the Controller, Admiral Henderson, was particularly perturbed by the comparison between the *Illustrious* (23,000 tons and 36 aircraft) and the USS *Ranger* (14,500 tons and 75 aircraft). "Apparently," he complained, "we cannot look at this."[57]

The decision to accept a reduced aircraft complement in return for very high standards of protection reflected several important Naval Staff assumptions about how carriers would be operated. First, in innumerable exercises of the period, carriers operating with the Battle Fleet had either been sunk by pre-emptive air strikes or had been ambushed by surface units when they had strayed from the protection of the battle line in order to operate their aircraft. Both of these dangers seemed to point at the need for carriers able to withstand damage. Also, British carriers would probably have to operate in the narrow North and Mediterranean seas, well within range of shore-based air power, and this too seemed to demand structural resilience. Second, the Royal Navy tended on the whole to be sceptical about the potential of fighter protection and so assumed that the carrier would look for defence against air attack primarily to its own and the Fleet's AA gunnery and to its own inherent strength. This policy would also have the advantage of increasing the proportion of carrier aircraft that were capable of significant offensive action against the enemy.

In fact, though, the potential aircraft complements of these vessels were not as low as the original raw figures seem to suggest. In the first place, it was always intended that the *Unicorn* would support the *Illustrious* class in a way which would have increased their effective aircraft operating capacity. *Unicorn* was however only completed in March 1943, having been delayed by the advent of other more urgent requirements. Various operational improvements and the extension of the flight deck also pushed the aircraft complement of the *Illustrious* class up to a respectable 50 or so by the end of the war. Finally, later examples were inevitably better than the original. Alterations to the armour arrangements of the last three armoured carriers allowed them to operate many more aircraft – 81 in the case of the *Implacable* – without appreciable loss of protection.

Although designed only to withstand 500lb semi-armour-piercing bombs, a requirement shared by other navies but undoubtedly on the low side as an estimate of what enemy aircraft would be able to attack her with, the *Illustrious* and her sisters proved able to survive much more. Their subsequent performance in the Mediterranean and Pacific theatres does much to justify their design philosophy, and many of their design features were adopted for later British and American carriers.

The armoured carrier programme showed that shortages of resources had not after all stifled the Admiralty's capacity to experiment and to make bold new departures in carrier design. It would have been much easier merely to have ordered some "repeat *Ark Royals*," but the Controller, Admiral Henderson, was adamant that the new vessels should be armoured. Henderson, who did more for naval aviation than any other Flag Officer of the inter-war period, was clearly the driving force behind the whole programme, and its rapid progress illustrated the extent of his energy, determination and preference for unorthodox methods. He cut the usual stately progress of carrier design from three years to three months. Although in the spring of 1936 there were neither staff requirements nor design studies for armoured carriers, the Admiralty Board was nevertheless able to approve the sketch design for the *Illustrious* in July of the same year. Bad health forced Henderson into a premature retirement in March 1939, and it was widely believed in the FAA that the programme slowed up in consequence, particularly affecting the *Implacable* (laid down February 1939) and the *Indefatigable* (November 1939). But, as we shall see, the urgent requirements of war production also played a part in this.[58]

In the last years of peace the attention of the Naval Staff turned to the question of carriers in the defence of trade. A need for convoys to operate their own air escorts had been recognised in the First World War[59] and the requirement surfaced in various guises from time to time during the 1920s and early 1930s. However, from the mid-1930s War College investigations and several exercises added weight to the argument. Estimates of the number of trade-protection carriers needed in peacetime usually hovered between four and six, but in October 1935 the Naval Staff argued that a simultaneous war with Japan and Germany would require no fewer than 16. "A carrier," it was concluded, "is essential to the successful conduct of every phase of the trade defence and is economical vis-à-vis cruisers similarly employed."[60]

There were three methods of producing carriers for this purpose. The first, also suggested in the First World War, was "for merchant vessels to be fitted and equipped for carrying machines of a suitable type." Shortly after the war the idea was taken up by the Director of Naval Construction, who prophetically suggested "Mercantile Aircraft Carriers," even to the extent of using grain ships and oil tankers for the purpose. In correspondence with the Chief of the Air Staff, he also outlined proposals for Mail Steamer Carriers capable of operating between 25 and 50 aircraft, which he thought would be "very valuable in convoys." But little was done about this idea, largely for reasons of cost.[61] It was nonetheless the Admiralty's declared intention to build and equip four Merchant Ship Carriers and a force of Armed Merchant Cruisers (AMC), with aircraft, once war had begun.

Trade-protection duties were also thought to be an appropriate occupation for elderly Fleet carriers. In 1942, for example, the Naval Staff told the Treasury that obsolescent Fleet carriers like the *Argus* and *Hermes* would be used

". . . eventually for the protection of our ocean trade routes". In October 1938 the First Sea Lord suggested that the *Eagle, Glorious* and *Furious* might be used for this once the armoured carriers to replace them had materialised.[62]

The third possibility was the purpose-built trade-protection carrier. One such vessel was originally included in the 1936 construction programme, and great effort went into the production of an appropriate design. Later it was planned to build seven 14,500-ton trade-protection carriers, each capable of operating 15 amphibious aircraft. The Naval Staff, however, had a distaste for the idea of expensive special-purpose vessels whose design seemed to rule out their effective co-operation with the Fleet. In addition, further investigation showed the notion to be prohibitively expensive, as small carriers were not as cost-effective as large ones. It was better, suggested Admiral Henderson, to have larger carriers operating many more aircraft, ". . . more possibly than in aircraft carriers attached to the Main Fleet. The ocean is very large and location of the enemy will need a lot of aircraft sweeping." Unfortunately, these considerations made the cost of each ship too high for peacetime planners to contemplate; and there the matter rested for the rest of the inter-war period.[63] The Royal Navy therefore went to war – knowing very well that the protection of trade would be its ultimate preoccupation – without a single escort carrier built, building or planned, although the requirement for such vessels had been known for 20 years.

Nonetheless, the Navy was not blind to the necessity of trade protection. The root of the Admiralty's failure lay in its conviction that Asdic and other developments had defeated the submarines, and that the main threat to shipping was once more posed by the surface warship. "Nothing," the Staff believed a month before the war, "would paralyse our supply system and seaborne trade so certainly or immediately as successful attack by surface raiders." To deal with surface raiders, Dudley Pound told the other Chiefs of Staff, "We will need all the aircraft carriers on which we can lay our hands. . . . The carriers will be required not only to find them, but also to strike and reduce their speed in order to enable our slower capital ships to catch and destroy them."[64]

This assumption coloured all recommendations for the protection of trade. One of the reasons, for example, why small purpose-built carriers were so expensive was that the Naval Staff wanted them to have armoured flight decks to protect them against surface ship attack on the high seas and air attack in the narrows. Even with the greater resources released by the war, it was only possible to produce escort carriers by making them as simple – and therefore as cheap – as possible. The apparent requirement for this standard of excellence in peacetime made the provision of such escorts quite impossible. Furthermore, the Admiralty based all its plans on the assumption that in any future naval war there would be a major engagement between the contending battlefleets. Since the results of this would be decisive, it was obviously necessary for the aerial needs of the battlefleet to take precedence over those of trade defence. If there were insufficient resources for both in the new construction programme, then the latter's needs would have to wait until the former's had been met. This had been the agreed and formal priority since 1936.[65]

It is probably also true that, even if the Admiralty had planned to build trade-protection carriers of one sort or another, the required aircraft would not have been available. The Air Staff reacted to projections of aircraft needs in this area with a ferocious hostility unusual even in the embittered atmosphere of the time. When the possibility of equipping AMCs with aircraft was discussed at a Chief of Staff meeting in December 1936, Air Marshal Sir Edward Ellington, the Chief of the Air Staff, stated flatly that "a decision to allocate aircraft solely for duties in connection with the protection of trade could not be carried out within a reasonable time while our capacity to expand the Air Force was fully required for the provisions already authorised." The same message was driven home a month before the war. "[It is] imperative," said Air Vice-Marshal Sir Cyril Newall, "to resist further inroads into a Metropolitan Air Force which would already be very hard put to it to carry out its responsibilities in war. . . . It would be preferable that we should face the risk of losses on our trade routes in the Atlantic than accept a further reduction of our Air Forces at home, which we could not afford."[66]

The difficulty really lay in the fact that the Admiralty's programme to build up its trade protection forces, and indeed the whole of its Naval Air Service, co-incided with similar efforts in the Air Ministry, which, as we shall see later, inevitably took up the majority of the country's air resources. In this way, one of the fundamental reasons for continuing weakness in the FAA lay in the even more obvious deficiencies of the RAF.

Although for the first few months of the war the FAA was indeed much involved in the protection of trade, the first real test of the quality of its carriers came with the Norwegian campaign of 1940. The all-important benefits of close air support were demonstrated in most of the land and sea battles of this campaign, but since Norway was substantially out of range of most of its airfields, the RAF could not provide it. The Navy had therefore to step in and try to meet the Army's needs. The usefulness of the German seaplanes, the endeavours of the naval Walrus flight operating from Harstad, the seaplanes of the British cruisers, and above all the extraordinarily valuable flight of the *Warspite*'s Swordfish at Narvik all did much to justify the Navy's inter-war faith in the worth of float-equipped aircraft. But it was primarily on the presence and efficiency of the air-craft carriers that success depended. The enormous value of the carrier in amphi-bious operations became clear for the first time off Norway.

The problem, however, was that the Navy simply did not have enough of them. The *Argus, Eagle* and *Hermes* were too old and slow for this kind of dangerous operation, which clearly required Fleet carriers of the best sort. Whatever its plans for the future, the Royal Navy only had four of these when the war began. One of them, the *Courageous*, was recklessly used and lost in a misguided anti-submarine operation within a fortnight of the war's beginning, and the *Ark Royal* very nearly went the same way. The Admiralty quickly realised that Fleet carriers were too valuable to risk in this kind of work and that, in the absence of purpose-built trade-protection carriers, some other way of taking aircraft to sea, which could defend sea communications without mortgaging the future security of the Battlefleet, had best be found. Even so, when the Norwegian campaign began, the British had only three Fleet carriers, two of which were away training in the Mediterranean, and the third only partly operational and not fully integrated into the Fleet. The Fleet's lack of a carrier in the first stages of the German invasion was undoubtedly a severe handicap to Forbes' attempts to intercept the German force at sea.

The value of the first carrier on the scene, the *Furious*, was limited by her age, low complement of 18 aircraft and lack of fighters, but her achievements in spite of these disadvantages gave a clear foretaste of what the well protected and complemented strike carrier force of later years would be able to do in such circumstances. The subsequent arrival of the *Ark Royal* and *Glorious* emphasised this message. Nevertheless, the campaign also showed that carriers were vulnerable. All of them were near-missed at some stage by enemy aircraft, and the *Glorious* was destroyed by gunfire. The campaign therefore emphasised the value of fighters and underlined the need for carriers capable of absorbing damage from bomb, shell and torpedo.

In the month before the Norwegian campaign began, the First Lord, Churchill, initiated a discussion of precisely this point. "It must be clearly understood," he wanted to argue, "that the role of the two armoured carriers in 1940 and 1941 must be the defence of the Fleet when at sea or at Scapa against shore-based aircraft. . . ." The *Illustrious* commissioned shortly after the Norwegian campaign ended. Carriers of this type might have been able to stand more closely into Norwegian waters and take on enemy aircraft and ships more confidently. But Churchill was also well aware of their Achilles heel: the lack of modern fighters. Without them, "these splendid vessels immune from the 500lb bomb can go into the the danger area but cannot do anything effective or indispensable when they get there."[67] For this reason, even had the armoured carriers been ready in time for the Norwegian campaign, the Royal Navy would probably not have had the men and aircraft for it to have made a decisive difference.

The Admiralty's carrier construction policy after the Norwegian campaign[68] was very ambitious by immediate pre-war standards. In addition to a large programme of escort carriers and AMCs of various kinds, the Admiralty was authorised to proceed with 31 new Fleet carriers (four *Ark Royals*, three *Maltas*, ten *Colossus*, six *Majestics* and eight *Hermes*), a programme which itself bears striking testimony to the central importance of this kind of ship to the war at sea.

The Admiralty continued its pre-war pursuit of excellence in carrier design

and construction. It recognised the importance of strengthening the carrier component of the Fleet and, in introducing the New Construction Programme
(NCP) of 1942, stated the need for a Fleet of 16 carriers with 48 aircraft each by
1946, a target well above the four new carriers and three old ones which, barring
losses, the Fleet would otherwise have had. In October 1941 the Naval Staff
argued that the Mediterranean and Atlantic wars had afforded "striking evidence of the value of carrierborne aircraft in finding and fixing the enemy and in
providing air protection for our forces operating in narrow waters."[69] In their
planning the Naval Staff had particularly in mind the enormous air efforts
which they would be required to make when the Royal Navy moved back into
the Pacific, but they also had an eye on the needs of a balanced Fleet after the
war.

The Navy's carriers came in three categories of descending excellence:
Armoured, Light Fleet and Escort carriers. The Armoured carriers – such as the
four *Ark Royal* class of 1942 (37,000 tons and 100 aircraft) and the three *Malta*
class (46,900 tons), arguably "the most advanced carriers of their day" – were
ships whose design amply illustrates this continued preference for excellence.
But since all three of the last class and two of the first had to be cancelled and the
survivors did not complete until long after the war, the cost of such a policy was
evidently too great to pay.

In fact, Britain's shipyards were at full stretch for the first two years of the
war and it was hardly possible for any new carriers to be started. The four *Illustrious* class (the *Illustrious, Victorious, Formidable* and *Indomitable*) were completing,
with the *Implacable, Indefatigable* and *Unicorn* following along. There was an urgent need, too, for small craft, especially landing craft and anti-submarine and
minesweeping vessels; for merchant ships, of which some one million tons were
supposed to be built every year; and for the repair of increasing numbers of war-
damaged ships. Carriers, battleships and cruisers would have to take their turn.

Nevertheless, there was an increasing anxiety that carriers were not getting
their proper priority. The lead in this seems to have been taken by Capt Charles
Lambe (the Director of the Plans Division and a future First Sea Lord) and the
Controller, Admiral W. F. Wake-Walker. Their efforts were much helped by
events in the Pacific, particularly the battle of Midway, which demonstrated the
value of the offensive and defensive capabilities that could only be provided by
fleet carriers. Suddenly, in the spring and summer of 1942, the carrier began seriously to challenge the position of the battleship as the Navy's capital ship.

As a result, there was a great surge of interest in carrier construction of all
kinds. All methods of increasing the air component of the Fleet were considered
afresh. Even the liners *Queen Elizabeth* and *Queen Mary* were examined to see
whether they could profitably be converted into super-carriers, a project only
abandoned when it was found that they could operate no more than 80 aircraft.
The main upshot of all this activity, however, was the ambitious construction

programme of Armoured and Light Fleet carriers which the Admiralty put before the War Cabinet in August 1942.

In the ensuing discussions and decisions there were interesting echoes of pre-war controversies, especially with the Air Ministry. "Is it certain," asked Sir Archibald Sinclair, the Secretary of State for Air, that "aircraft carriers have been proved successful, particularly when operating within range of enemy land-based aircraft, as at Midway?"[70] Old prejudices, it seems, die hard. Sinclair went on to insist that the aircraft these carriers would require should not be produced at the expense of any reduction in the offensive capacity of the RAF. Other members of the War Cabinet were more sympathetic. The Minister of Production, for example, did not see why the Admiralty should cancel four cruisers to get its carriers. "In my view," he said, "the proportion of national effort devoted to shipbuilding is too small."[71]

Eventually, the Admiralty were authorised to proceed with four Armoured carriers (the *Ark Royals*), 16 Light Fleet carriers (the *Colossus* and *Majestic* classes) and, later, another eight Improved Light Fleet carriers (the *Hermes* class). The Light Fleets were initially intended as stopgaps to strengthen the carrier fleet at the earliest moment, being small, fast enough to operate with the Fleet and simple enough to be handed over to civilian contractors. With their lower complements and running costs, they proved to be very successful as fleet carriers and were retained to become "the backbone of the post-war British Commonwealth Fleet".[72] The first four of them passed through Trincomalee in the summer of 1945, ready for operations in the Pacific but in fact arriving too late to take part. Less ambitious specifications made possible the speedy construction of effective ships whose more timely arrival would certainly have eased the Royal Navy's problems earlier in the war.

The same problem of relative priority was also evident in the Escort Carrier programme, another response to the need for large numbers of relatively unsophisticated carriers. The war showed that the Naval Staff had paid insufficient attention to the needs of trade protection, and that its emphasis on the AMC was probably misplaced. Early in 1941 a "panic yellowjacket" (a docket put in a yellow cover for top-priority treatment) went round the Naval Staff about the urgent need to deal with the depredations of the U-Boat and the Fw 200 Condor on the trade routes. This requirement inspired a series of such expedients as Fighter Catapult ships, CAM (Catapult-armed Merchantship) ships and, later, MAC (Merchant Aircraft Carriers) ships. It also led to the celebrated Escort Carrier, another new departure in the development of the aircraft carrier.

In early 1941 the Admiralty turned its attention to the provision of special carriers for the protection of trade, only to run into opposition from the Ministry of War Transport, which was reluctant to release valuable large merchant hulls for this purpose. All the same, the construction of five was initiated in May 1941 and another six were ordered from the US. In September that year the very makeshift *Audacity* sailed on her first convoy and, as we shall see later, did very well. This success showed that the task of providing convoys with air cover could be effectively carried out with ships of the most simple and austere kind, so large numbers became possible after all.

In fact 44 escort carriers entered service with the Royal Navy, the great majority of them built in the US. Their incorporation into the Fleet was delayed, to the irritation of some US Navy officers, by the Admiralty's insistence, especially after the *Avenger* was sunk by a single torpedo and the *Dasher* gutted by an internal explosion, on extensive improvements to the fuel storage systems, the lengthening of the flight decks and, in some cases, the installation of fighter direction facilities. The British-built Escorts were more refined still, even having the by now traditional integral hangar, with accordingly reduced aircraft complements. Here again, "Admiralty standards" imposed delays, usually of about three months, but were clearly justified by subsequent events. American Escort carriers were soon shown to be much more vulnerable to submarine and air attack, several of them consequently sinking with heavy loss of life. Even thus improved, the Royal Navy's Escort carriers were still relatively cheap and simple ships. But they provided a very effective response to the trade-protection problem, and also turned out to be surprisingly good as assault carriers in the many amphibious operations that followed their arrival in the Fleet.[73]

Ship design and production policy is always a compromise between quantity and quality. The Royal Navy attempted to reconcile these inevitably conflicting attributes by reducing its Armoured Fleet Carrier programme, stepping up production of Light Fleets and producing a series of modified Escorts. This was not easy. The increasing performance of aircraft, for instance, caused the Naval Staff to argue that the *Colossus* class of Light Fleet carriers would not be able to operate modern aircraft beyond 1947 and so would then have to be redeployed to the trade-protection role. Instead it would be necessary to press for the heavier and more expensive *Hermes* class of 1943, ships which it would be possible to retain after the war. The technology of naval aviation was advancing so rapidly that it caused frequent adjustments to existing plans. Like this one, such revisions were virtually always in the direction of increased size and expense.[74]

In addition to the general problem of reconciling quantity and quality, the Navy's carrier construction programme had to compete with other equally voracious demands on British shipbuilding and general war-fighting resources. The Fleet carrier programme seemed especially profligate of money and manpower in that it was intended for a force which, according to Churchill, "is only occasionally and very slightly engaged with the enemy and which is a direct subtraction from our immediate war effort.'"[75] The trouble lay at least partly in the fact that the Naval Staff based its construction programme on the requirements of an approaching war with Japan and on their perceptions of what a balanced post-war Fleet should be like, while the Prime Minister and the other services wished to concentrate the country's slender resources on the needs of the current war in Europe. This strategic division had in fact existed long before hostilities began, and it was one that inevitably retarded and reduced the Navy's carrier construction programme.

After prodigious efforts, the British eventually emerged from the Second World War with a total of 19 Fleet carriers built or building, roughly half the US total. During the war it took the British an average of $38\frac{1}{2}$ months to complete each Fleet carrier, while American shipbuilders managed to complete the *Essex* class in an average of some 18 months. In short, the vicissitudes, size and quality of the British carrier construction programme when compared to that of the US Navy symbolised the growing disparity in the industrial resources of the two countries.

CHAPTER FOUR

THE AIRCRAFT

*"Our Fleet Air Arm aircraft are hopelessly outclassed
by everything that flies. . . ."*

ADMIRAL SIR CHARLES FORBES
C-in-C Home Fleet, July 1940

The First World War saw an enormous increase in the number and quality of aircraft deployed for naval purposes. At the outbreak of war the RNAS had 93 machines, of which only about 50 were actually usable and fewer still capable of working with ships. By the time the RNAS was absorbed into the RAF four years later, it had become a large and effective force of over 55,000 officers and men deploying nearly 3,000 land and seaplanes. While in raw numbers the US Navy, with its 1,865 flying boats and seaplanes and 242 landplanes, was not far behind, the two navies differed widely in their experience of operating aircraft with the Fleet[1].

The most significant aspect of this experience was the Royal Navy's work with wheeled aircraft in support of the Fleet. Much of the pioneering work in the development of air power at sea had actually been done by seaplanes, but by 1916 it was clear that the war potential of these aircraft was limited. Landplanes were needed to deal with Zeppelins, to carry out extended spotting and reconnaissance flights and, perhaps above all, to lift and drop effective torpedoes and return to the decks of the ships that had launched them. After the flight of a Bristol Scout from the deck of the *Vindex* on November 3, 1915, the future evidently lay with aircraft like the Sopwith Pup and Camel (fighters), the 1½-Strutter (reconnaissance) and the Cuckoo (torpedo-bomber). At the Armistice there were nearly 300 of these machines serving with the Fleet and, according to Admiral Phillimore, had the Navy fought its "great sea battle of 1918," about 100 aircraft would have taken part[2].

War had stimulated enormous progress in aeronautics, a good deal of which had been carried over into naval aviation. The rate of technical development was very rapid, with one breakthrough following another with extraordinary speed, and it is not surprising that in this rush there were mistakes and oversights. The prototype of the Sopwith Cuckoo, for example, was allowed to moulder away in a forgotten corner of the factory until a visiting airman chanced to ask what it was. The inspiring genius behind this aircraft was Capt Murray Sueter, who later wrote angrily: "The stupidity in blocking torpedo aircraft when they could have been of some use and then ordering several hundreds which were delivered too late to be used in the war is quite beyond all comprehension." Advancing from the particular to the general, he claimed after the war that "the former Board of Admiralty did everything possible to prevent the RNAS doing their real work in the war."[3] Nevertheless, there can be little doubting the great store of aeronautical expertise built up in the Admiralty by the time of the Armistice, although a fair amount of it had admittedly been directed to such non-naval tasks as bombing Germany or defending Britain against air attack. "Owing to the precedence given to the demands of the Army during the war," commented the C-in-C Atlantic Fleet, Admiral Madden, "the development of the use of aircraft progressed more slowly at sea than on land. . . ."[4] Even so, the Admiralty had built up such close and abiding links with the aircraft industry that the interests of the RFC were felt to be swamped by those of the RNAS (especially where the latter service was doing the former's work), and this contributed greatly to the creation of the RAF in April 1918. Certainly, in the development of land aircraft the US Navy trailed far behind the British when the war ended, and in fact a large proportion of the American service's aircraft were either British or French in origin.

In the immediate post-war period, however, the number of aircraft deployed with the Fleet fell very sharply. Although in such fluid and uncertain times it was difficult to arrive at precise estimates, the number was not above 50 by the winter of 1919–20. Thereafter the total gradually rose to about 105 seaborne aircraft in 1924, where it remained for several years until the inauguration of the catapult programme and the commissioning of the *Glorious* and *Courageous* raised it to about 150. The efforts of the 1930s added another 80 or so front-line aircraft to the total by the time the Second World War began.

This unhurried rate of advance allowed the US Navy easily to overtake the British in terms of number of aircraft deployed at sea. Although the existence of the RAF makes straight comparisons awkward, the US Navy was certainly ahead by 1926. In that year, also, the lily was gilded by the report of the Morrow Board, which led Congress to authorise a programme designed to produce 1,000 naval (i.e. including land-based) aircraft by 1931. As a result of this programme the US Navy was able to deploy some 300 aircraft at sea by 1930, producing a naval air service that was twice as big as its erstwhile rival. The contrast was even greater by the end of the post-war period.[5]

This numerical inferiority was very serious indeed for the Royal Navy's aerial pretensions, as the quality of naval aviation was much bound up with the quantity of aircraft involved. Large numbers compensated for the relative inadequacies of individual aircraft, and low numbers made it difficult for the British to launch massed attacks of the kind used by the US and Japanese navies to convince the sceptical that air power could revolutionise war at sea. Having too few aircraft, the FAA was less able to make the dramatic impressions required to stimulate the kind of growth in size, quality and perceived importance which would be needed if the British were to keep up with their competitors. Neptune was plainly on the side of the big squadrons.

What were the reasons for this very disappointing performance? Naval plans for expansion were of two kinds: short-term, in which the carrying capacity of the existing Fleet tended to play a particularly important role, and longer-term, in which ultimate tactical and strategic requirements moved more to the centre of the stage. In the immediate post-war period the dividing line between the two categories of plan was usually taken as the commissioning of the *Glorious* and *Courageous*, by which time the Fleet was expected to be equipped with 161 aircraft. During this period plans were in a state of constant flux, but the changes almost invariably lowered the total of aircraft to be provided, or stretched out the date of the plan's completion, or both.[6]

One of the main reasons for the general lowering of sights was the impoverished state of the RAF at the time and the effects that this had on its offshoot, the FAA. The RAF owed its beginnings at least partly to the belief that a centralised organisation would be more efficient as a supplier of aircraft than the Admiralty and War Office had between them proved to be in the First World War. At first this seemed to be far from the case, and there were soon loud and angry complaints from the Fleet about the quality and quantity of the aircraft provided for the naval campaigns in Turkey and Russia.[7] Rather disappointingly for those who wished to use this as ammunition in a struggle to regain control of the naval air service, the Naval Staff was obliged to admit that "it would appear that the Air Ministry have done their best with the limited finances at their disposal." Looking back on the period, Bell Davies wrote: "I have often thought since that if the RAF at this time had been numerically stronger, the Air Staff would have been much more willing to meet the wishes of the Naval Staff. As it was, they felt they simply could not afford to."[8]

The development of the torpedo aircraft is a good instance of the Navy's tribulations at this time. The slow appearance of the Cuckoo had already produced complaints from the Naval Staff, and in the autumn of 1919 Capt the Honourable Arthur Stopford had warned that "with the Air Ministry looking after it, [the] torpedo machine will die from stagnation," and there seemed much substance behind this anxiety. "In fact," wrote one ex-RNAS RAF officer, "no progress at all has been made. Nothing has been done. It is necessary to point this out as a typical example of the way in which the development of this arm has been treated since its conception. There is no real support. The potential value of the weapon is universally recognised. The department [producing it] is however almost universally neglected. The Admiralty recognise the need for torpedo squadrons and rely on the Air Ministry to provide them at the earliest possible date. It is necessary that the development should be taken seriously."[9]*

Nevertheless, most naval officers still continued to believe that the present perilous state of the Royal Air Force was not a complete explanation of present deficiencies. They believed, on the contrary, that a system that made the Navy so vulnerable to the frailties of the RAF and the caprice of its leaders was fundamentally unsound and bound to produce such situations. There can be little doubt that their early sufferings in this period played a large part in persuading the Admiralty to begin the campaign for the repossession of the naval air service that so bedevilled the inter-war period. The more immediate outcome, however, was a significant contribution to the retardation of the Navy's aircraft expansion programme.

The financial circumstances of the times and the slow progress of the carrier construction programme also did much to limit any increase in aircraft numbers. The tardy completion of the old carriers and their low aircraft complements, the delays in the conversion of the *Glorious* and *Courageous,* and the meandering catapult programme all reduced the carrying capacity of the Fleet and led to delay in the formation of the units originally intended for it. It was assumed that the Government would not authorise the provision of aircraft for which no ships existed, as these, almost by definition, would be "surplus to the requirements of the Fleet". Thus when *Glorious* and *Courageous* fell behind schedule, the ACNS, Admiral Dreyer, realised that this meant abandoning the aircraft too. "In view of the Cabinet's '10-year formula'," he wrote, "I do not consider that we could possibly hope to overcome the temptation to the Cabinet of the £134,000 saving. . . ."[10]

As has been said earlier, the assessment of future strategic and tactical needs in aircraft played a more important part when it came to formulating plans for the more distant future. One of the first essays in this area was by Admiral Madden, who calculated in December 1919 that the Fleet would require at least 233 aircraft in 11 carriers, but a Joint Staff Conference the following summer believed that this exaggerated the need for spotting aircraft.[11] Various other suggestions were made at this time, but the next major attempt to define future policy was made in the Tentative Ten Year Programme. First sketched out by the Plans Division in July 1924, the programme suggested the four new 17,000-ton carriers described earlier and found that, with the completion of the first of these by 1929, the carrying capacity of the Fleet would then be 350 aircraft. There were many consultations between the Fleet and the Naval Staff at this time, but the

* The timely arrival of the Blackburn Dart eventually saved the day. The confusion of these times and the need for torpedo aircraft for operations in the Baltic nearly led to the revival of the Short Shirl, for "though too slow and unhandy for severe work these machines would be good enough against Bolsheviks." (Air Staff Conference, January 3, 1919; Air 2/122/B9969)

participants knew that they were bound to be speculative as there had been "so little sea experience owing to the unavoidable delays which have occurred in the completion of aircraft carriers for work with the Fleet."[12] Eventually, though, a policy calling for 275 aircraft with the main Fleet and 59 for subsidiary operations – a total of 334 aircraft – was laid before the Cabinet in March 1925. The Cabinet ruled however that no major war against Japan was to be expected for 10 years and so this programme was reduced by cancellations and postponements in the carrier programme to a total of 241 aircraft by 1935.[13]

Admiral Dreyer, however, was anxious about this programme as it made no provision for ships other than carriers. Accordingly, he suggested that some of the aircraft intended for the carriers should be temporarily allotted to cruisers and battleships for the period up to 1935. Then, having gained useful experience of all kinds of naval aviation, the Admiralty would be in a very good position to make up the carrier complements, thereby producing a total air service of 346 seagoing aircraft.[14] This policy was adopted by the Board.

The next ACNS was Admiral Pound (a future First Sea Lord), who was to be responsible for a drastic reduction in the ultimate projected strength of the FAA. In the early summer of 1927 he took another look at the tactical requirements of the Fleet and concluded that a total of 289 aircraft would suffice. In the following year he reduced this again to a total of 251 aircraft by 1938, a level which the Board approved in November. Soon after, a slight change in the catapult programme led to the final aircraft total dropping to 241 (of which 65 would be in ships other than carriers), and this figure was reported to the Treasury on the appropriately portentous date of September 3, 1929. Dreyer and Pound had therefore effectively delayed the completion of the original 1925 programme by exactly three years.[15]

How is this important and ultimately very damaging reduction in the Admiralty's target to be explained? Of course the collapse of the 1925 carrier replacement programme and the modest nature of the British catapult effort played an important part, as they much reduced the carrying capacity of the Fleet. Against this, though, Pound himself noted "that for reasons of economy, it is not proposed to provide aircraft up to a full carrying capacity." So limited capacity is obviously only a partial explanation. The manpower situation also played a part, for, as has already been shown, demand much exceeded supply and Pound was quick to see that "by reducing the total number of machines in the Fleet Air Arm, the difficult problem of finding the 70 per cent of pilots from naval personnel will be eased."[16]

To a certain extent, any reduction in aircraft total targets also represents a reduction in the perceived importance of the tasks the aircraft would have performed. If the kind of aircraft envisaged in the various proposals is examined, it becomes clear that Pound was prepared to contemplate reductions in all categories. But he was especially hard on fighters, which he reduced by rather more than a third, perhaps reflecting the current faith in the efficiency of AA gunfire in protecting the Fleet from air attack. Nevertheless, the overwhelming impression gained from these various dealings is of an absence of policy rather than of a series of mistaken judgements. In December 1919 Madden's suggestions for the future of the Fleet naval air service were accompanied by an observation to the effect that "the first step . . . is to settle the air policy of the Fleet," but unfortunately no such settled policy emerged. The contrast between the Royal Navy and the US Navy in this is stark, for the Americans had a clear-cut programme of expansion which was authorised by Congress in 1926 and which "cleared the way for a rational programme of aircraft procurement [and] gave recognition in precise detail to the special place fleet aviation should occupy in the years ahead."[17]

This should be compared to the fainthearted policy described by Capt Roger Bellairs, Director of the Plans Division, in October 1928. He emphasised how very tentative the 1924–5 policy had been, explaining this by pointing to the paucity of experience to date, the difficulty of forecasting aeronautical developments over the next decade, and the necessity of taking the as yet unknown policy of the other powers into full account. It was impossible, he said, to frame a definite policy.[18] Nothing could more clearly demonstrate the readiness of the Royal Navy to surrender the initiative in air development at this stage. This abdication meant that the Admiralty had no long-term vision of the future of naval aviation to set against current difficulties and uncertainties. A loss of momentum became almost inevitable.

Another reason for the Admiralty's lack of urgency was a quite noticeable tendency to underrate American achievements in naval aviation. It was recognised that they had forged ahead in the aircraft equipment of cruisers and battleships because of their early development of catapults, and this was certainly one reason for Dreyer's recommendation to switch a certain amount of effort away from carriers. "In a recent exercise", he wrote, "the American Fleet discharged 16 aeroplanes from 16 ships simultaneously prior to a target shoot. We are a long way behind. . . ." However, he thought there was a silver lining to this particular cloud, for "the handicap under which the US Navy must be labouring as regards the development of the tactical use of aircraft in action must . . . be very great as they concentrated on catapults and are far behind as regards carriers 'in being'. As regards working with the Fleet," he concluded, "we must be a long way ahead of the Americans."[19] The British were sceptical about the actual levels of excellence attained by the US Navy and, more specifically, about the number of aircraft they seemed to deploy at sea. Supported very strongly in this by the Air Staff, the Admiralty tended to argue that the unduly high complements of the few US carriers and the American habit of carrying several aircraft per catapult led to a confusion between stowage and operational capacity. The US Navy, they thought, could certainly carry large numbers of aircraft but would not be able to operate them efficiently.

American efforts in the field of aircraft procurement were perfectly well known, and the British Naval Attaché in Washington (Capt the Hon Arthur Stopford, a keen air enthusiast) reported in 1926 that the Bureau of Aeronautics considered that "more has been accomplished in aviation in the Fleet than in any previous year, and such results are particularly gratifying." He noted that the US Navy was aiming to have 1,000 aircraft by 1931 and intended training about 140 pilots a year. The Naval Air Section believed that the US Navy had gone ahead by 1928 and that the gap would grow.[20] While their presumed tactical disadvantages could offset some of this numerical inferiority, no-one believed that it would do so entirely. Pound reduced the US total by 169 aircraft for such reasons, but was still willing to advocate a situation in which the US Navy would have 303 "operable aircraft" by 1934 against the FAA's projected total of 213. This memorandum and the Board's ready acceptance of it shows that the British were prepared to acquiesce in the loss of their lead.[21]

The reason for this is not hard to find. In June 1929 it was recorded that as a "Basis for Preparations for War" the "United States is not considered in this respect. Japan being the next strongest naval power, requirements in the event of war in the Far East form the general basis on which preparations are made." In the following year, the Controller (Backhouse) noted in similar vein: "As regards the United States, our policy does not consider this country, and our weakness in regards to her lies not so much in the naval as in the financial sphere."[22] War with the United States was unthinkable, and so the maintenance of equality with the US Navy was no longer the vital necessity that it was once felt to be. At least in this area of naval preparation, the Admiralty had effectively abandoned the One Power Standard.

Japan, however, was not a very satisfactory substitute in some ways, at least as far as the development of British naval aviation was concerned. The Cabinet had ruled in May 1925 "that in existing circumstances aggressive action against the British Empire on the part of Japan within the next 10 years is not a contingency seriously to be apprehended."[23] This Ten Years Rule became formally self-perpetuating in July 1928. More to the point, the Royal Navy did not take the Japanese threat very seriously in the late 1920s, despite the early warnings of Beatty. Backhouse, for example, was quite sanguine about the prospects of war with Japan, for ". . . the geographical position of that country, and the vast distances of the Pacific Ocean render aggression on her part a matter of difficulty. Provided we have the power to send a fleet to the East, equal to that of Japan, and provided we undertake the adequate defence of the key positions of Singapore, our security is not endangered. Both these considerations the Admiralty have had in mind in their preparations."[24] Japanese naval aviation was of course thought to be in a particularly poor state. For all these reasons, the distant threat of an apparently weak Asiatic foe proved an inadequate weapon for the Admiralty to use in self-defence against the Treasury's unceasing campaign for strict economy.

Although the restrictions imposed by the Treasury most certainly had an extensive effect on defence expenditure as a whole during the inter-war period, they cannot be held exclusively responsible for deficiencies in a particular weapons system. Economic cuts force Departments to make choices and form priorities, a process in which many other considerations come into play. Nevertheless, Treasury pressure distinctly limited the expansion of naval aviation.

It delayed the completion of short and long-term plans, as it had done in 1925. In some cases it resulted in the blocking of specific proposals. The very modest expansion scheme put forward by Pound, for instance, had envisaged the addition of a steady two flights (12 aircraft) a year to the FAA total, but even this proved impossible. "I shall need," Chancellor Philip Snowden wrote, "a great deal of convincing that any expansion at all of your existing strength is necessary at the present moment." He did not find the Admiralty sufficiently persuasive and the formation of the two flights intended for 1930–1 was postponed.[25] It is difficult to believe that larger plans would have produced better eventual results, for the Treasury believed that even "the present state of naval aviation . . . and the marked lead already possessed by this country justified substantial reductions."[26] But some of the effects of the campaign for retrenchment were more intangible though no less profound. The expectations of the senior officers of the Admiralty were conditioned by the atmosphere of the time. Thus when the Naval Staff proposed the formation of four new flights (24 aircraft) for completing carriers, Madden gloomily responded: "There is no chance of obtaining *this large increase,* especially since the extended ten-year safe period has been adopted." Later, the Board's ready acceptance of Pound's reduction proposals almost suggests that economy in naval aviation had become a habit of mind.

The dangers of acquiescience in this policy of downward drift were however becoming increasingly apparent. "The United States is more advanced than we are in naval air matters, due to unity of purpose and control," wrote Madden anxiously in February 1930. "From conversations I have had with Rear-Admiral Moffett, the head of the US Naval Air Service, I find they put a higher value on the Naval Air Arm than do the Admiralty and they are determined to increase it both in terms of number and efficiency. We cannot afford to drop further behind." This anxiety was increased shortly afterwards by a report written by Lt Cdr R.St J. Prentice, who went as an observer to the USA in the airship R100. He was taken round the principal US Naval Air Stations and his account of various American superiorities shattered a good deal of Admiralty complacency. The US Navy, in fact, was known to be already working on a programme designed to give it 750 seaborne aircraft by 1940.[27]

The urgency of the Admiralty's need for a thorough revision of its attitude to the expansion of the FAA was also emphasised by the imminence of the General

Disarmament Conference at Geneva in 1932, for which the Admiralty had clearly to prepare a departmental case. More ominously, there were early indications that with the growth of its naval power, Japan would very likely prove more of a menace than previously thought, especially if this were exerted in conjunction with trouble from a European power. The invasion of Manchuria indicated the possibility of menace, and the patterns of Japanese naval spending its dangers. "I notice," wrote Dreyer (now DCNS) to Hankey, the influential Secretary of the Cabinet and CID, "that the Japanese are going to expend the money which they save as a result of the London Naval Treaty in order to largely strengthen their Fleet Air Arm. We, of course, are taking the opportunity of reducing ours. . . ."[28] This warning proved very well founded and the Air and Naval Staffs were soon to make the alarming discovery that the Japanese Naval Air Service had overtaken the British, in size at least, by 1933.[29]

The Air Staff, meanwhile, were making their own reappraisal of the future of naval aviation, at least in so far as it affected the well-being of the RAF. Their special problem was what came to be Article 25 of the draft Disarmament Convention: the notion that all powers be allotted a single aircraft quota. This put the interests of the Navy and the Air Force in direct and undisguised opposition. If the Admiralty was eventually allowed to proceed with its new carrier construction programme, and achieved modern ratios between tonnage and aircraft complement, the Air Staff saw that an FAA of some 350 aircraft might well be possible. The French, however, had no significant naval air service, and if a common total of 1,300 aircraft was indeed accepted by both countries, as some officers thought it might be, then the FAA would take up over a quarter of the British allotment and severely jeopardise British air security. Each aircraft deployed by the Navy meant, quite literally, one less for the Air Force. In their view, the Admiralty's vainglorious desire to compete with the US Navy could therefore imperil the security of the country against a European enemy. It was this fear which led Lord Thomson, the Secretary of State for Air, to write a remarkably candid letter to the Prime Minister in January 1930. "The Fleet Air Arm," he said, "is an integral part of the RAF; the machines allocated to it are part of our total strength, and each machine so allotted means one less immediately available for home defence against attack by the shore-based aircraft of European powers. The Navy, of course, needs some aircraft, and an adequate number can always be made available in case of emergency, but the principal danger we have to guard against is air attack by shore-based aircraft."[30]

The Air Staff's anxiety on this point also helps to explain their readiness to co-operate with the Treasury in their various attempts to limit the growth of the FAA. "Surely," suggested one Treasury official, there ought to be ". . . some proposal for the limitation of the size of the FAA. Have you considered this, and if so, what form had you in mind? Should we go too far if we proposed boldly 'that there should be no increase in the number of aircraft used for flying off and on ships of war'? That would still leave you free to develop your flying boats, would it not?" Eventually such considerations led the Chancellor of the Exchequer to suggest for the forthcoming Disarmament Conference the complete abolition of all seaborne aircraft.[31]. Although there was little chance of this being accepted by the other powers, there was much to be said for it from the Air Ministry's point of view.

The Air Ministry, in fact, had already antagonised the Admiralty by its opposition in the past to various proposals for expansion. For instance, the Navy's 1925 plan, for 241 aircraft by 1935, was considered to be "out of proportion to the present financial stringency," which made 144 aircraft a more reasonable target. The Air Staff were sceptical of the large carrier complements proposed and made the rather startling observation that "the programme has evidently been drawn up with the idea of cramming aircraft into every possible space which can take them in every possible ship in the British Navy." Trenchard argued that, as a result of the 1925 Cabinet ruling, "we know things are safe up to 1935" and that it would be better to concentrate on shore installations and training. This was in line with the Air Ministry's long preference for maintaining a flexible and generalist peacetime force capable of rapid and substantial expansion in war, a policy which ran counter to the specialist requirements of the Navy.[32] For all these reasons, the Air Staff had been very cool about even the reduced programme proposed by Pound and could be relied upon to give a hostile reception to any more ambitious plans from the Naval Staff.

Conflict was bound to arise, however, because the Admiralty was indeed having second thoughts about its rather modest plans for expansion, which were intended merely to provide 241 aircraft by 1939. The renaissance seems to have begun in the spring of 1931, when the Naval Staff decided that "our limitation figure should be based on the carrying capacity of all carriers, heavy ships and cruisers allowed by treaty." Present targets, such as that for 241 aircraft, were merely temporary arrangements, much influenced by political and economic circumstances. Instead, the Director of the Naval Air Division (DNAD), Capt C. E. Turle, conjured up a figure of 502 aircraft, and this was further discussed with the other Staff Divisions. Eventually the Director of Plans suggested that the Air Ministry be told that the Royal Navy could not accept anything less than parity with the US Navy as a matter of principle, but as a concession would be prepared to go down to a capacity requirement of 575 aircraft! At the same time, DNAD also found that the Fleet had an irreducible tactical requirement for 346 aircraft, which could in turn demand the maintenance of a front-line strength of 433 or, a little later, 405 aircraft.[33] The Air Ministry was appalled by all this and some members of the Air Staff wanted to force a Government inquiry into the matter. It certainly persuaded the Air Ministry into supporting the Snowden suggestion described earlier, and although the Chief of the Air Staff admitted that the complete abolition of all seaborne air forces was probably too much to hope for, he nevertheless urged "that negotiations should be opened as early as possible with the USA for the drastic limitation of the aircraft-carrying capacity of the fleets of the two countries on the basis of parity and at as low a level as can be secured."[34]

The Admiralty's new-found ambition in aircraft totals had little chance of making headway against the combined effects of current hopes for disarmament, needs for economy and Air Staff hostility. But even though only 18 aircraft were finally added to the FAA total over the whole period between 1929 and 1934,[35] the pressure for expansion was kept up. Although, wrote the ACNS, "we probably know more about [the tactical handling of aircraft carriers] than anyone else does . . . we have been slow to arm our fleet with aircraft and to complete the carrier complements of aircraft and to become air-minded. . . . Again with aircraft, as with other weapons, numbers are a predominating factor in active operations."[36] The decision to build and equip the *Ark Royal* was the next move in this direction.

The Air Staff made their normal objections to this proposal but were over-ridden relatively easily. In the preliminary preparations for the London Naval Conference of 1935, they made again their usual plea for a reduction of carrier tonnages and consequent limitations on the number of seaborne aircraft. The point seems largely to have been made for form's sake, as much of the fire had gone out of the issue. The spectre of a single aircraft quota had largely receded and there were now officers in the Air Staff, though they were still in a decided minority, who argued that the Admiralty ought to be encouraged to expand the FAA, especially if this was at the expense of its guns. The more aircraft there were, after all, the better.[37]

Any hopes, however, that "the days are forever past when the Air Force and the Navy looked suspiciously at any increase in each other's strength," in the words of the First Lord when he introduced the Naval Estimates for 1937, rapidly proved illusory. In its desperate attempt to keep pace with the threatening growth of German air power, the Air Ministry was in no mood to dissipate air resources on subsidiary and subordinate purposes. "The problem [of expanding the FAA] is aggravated at every point," said the First Lord in 1936, "by the strain put upon the national resources by the much larger expansion of the RAF that is taking place over the same period."[38] British aircraft manufacturers had been run down to such an extent that they were incapable of meeting all orders and schedules, and first priority inevitably went to the RAF. When, for example, the Naval Staff wanted to place more orders for Swordfish, they were told this would only be possible if they found the necessary factory and materials. The Air Member for Supply, Air Marshal Sir Wilfred Freeman, was very sympathetic but made it clear that this was the Navy's problem. In the end, a new factory was built at Shelburn-in-Elmet with the aid of Blackburn, a local garage, and Hudsley Clarke, the locomotive builders. The results of this arrangement and a great deal of steel bicycle tubing was the "Blackfish," Blackburn's version of the celebrated Swordfish.[39] In the circumstances of the late 1930s naval aircraft procurement had often to be a matter of great improvisation.

In some ways, however, the times were a little easier for the Admiralty. The clear deterioration of the international situation led to the creation of the Defence Requirements Committee (DRC), which was soon persuaded that recent economies meant that the Fleet was some 51 aircraft short of authorised capacity and that the new target should be 357 aircraft by 1939 and 504 aircraft by 1942. No specific programme of expansion was worked out at this time, for there was still a great deal of uncertainty in the Staff and in the Fleet about the kind of aircraft that had best be ordered. This was the result of the continuing wide differences of opinion about the relative importance of the various tasks that aircraft could perform for the Fleet. The basis on which estimates of the required strength of the FAA should be worked out was also by no means clear. Should they be based on some theoretical "absolute" tactical requirement or upon the forces of possible enemies? Because of this uncertainty, there remained in some quarters a certain tendency to put the cart before the horse by basing estimates of the Navy's air requirements mainly on the projected carrying capacity of the Fleet.

In 1934, as we shall see later, the DNAD started a fairly determined campaign to get a settled policy on all these points, but much time passed before success was achieved. One unfortunate result of all this was a certain reluctance to seize the nettle and to place definite war orders with the Air Ministry. The new Director of Air Materiel (Capt M. S. Slattery) was so alarmed by this that he placed orders worth several million pounds with Fairey and Blackburn entirely on his own initiative. Fortunately, the new First Lord (Churchill) backed his judgement.[40]

The final problem was financial. In its aircraft procurement programmes the Navy was only authorised to prepare for war at some time after 1942, the date originally settled on by the DRC, and its plans were carefully scrutinised to see that they conformed with this ruling. "Financial rationing overrides considerations of strategy, etc," remarked the ACNS in 1938, "and all we need to know is how many first-line aircraft the Fifth Sea Lord can support on his ration. When this is settled, it will not be difficult to fit the aircraft available to the framework of the Report."[41] It rapidly proved impossible to achieve the DRC target of 504 aircraft within the financial ration allowed. A conference was held in September 1938 to consider the problem, the upshot of which was a decision promulgated to the Fleet in May 1939. It was expected that by March 1942 the FAA's first-line strength would comprise 480 aircraft, 300 in the seven fleet carriers (including the first four Armoured carriers), with the remainder distributed between other older carriers, cruisers and battleships.[42]

The war started a few months after this projection was made, however, and in the event the Royal Navy entered the conflict with 147 TSRs, 41 amphibians and 30 fighters, a mere 218 aircraft. A further 192 aircraft of various kinds were ashore, some of which were also regarded as "first-line aircraft".[43]

Even had the 1939 programme been fully achieved, it would still not have been enough to bring the Royal Navy up to the standards of relative strength originally envisaged at the beginning of the inter-war period. The Admiralty had also been forced to abandon hope of recapturing parity with the USA, and was now obliged to accept that the US Navy was "definitely ahead of Great Britain in respect of the FAA. It is bigger, has better types of machine, which are replaced by the latest types more quickly. Its training is better and a much higher proportion of American naval officers have experience of flying than is possible under the present British arrangements (i.e. Dual Control)."[44] In 1938 Congress had passed legislation for a "Two Ocean Navy" capable of fielding 3,000 aircraft. When the Second World War began, contemporary British estimates already put the US Navy's total at 811 aircraft. Some comfort could be taken from the fact that, pride apart, the "disparity [has] not been regarded as a factor of the first importance on account of the remoteness of the risk of war with the USA."[45]

But there was no such consolation to be had when comparisons were made with the naval air strength of Japan. The Admiralty had always emphasised that Japan rather than the USA was the yardstick by which naval air requirements should be measured. Just before the war, however, the Admiralty had come to the melancholy conclusion that national resources did not allow Britain to take the appropriate measures, at least to the level required. 1938 estimates put the Japanese seaborne aircraft total at 377, rising to 503 by 1942. These levels of strength were superior to current FAA totals and to the aspirations of the May 1939 programme. Tacitly, the British had accepted the present impossibility of maintaining strict parity with the Japanese.

This was particularly ominous in that the Staff had recommended in 1938 that Britain should seek to maintain parity in naval air power with both Japan and Germany, whose total naval air effort was expected to be 677 by 1942. The First Sea Lord, however, felt obliged to note that "while I do not accept this [proposal], as I consider it involves putting too large a proportion of our money into the very costly air arm, we shall have to arrive at a ratio which I am inclined to think should be the same as for the relative capital ships vis-à-vis these two powers."[46] The Royal Navy resigned itself to being much inferior in numbers to the combined naval air strengths of its two anticipated enemies.

The Admiralty could also find little comfort in the present strength of British land-based maritime air power, for as the Director of Naval Intelligence had argued ten years previously, ". . . in aircraft for use in naval operations conducted from shore or harbour, we are a long way behind." He added, most perceptively, "between the Devil and the deep blue sea – if I may thus refer to the Air Ministry and the Admiralty respectfully and respectively – the matter has lain undeveloped."[47] At the end of the First World War some 1,062 shore-based aircraft were available for distant reconnaissance and anti-submarine patrol work. "Coastal Area" was formed in 1919 but had a mere 29 aircraft, of which only 11 were usually available for naval co-operation. In July 1924 the Naval Staff opened the question of the strength of this force, suggesting an increase to a total of 72 by 1929, a target later changed to 49, and then to 60 by 1935. None of these levels were achieved, and by 1930 Coastal Area still had only 26 operational aircraft. The process continued through the 1930s, although some slight progress was made. Coastal Command, as it had by now become, deployed some 200 operational aircraft by 1938, a level contrasting badly with contemporary US and Japanese shore-based maritime air power.

In theory at least, all concerned were convinced of the necessity of maintaining large numbers of shore-based maritime aircraft. A Joint Staff Conference in March 1927, for instance, concluded that some 350 shore-based aircraft would be needed for convoy escort work in a war with a European power, a target not much at variance with the 339 thought necessary ten years later.[48]

To a certain extent, of course, the failure to achieve these targets reflects the low priority assigned by both the Admiralty and the Air Ministry to this particular form of air power. The Admiralty concentrated its aerial ambitions on the FAA, and the Air Ministry naturally tended to be preoccupied with Fighter and Bomber Commands. All this can be reasonably inferred from the extraordinary lack of urgency with which the strength of the force was discussed from time to time during the inter-war period. For instance, the Naval Staff suggestion for a force level of 49 aircraft was made in March 1925, but no action of any kind was taken for two years until the next request – for 60 aircraft – appeared in 1927. Again, no action was taken until January 1929, when the Admiralty suggested another conference. A month later the Air Ministry argued that there would be little point in such a conference: four months later the Admiralty replied, agreeing.[49] No further action seems to have been taken until the mid-1930s. By any standard, this was a leisurely campaign. The coincidence of estimates between 1927 and 1937 would therefore suggest an absence of thought in the meantime rather than a pleasing firmness of purpose.

Unfortunately, the issue of shore-based maritime air power was politically very sensitive, something which did not help mature consideration of its possibilities. The Air Staff had many reasons to doubt the purity of their naval colleagues' intentions in this area, as they knew that many of them were actively campaigning for the Admiralty's repossession of the whole organisation. "Eventually," wrote Capt Tom Calvert, Chief of the Naval Air Section, "both the FAA and Naval Co-operation Units should be amalgamated and come under the complete control of the Admiralty as an integral part of the Navy."[50]

Knowing such views were common, the Air Staff were consequently on their guard against what they imagined to be overt or covert moves in this direction. For their part, the Naval Staff believed that the standards of Coastal Area left much to be desired. An exercise of 1931 showed, thought Chatfield (C-in-C of the Mediterranean Fleet), "little, if any, advance in the efficiency of flying boat squadrons to carry out naval duties, ten years' intermittent experience notwithstanding."[51]

Naval officers tended to attribute this indifferent performance not only to inadequate numbers of aircraft and poor training but also to an Air Staff reluctance to accept that naval co-operation was indeed Coastal Command's primary function. "I fully recognise that flying boats can be of great use in co-operation with the Navy," wrote Trenchard. "At the same time, it is essential to investigate what flying boats can achieve independently, as the more they do on their own, the more useful they will be in co-operation with the Navy or with the Army when the time comes."[52] Hidden within this typically Delphic utterance was a suggestion that flying-boats might prove cheaper and more efficient in the performance of certain maritime duties and might therefore replace the naval units originally tasked with such work. Hence, in 1929, a flying-boat squadron was sent by the Air Ministry to practise "air control" in the Persian Gulf. The Admiralty was neither consulted nor informed about this and local representatives of the two services spent much of their time spying on each other. As far as the Navy was concerned, it all showed that "the only way . . . flying boats can be made use of . . . is in conjunction with H M ships."[53] It is perhaps not surprising that in an area so strewn with semantic, administrative and operational subtleties, inter-service co-operation should be so meagre and British shore-based air power so limited in extent and too often divorced from naval operations.

If the low numbers of maritime aircraft deployed on land and sea was a serious problem for the Admiralty at the onset of the Second World War, the quality of these aircraft was no better. Immediately after the First World War it was not entirely unreasonable for the Air Ministry to claim that it supplied the Navy with "ship planes for purely naval purposes which are vastly superior to anything [else] of their kind in the world."[54] By 1939, however, the British had slipped to a position of clear inferiority and were well behind both the US and Japanese navies in the quality of their aircraft. Only the Royal Navy went to war with large numbers of biplanes in its front-line forces. Its basic aircraft was the Fairey Swordfish, production of which was behind schedule and which did not perform as well as the types currently coming into service with the US and Japanese navies, such as the Douglas TBD Devastator and the Nakajima B5N2 Kate. The fighter situation offered little comfort either. Neither of the Navy's first two monoplanes, the Blackburn Skua fighter/dive bomber and the Roc, its turreted version, lived up to expectations. The FAA was accordingly forced to improvise with a few obsolescent Sea Gladiator biplanes for a few years more. Moreover, there were no designs in hand for the kind of single-seat high-performance fighter that was beginning to enter service with the US and Japanese navies. "There is," concluded the First Lord in January 1939, "a serious deficiency in fighter aircraft, of which the FAA has virtually none."[55] By the beginning of the Second World War it was evident that something had gone seriously wrong with British naval aircraft design.

Under the terms of the Dual Control agreement, it was agreed "that the Air Ministry shall provide all the material which they [the Admiralty] demand," while the Air Staff were to be responsible for aircraft design and production. Originally the Navy was very worried that with the "increasing divergence of type from the standard land machines . . . priority will not be forthcoming at the critical moment, when all that is best in the Air Ministry will be devoting their utmost energy to furthering their own interests."[57] There is certainly something to be said for this view. Preoccupied with their own problems, priorities and shortages, it was only natural that the Air Staff should concentrate their efforts on their own requirements. As a result, there was a tendency to adapt land-based designs for naval purposes, rather than to design naval aircraft from scratch. All this raised something of an echo in the aircraft industry. Some firms, such as Rolls-Royce and Hawker in the late 1930s, decided for themselves that the RAF was a more important customer and resisted the suggestion that they should make aircraft and engines for the FAA.[58]

The Air Staff sometimes seemed to be unnecessarily defeatist as well, maintaining that the ambitious specifications sometimes produced by the Naval Staff were impossible to reconcile with the requirements of carrier operations. Perhaps the Navy should just concentrate on air fighting and spotting, "and the rest of the naval requirements in aircraft, such as bombing, should be provided by shore or land-based aircraft."[59] The Air Staff were particularly defeatist over those projects in which they had little or no departmental interest. This was certainly the case in the prolonged controversy over the Navy's dive-bomber requirement. While the Naval Staff had discovered an enthusiasm for this method of attack in the early 1930s, the Air Staff were always politely unreceptive, preferring to pin their faith on high-level bombing. This made them sceptical and generally unhelpful about the production of the necessary equipment. In the end, the Admiralty had to short-circuit the normal procedures by ordering the Blackburn Skua straight off the drawing board and, after the failure of its determined six-year campaign to prise a good dive-bombing sight out of the Air Ministry, sending it to war without one.[60]

Needless to say, the Admiralty was also not entirely blameless in the matter. When the question of aircraft procurement was discussed in 1936, for example, Air Marshal Dowding pointed out that specifications were agreed between the Air Ministry and the Admiralty before they were issued to the trade, so it was not a case of the RAF foisting inadequate aircraft onto the

Navy. "In my opinion," he added, "the fundamental trouble is that no agreed policy exists as to the strategical and tactical requirements for the FAA." Uncertainty over the ultimate purposes of naval aviation, aggravated by constant changes in personnel, certainly played a part in the adaptations and delays in aircraft procurement which constantly occurred. Occasionally the Admiralty chose to ignore "professional" advice, and this could cause problems too. Difficulties of this kind seem to have beset the early stages of the development of the Blackburn Shark torpedo-bomber, for example.[61]

The Admiralty undoubtedly had itself partly to blame for the problem which worried it most in 1939. That was, said the First Sea Lord, ". . . the position regarding fighters in the FAA. They only have a handful of old-fashioned aircraft and nothing to replace them."[62] The problem began to arise in the early and mid-1930s, when the highly successful Fairey Flycatcher and its successor, the perfectly adequate Hawker Nimrod, were approaching the end of their operational lives. Instead of proceeding with a new high-performance single-seat fighter, the Navy shifted over to the concept of a two-seater capable of doing something else as well. There followed the fighter-reconnaissance Hawker Osprey, the Blackburn Skua fighter-dive bomber and the Fairey Fulmar fighter-reconnaissance aircraft, none of which were as good as the single-seat high-performance fighters of the US and Japanese navies.

There were good reasons for this penchant for two-seat fighters. This was before the days of good homing devices, and R/T communications were very restricted, having a range of barely 40 miles. All this made it hazardous for single-seat fighters to stray too far from their carriers. Two-seaters, however, could carry an observer who could provide the necessary accurate over-sea navigation and so allow the fighters to escort long-range attack aircraft to their targets. The status of observers within the FAA is often held to be associated with its predilection for two-seaters. The paucity of aircraft also encouraged the Naval Staff to make each machine as versatile as possible. Finally, "the Admiralty idea appears to be," the Air Staff warned, "that they will be able to operate in war without interference from land-based aircraft. What would they do if the Germans employed large numbers of land-based aircraft of higher performance against the British Fleet. . . ?" A good question, as it very soon proved.[63] Basically, the Navy thought it would generally operate outside the range of shore-based enemy fighters and that two-seaters would be adequate against enemy bombers.

Although the advantages of two-seaters certainly seemed attractive, the penalties eventually proved too great. The Blackburn Skua, for example, went into service in September 1938, three months *after* the new Air Materiel Department proposed its cancellation on the grounds that it was already obsolescent. The NAD resisted this idea, arguing that any fighter was better than none.[64] The point was that the Skua was a good dive bomber but a poor fighter. The staff requirement had proved too all-embracing, and the ideas behind it too unsettled. The whole evolution of the Navy's fighter aircraft seems in fact to illustrate that "there were," in the temperate words of the FAA Committee report of 1935, "no clear ideas on the subject."[65]

The Naval Staff's attitude to fighters was also influenced by its more general preference for multi-purpose aircraft. The compressing of all air functions into two types of aircraft (the TSR and the fighter) "is attributable," said the FAA Committee proudly, "to the insistence of naval officers on the operational desirability of so doing."[66] It was however a controversial and finally dangerous policy. The variety of their intended functions made it difficult for multi-purpose aircraft to reach the standards of foreign specialist types. There were plenty of naval officers who recognised the problem. "It seems to me," wrote the Controller, Admiral Backhouse (a future First Sea Lord), in 1931, "that if we continue to provide in one aircraft for every possible duty we shall merely defeat our object of getting a type which is of utility at sea, having regard to what we want them to do and what they are likely to meet in the way of enemy aircraft."[67] These words proved to be entirely prophetic.

The drive for multi-purpose aircraft seems to have begun with a paper written by several FAA officers in the *Courageous* in 1930. The FAA's limited expansion programme meant that there were only very low numbers of aircraft available. The notion of combining several tasks in one machine therefore seemed particularly attractive, since it would greatly increase the flexibility of the force as a whole. If, for example, every aircraft embarked for reconnaissance or spotting could carry a bomb or torpedo and so have a "sting in the tail," the offensive potential of the FAA would be much increased. The idea attracted a good deal of interest and it was followed up by the new DNAD, Capt H. C. Rawlings. The Air Ministry was not at first enamoured of the idea, but Rawlings persuaded his friend Richard Fairey to work out the details of such an aircraft. The eventual result was the Fairey Swordfish, an obsolescent-looking aircraft which actually did sterling service all through the war but which nevertheless set a precedent that was in some ways unfortunate. Although the multi-purpose idea made sense at the time, it appears with hindsight that the airmen would have been better advised to press more strongly for larger numbers of specialist aircraft.[68]

Although it is possible to find individual misjudgements either in the Admiralty or the Air Ministry, or indeed in both, the system of aircraft procurement was probably more at fault than either of its main components. One of the Navy's most sacred doctrines on the procurement of materiel was that the producer and the user should be in the closest touch. "It is desirable," wrote Capt Roger Bellairs, "that the supply of these special types should be centralised in the authority responsible for their use, making that authority completely responsible in regard to requirements being met and that machines are up to specification.''[69] Only by such a means, thought the Navy, could the technical and operational sides of the problem be satisfactorily reconciled. In the case of naval aircraft, however, this did not apply. The Air Ministry was good on the first of these perspectives and the Naval Staff on the second, but the two did not always meet as they should. In consequence, says Admiral Sir Caspar John (who spent much time in the MAP), "The Admiralty was not competent to say what it wanted and the Air Ministry was not competent to advise."[70]

Although there gradually developed on both sides an awareness of how the other saw the problem, it took some time. The loss to the RAF of its first generation of flyers, and the *entrée* into and informal contacts with the aircraft industry that they had gained, left the Navy with a shortage of technical expertise that was difficult to make up. Aero-technical experience grew slowly, of course, even though the Royal Navy lacked the airfields, testing establishments and general infrastructure enjoyed by the US Navy. Only after the Inskip Report, for example, did the Navy seriously try to build up a nucleus of FAA air engineer officers who could help it to bridge the gap between the operational and technical sides of aircraft design and production.

The results of all this were sometimes plain to see. "The Naval Staff," suggested the Secretary of State for Air, "had the tendency to ask for machines which would do the impossible."[71] The Admiralty was well aware of its shortcomings and disadvantages in this area, frequently complaining that it no longer possessed "the necessary practical knowledge to intelligently criticise the design of aircraft in a similar manner to that of all [other] naval equipment." When, for instance, the Air Staff very wisely suggested the abandonment of the Blackburn Roc, the NAD observed pointedly: "Since the Admiralty has no technicians to advise them in this matter, we are not competent to insist on pressing forward with the contract [and] must accept Air Ministry advice."[72]

By the end of the Second World War the Navy had built up a strong body of technically minded officers and had re-established the close links with both the American and British aircraft industries which it had enjoyed in the First World War. In the meantime, however, the Navy was forced to rely on the Air Ministry for technical advice, and there were inevitable delays and confusions. Interdepartmental bodies like the Advisory Committee on FAA Aircraft, and its Technical Sub-Committee, worked increasingly well during the inter-war period. But it still worked slowly and it was often virtually impossible to track down ultimate responsibility for design decisions. With the best will in the world, two departments could hardly have worked as well as one. As a result, the production of naval aircraft all too often lacked the drive it needed if the FAA's requirements were to compete with those of Fighter and Bomber Commands in the country's aircraft industry.

Nevertheless, even if the Admiralty chiefs knew the present system to be unsatisfactory, they also knew that they could not hope to replace it with one in which they would be solely responsible for the design and production of their own aircraft. The political wisdom of the time was that aircraft procurement had failed in the First World War because of the existence of two competing sources of production. Air research was one and indivisible and best rooted in the Air Ministry. As Chatfield recognised, it would have been politically suicidal for the Admiralty to seek to be the supplier of its own air needs. "Any attempt to run research, experiment and supply by the Navy alone," he wrote in 1922, "will meet with great opposition. . . ."[73] The same was true during the 1930s, when so much attention was devoted to the urgency of air rearmament, and so the Navy neither claimed nor was awarded the authority over aircraft design which it had enjoyed up to 1918. The basic problem therefore persisted even after the Admiralty regained control of the FAA.

The deficiencies of British aircraft were clearly revealed during the Norwegian campaign. First of all, there were not enough of them. *Fliegerkorps X* deployed something in the order of 500 fighters, bombers and reconnaissance aircraft, with a similar number of auxiliaries of various kinds. While RAF aircraft were intermittently present, the Luftwaffe's main regular adversaries were the aircraft of the Fleet, of which there were rarely more than a hundred present at any one time. These odds were severe for a force operating mainly at sea, in unfamiliar terrain and in support of two expeditions well over two hundred miles apart. Low numbers meant particularly that the FAA was not able properly to follow up the success achieved in such operations as the Second Battle of Narvik or the carrier attacks on Vaernes airfield. The Luftwaffe, on the other hand, was able to keep pounding away day after day. As a result, despite the establishment of a generally satisfactory tactical kill ratio, the FAA was strategically defeated by *Fliegerkorps X* in Central Norway.

The situation in the North was less clear because the Luftwaffe was not so well placed and because, towards the end of the campaign, modern high-performance fighters at last appeared on the Allied side. Significantly, though, these were RAF aircraft. Throughout the campaign British naval aircraft were just as deficient in quality as they were in quantity. The Skuas, which sank the *Konigsberg* but missed the German destroyers at Narvik and the *Scharnhorst* at Trondheim, compared reasonably well with the Ju 87 Stuka but had no bombsights and were expected to double as fighters as well. The stately Swordfish did everything: it launched torpedoes, did reconnaissance, spotting and transport work, carried out level and dive-bombing tasks ashore and afloat, and on some occasions even acted as a fighter. Its ability to act as a kind of one-aircraft air force in some ways justified the pre-war faith in multi-purpose aircraft, but its performance could obviously not match that of its specialist German adversaries. Lastly, even the unlikely Walrus entered the fray. One chased a Heinkel unavailingly up and down a steep-sided fjord for half an hour, and another even attempted to act as a dive bomber. The fact that the FAA was able to achieve much with such aircraft is striking testimony to the élan and skill of its pilots, but says much less to the credit of those ultimately responsible for aircraft procurement before the war.

But undoubtedly the main lack was that of high-performance fighters. Apart from a few Sea Gladiators, the FAA placed chief reliance on the Blackburn Skua. A reasonable dive bomber, it was inadequate as a fighter. It was 50 mph slower than the He 111K bomber, 125 mph slower than the Me 110 twin-engined fighter and entirely outclassed by the Me 109. Its rate of climb was often too low for it to reach the He 111 or the Ju 88 if these aircraft were bombing from high levels. It was armed only with four 0.5in machine guns, against the 20mm cannon and four machine guns of the He 111. To a certain extent pilots could attempt to make up for these technical deficiencies by out-flying their opponents as far as their aircraft allowed, but they had always to remember the well known tag of the time, to the effect that the Skua after all was "a bird that folds its wings and dives into the sea".

These deficiencies in fighter protection had been realised even before the Norwegian campaign, not least by the First Lord, Winston Churchill, who was much exercised by the lack of good fighter aircraft for the new Armoured carriers, a shortcoming that was not always recognised. Even Admiral G. C. C. Royle, the Fifth Sea Lord and Chief of the Naval Air Service, was prepared to argue a bare two months before the Norwegian campaign began: "The Fleet when at sea with its destroyer screen in place presents quite the most formidable target a formation of aircraft could attack and the presence of fighter aircraft to protect the Fleet is by no means a necessity. They should be looked upon as an added precaution *if available.*"[74] The Navy very rapidly realised the unwisdom of this view, and set to work to obtain the aircraft that Fleet defence required. The idea that in some circumstances single-seat fighters might be best had already played a role in the Navy's pre-war decision to order a few Gloster Sea Gladiators. In February 1940, also, the Admiralty asked for some Spitfires but agreed to waive its claim as it would have interfered with the urgent task of re-equipping Fighter Command. The Navy therefore looked across the Atlantic for an alternative supply of modern single-seat fighters and intercepted about 50 Grumman Martlets (the equivalent of the US Navy's F4F-3) originally intended for France. Reaching the UK in July 1940, they did not solve the problem, however, as they could not fold their wings and could not therefore be embarked in Fleet carriers.

Even in the desperate days of the summer of 1940 the Admiralty had to look well ahead. In June the First Sea Lord begged Lord Beaverbrook at the Ministry of Aircraft Production not to let present concerns too much endanger the delivery of naval aircraft. In July the Admiralty ordered 100 folding-wing Grumman Martlets and authorised the development of a new high-performance single-seater, the Blackburn Firebrand. It soon became obvious, however, that this orderly progression would not meet the requirement. In November 1940 the Prime Minister charged the Admiralty with not expanding the Fleet Air Arm properly, a view reinforced by the urgent demands that soon began to arrive from the Fleet for a fighter offering more performance than the two-seat Fulmar. Under an "Action This Day" appellation, Churchill wrote: "It is absolutely necessary to have a comparatively small number of really fast fighter aircraft on our carriers. Without these the entire movement of our ships is hampered."[75]

The urgency of the Fleet's need, production delays at Grumman and the expanding requirements of the "cata-fighter" trade-protection scheme obliged the Admiralty to ask for the Sea Hurricane I. These aircraft, which began arriving in January 1941 and in July joined the *Furious*, were a great advance on previous naval types and were the first single-seat monoplane fighters to be used in British carriers. However, their wings did not fold, greatly hindering carrier operations. Worse still, many of them were old aircraft reconditioned for the Navy's use. Indeed, one of them was reported to have force-landed once and been shot down twice during the Battle of Britain over a year before.[76]

In June 1941 the Admiralty decided, after learning of yet more delays in the arrival of Martlets and Firebrands, to ask for the Seafire, a naval version of the Spitfire. Early versions of this aircraft also could not fold their wings, and only in the spring of 1943 did large-scale production of folding-wing Seafire IIIs begin. In September 1941 Churchill visited the carrier *Indomitable* and was appalled to find it still equipped with Sea Hurricanes. "I trust it may be arranged," he wrote, "that only the finest aeroplanes that can do the work go into all aircraft carriers. All this year it has been apparent that the power to launch the highest class of fighters from all carriers may reopen for the Fleet great strategic doors which have been closed against them. The aircraft carriers should have supreme priority in the quantity and character of suitable types." For this reason it was formally decreed on December 9 that fighters for Armoured carriers should have the highest possible priority, "even . . . over the bomber programme". This decision was in fact taken by the Minister for Aircraft Production to apply to all Armoured carrier aircraft.[77]

The shattering disaster of the sinking of the *Prince of Wales* and *Repulse* by unopposed Japanese aircraft the day after this decision was made underlined the urgency of the requirement. The burgeoning demands of the Japanese war combined with the great urgency of the need for aircraft in the U-Boat campaign to produce a crisis in aircraft procurement in the early summer of 1942. "The gap that has opened between the end of the Fulmars and the beginning of the Firebrands," wrote the First Lord, "is a most dangerous one for the naval air arm." He added that the Navy must have another 500 Seafires and 250 Sea Hurricanes to keep going until the new aircraft arrived. The consequences of having inadequate aircraft were made very clear by a series of signals from a hard-pressed

Admiral Somerville as he faced the Japanese in the Indian Ocean that summer. The British fleet had no choice but to adopt cautious and defensive tactics in the air as ". . . our Fleet Air Arm, suffering as it does from arrested development for so many years, would not be able to compete on all-round terms with a fleet air arm which has devoted itself to producing aircraft fitted for sailors to fly in."[78] Although there were signs that the Prime Minister and the MAP were losing patience with the Admiralty by this time, naval demands were adequately met, and in December 1942 naval aircraft of all kinds were given top priority. The problem thereafter became more manageable, especially with the provision of American aircraft under Lend-Lease and with the large-scale production of folding-wing Seafires from April 1943.

Even this quick survey of the first years of the Navy's wartime fighter programme suggests that some of the pre-war problems of aircraft procurement were still present. The Admiralty was much criticised by the Prime Minister in August 1942. "In my opinion," Churchill wrote angrily, "the Admiralty themselves are very largely to blame for the present very unsatisfactory condition of the aircraft of the FAA . . . by not having a clear view of what was wanted, by repeated alterations and by attempting to pile up inordinate reserves you have crippled yourselves."[79] There is justice in at least some of this. Occasionally the Naval Staff asked for the impossible, dismissing technical objections with phrases such as "well, nevertheless, it remains a Naval Staff requirement". Sometimes, too, they varied their specifications and were consequently accused of causing endless delays, especially at times when cumulative shortages of components rendered schedules difficult to keep. "Every such change," said the MAP of the Barracuda programme, "inevitably leads to delay and so retards the date at which the aircraft can be delivered to the services." The Fifth Sea Lord, inspecting a prototype of the Firefly at Fairey, once asked what was the intended use of the space between the first and second cockpits. An officer – evidently something of a wag – who had seen everything come and go in that area, told him that in the end it would probably be filled with copies of King's Regulations. In fact, Fairey was waiting to fit a more advanced radio, but the story nevertheless illustrates the point. The Naval Staff do not however seem to have been any worse at this than the other constituents of the aircraft design and production system.[80]

More seriously, some unfortunate pre-war assumptions seem to have lingered on. There was still something of a preference for what Churchill called "knockabout machines for general purposes," and a consequent reluctance to opt wholeheartedly for specialist aircraft. The Navy also perversely stuck to the idea of a two-seat fighter, a formula which the First Sea Lord surprisingly believed had been "vindicated in the Norwegian campaign".[81] This loyalty seems in retrospect to have been misplaced, since it inevitably led to such aircraft as the Fairey Fulmar, which as the direct descendent of a light bomber could hardly fail to be a mediocre fighter. Nevertheless, the continued preference for a second seat was not the whole story. The single-seat Blackburn Firebrand, for example, originally intended as a short-range interceptor, proved so cumbersome and unmanoeuvrable when first deck-landed in February 1943 that it was shelved, eventually to reappear as a "torpedo-carrying strike fighter" just as the Pacific war ended.

The Admiralty also suffered from influences beyond its control. The prior claims of the RAF up to the second Christmas of the war had delayed all development. The needs of Fighter Command before, during and after the Battle of Britain had overridden the Fulmar programme and put back the Seafire and Sea Hurricane because even such indifferent aircraft as the Defiant and Botha took precedence over naval types. By August 1942 the apparent need "to contain enemy air forces away from the Russian front" was held to justify Fighter Command's operations over France and consequent consumption of new aircraft. For such reasons the Admiralty did not feel that it was getting its fair share of the nation's air resources. "It appears," the First Lord (Alexander) stated in January 1943, "that only seven per cent of the entire aircraft industry was directed at satisfying the needs of the FAA."[83]

Possibly because they had the same priorities, the technical staff at the Air Ministry, and later at MAP, were in the navy's opinion sometimes neither as sympathetic to naval requirements nor as willing to solve particular problems as they might have been. As we shall see later, this was borne out by the delays in the introduction of the Seafire. It also certainly played a part in the disappointing failure to provide a prompt successor for the Skua dive bomber. "The dive-bombing success obtained in Norway by the Skuas and the Junkers 88s has raised in the mind of the Air Staff," said one Air Ministry official with massive understatement, "the suspicion that perhaps the pre-war policy of neglecting the dive bomber was not entirely sound." The design failures and tardy arrival of the Fairey Barracuda owed much to such attitudes.[84]

Churchill's sympathy for the Admiralty was somewhat strained by his conviction that it was obsessed with the desire to build up over-large reserves. "The Admiralty," he wrote, "always want not only to win the game, but to go to bed with the ace."[85] This contention, supported by the Air Ministry, paid too little attention to the fact that carriers had to operate all over the world. Nevertheless, as the war went on, the situation improved and the FAA's aircraft requirements attracted more favour – even to the extent, sometimes, of taking priority over Bomber Command. In 1942 Churchill wrote: "Having regard to the fact that the bombing offensive is necessarily a matter of degree and that targets cannot be moved, it will be right to give priority to the fighter and the torpedo-carrying aircraft required for the numerous carriers and improvised carriers which are available or must be brought into existence. . . . It must be accepted that the priority given to seaborne aircraft of suitable type will involve a retardation in the full-scale bombing offensive against Germany.'[86]

The result of this increase in effort and growth of aerotechnical expertise was a steady improvement in the quality and size of the Navy's aircraft procurement programme. When the war started it was widely believed that naval aircraft could not equal land-based aircraft in performance. There was more than a hint of this in General Auchinleck's final report on the Norway campaign when he said: "The vigour and daring of the pilots of the FAA when they were able to engage the enemy earned the admiration of the whole force but even their strenuous efforts could not compensate for the absence of land-based aircraft owing to the *unavoidable* relative weakness in performance of carrier-borne aircraft.'[87] The success of Gp Capt Cross in bravely landing on the heaving deck of the *Glorious* with a squadron of Hurricanes which were not modified for naval operation, and whose pilots had never attempted such a thing before, destroyed once and for all the all too prevalent myth that high-performance aircraft could not operate from carriers.

By the end of the war the gap in performance between land-based and sea-based aircraft had been largely closed, partly as a result of the realisation that this was as much a psychological as a technical barrier. The operation of aircraft like the Mosquito and the Spitfire 21 from carriers in 1944, the construction of such aircraft as the Hawker Sea Fury and Sea Hornet, and the carrier landing of the world's first naval jet fighter, the British de Havilland Vampire in 1945, all showed in the end that given adequate support British naval aircraft could compare very favourably with the world's best land or sea-based aircraft.

Nevertheless, the FAA's problems could not have been solved by British efforts alone. Although there was much point in the observation made in October 1943 by Admiral Slattery that "it would be preferable to equip the FAA entirely with British aircraft as these were expected to be better than American aircraft in the coming years and we should know where we stood if we were relying on our own production,'[88] he accepted that in the circumstances this was an unattainable ideal.

The US Navy and aircraft industry responded to British requests for help with great generosity. There were occasional difficulties as the demands of the USN's own war in the Pacific became clearer, and perhaps as its need for allies against the demands of the USAAF declined, but American help was indispensible. This was because US aircraft tended, initially at least, to be better than anything produced for the FAA in Britain, no doubt because the American industry was much bigger and more competitive. For their particular task the F4U Corsair and the F6F Hellcat were much better than the Seafire or the Firebrand, and the Grumman TBM Avenger outperformed the Fairey Barracuda. The American contribution was equally important from the quantity point of view. By March 1943 the US was providing 22 per cent of the FAA's torpedo bombers and 58 per cent of its single-seat fighters. By the end of the war over half the

FAA's aircraft were US-built. It was entirely appropriate that the FAA's last victory over German fighters came on March 26, 1945, over Norway, where in one sense it had all begun, and that the aircraft responsible were Grumman Wildcats supplied by the United States.[89]

During the war, and with much help from the US, the FAA grew into a force deploying 44 carriers of various kinds, 1,336 front-line aircraft, 2,790 training aircraft, about 84,000 officers and men and 45 shore stations. By comparison, in 1945 US Naval Air's 100 or so carriers were sustained by a huge infrastructure of over 41,000 aircraft and 400,000 officers and men. Nothing could more aptly symbolise the extent to which power at sea depended on manpower and industrial resources at home, and the gap that had consequently opened between the US and Royal navies.[90]

CHAPTER FIVE

POLICY, DEBATE AND DECISION

The efficiency of naval aviation in this period depended at least as much on the nature of its administration as it did on the number and quality of its personnel, ships and aircraft. Naval air power needed an effective bureaucracy to help it formulate and execute policy, secure adequate equipment and, perhaps most important of all, win it friends in high places.

In the early pre-war pioneering days all was unproved and experimental, dominated and driven by the personalities of the first generation of air enthusiasts, of whom the brilliant and restless Capt Murray Sueter was undoubtedly the leading light. He was made the Director of the Admiralty's Air Department (DAD) in the late summer of 1912 and was responsible "for all matters connected with the Naval Air Service,"[1] being subordinate to no particular member of the Board of Admiralty. Tireless in his endeavours to build up the Naval Air Service, Sueter was determined to keep as many as possible of the strands of policy in his own hands. He insisted: "It is essential for the rapid development of this new arm that a steady line of policy, training and internal organisation should be followed, and this can only be achieved by the maintenance for the present of a central authority which shall remain in close touch with, and in control of, all the details of material and personnel, and their work and training."[2] As a measure of the authority and autonomy he sought and at least temporarily gained, he was put in overall charge of all aircraft, carriers and stations in such a way that if a local Commander-in-Chief wanted the services of an air station within his command, he had normally to request it through the good offices of the DAD[3].

Sueter also realised the importance of drumming up support from senior officials and officers and was soon able to enlist some influential allies. The most important of these was undoubtedly the young First Lord, Churchill, who had demonstrated a keen interest in the air from the start. "You told me," wrote Admiral Fisher, "you would push aviation – you are right. . . ." Churchill's enthusiasm was soon translated into action. This may have been rather to the relief of the rest of the Board, for "it was common gossip amongst junior officers, no doubt with very little foundation, that the Sea Lords had gladly given the forceful young First Lord a free hand over air matters in order to divert him from interfering with the Grand Fleet."[4]

Whatever the truth of the rumour, Churchill certainly took an active and personal interest in every aspect of this new dimension of naval warfare. A stream of sometimes remarkably far-sighted directions and exhortations poured out of the First Lord's office. He often concerned himself with the most detailed and technical matters and went flying as much as he could. In October 1913, for instance, the Admiralty yacht *Enchantress* arrived at Cromarty Air Station and for the next few days Wg Cdr A. M. Longmore's seaplanes took the First Lord and the Secretary of State for War (Colonel J. E. B. Seely) up for flights, and Admirals Colville and Jellicoe as well. Future air policy was discussed over dinner in *Enchantress*, and the young aviators soon discovered that they had a friend and ardent champion in the new First Lord, who despite the Irish crisis "had been able to appear carefree and happy, displaying a kind of schoolboy humour and entertaining us on board *Enchantress* as though the only thing he was interested in was naval aviation."[5]

Churchill's enthusiasm did not blind him to the necessity of maintaining some order in the RNAS's affairs. "Captain Sueter," he wrote, "requires supervision," and proposed that Admiral Sir John Jellicoe, the then Second Sea Lord, be put in charge of the RNAS because he was "the very man to shake the whole thing together."[6] There was no doubt, as Sueter admitted afterwards, that the new service attracted the less conventional kind of officer, and "our over-impatience to push things with the greatest rapidity possible" certainly began to lacerate the sensibilities of the orthodox.[7] Their opportunity to regularise the situation occurred with the resignation of Churchill and of the equally controversial First Sea Lord (Fisher) in the spring of 1915 over the debacle in the Dardanelles. The new regime of A. J. Balfour and Admiral Sir Henry Jackson was in all respects a pale shadow of its predecessor and was determined to bring the airmen to heel. Jackson evidently believed that the RNAS had become too large, wasteful and undisciplined[8]. After the war Sueter complained that "lack of foresight, blocking tactics, and disgraceful persecution of the naval airmen was the unfortunate policy of the British Admiralty in the administration of their own air service in war,"[9] and he probably had this period most in mind.

The upshot of all this was a directive of July 29, 1915, which began: "The Royal Naval Air Service is to be regarded in all respects as an integral part of the Royal Navy. . . ." Air stations were taken away from DAD and returned to the local C-in-Cs.[10] Responsibility for the design of air materiel was later redistributed around existing technical departments, and it was decided that a large proportion of the personnel of the RNAS should be regular officers who would return to general service after their time in the air wing. There were also many administrative appointments of men who could claim no acquaintance with the air, but who were noted, in the words of the Official Historian, for their "power of organisation, their strict sense of discipline, their untiring energy and their pride in the ancient service to which they belonged." Finally, responsibility for the RNAS was taken away from Sueter and given to a Flag Officer, Admiral

C. L. Vaughan-Lee, who became the Director of the Air Service[11].

Vaughan-Lee "was a nice rather tubby little man who had been put in charge of the Air Department as being of suitable rank and presumably well thought of by the Board of Admiralty, though he knew nothing about aircraft and flying."[12] His appointment set the seal on a policy designed to integrate the Air Service within the Navy and to keep it in order. "Commodore Sueter was no longer in command of the RNAS," wrote one of its pioneers afterwards. "At once I felt a different atmosphere. The RNAS was in the hands of those that knew it not, and the prevalent idea seemed to be that the active pilots were a wild sort of people who should be kept well under."[13]

The airmen clearly resented all this, grew increasingly anxious about recurrent delays in various technical projects and complained of the poor use being made of air power at sea. In June 1916, for instance, Admiral Jellicoe (C-in-C Grand Fleet) told the Admiralty of his requirements in the way of aircraft at sea. An Air Department committee chaired by Sueter described this as "the only statement of requirements which has reached the Air Department." The Admiralty, on the other hand, had not studied the matter. "A recommendation or expression of opinion should be obtained from the War Staff," added Sueter, with perhaps more than a touch of sarcasm," as such an opinion would be a guidance to this department."[14] Things were certainly not as they had been in the dynamic Fisher-Churchill era.

In September 1916 agitation in the press and Parliament about the Admiralty's apparent indifference to the air led to the appointment to the War Staff of Cdr H. A. Williamson, an enthusiastic and experienced aviator. He encountered some hostility from some of his new colleagues, particularly Capt Thomas Jackson of the Operations Division, who was activated, wrote Williamson later, ". . . by unreasoning opposition to anything and everything to do with the air." Some senior officers, such as Admirals Oliver (the DCNS) and Wemyss (the Deputy First Sea Lord), were much more sympathetic, however.

"Air matters," wrote Williamson afterwards, "had become of importance to the Grand Fleet, and still more concerning the protection of merchant shipping convoys around our coasts, and should have been dealt with by a senior War Staff officer; but as not one of them knew a thing about it, I had to deal with all air matters, both heavier and lighter than air, though I was a very junior officer." Because the RNAS was so slightly represented on the Staff, wrote the somewhat censorious Capt H. W. Richmond in his diary later, "no initiative is ever shown in the use of aircraft."[15]

For this reason the airmen were inclined to look with a rather more kindly eye on the mounting agitation outside the Navy for a separate, independent, united air service which would be able to co-ordinate air policy and operations of Army and Navy and regularise the vexed and controversial matter of aircraft supply. In retrospect it appears quite extraordinary that the Admiralty should not have realised how dangerous it was to antagonise its own airmen at the very time that this campaign was reaching its climax in the deliberations of the Derby Joint War Air Committee and Curzon Air Board of 1916. One of the main planks in the argument of the latter, for example, was that the Admiralty had demonstrated its patent inability to comprehend the new strategic realities by failing to give naval air power due weight within the Admiralty organisation. Responsibility for the Naval Air Service, said Curzon, was diffused in the interests of assimilation. "It has no representative on the Board of Admiralty, the members of which, and the chief officers of which, have in no case any personal knowledge of aeronautics." The Air Service was novel and *sui generis* and it needed the special consideration accorded it in the Army.[16] In the course of an extraordinarily venomous report, the argument was put forward that the deficiency in understanding and imagination revealed in the Admiralty's treatment of its own flyers was all of a piece with its hostile attitude to the suggestion that Army and Navy efforts be better co-ordinated. The Admiralty was in effect behaving like the proverbial dog in a manger.

The Admiralty's case was further weakened by the fact that some of its own flyers, most notably Sueter himself, publicly agreed with the Curzon Report in the discussion held on November 27, 1916. Flatly contradicting Admiral F. C. T. Tudor (Third Sea Lord) and Vaughan-Lee (DAS), Sueter stated that after seven years' experience of the RNAS he was "entirely in sympathy with the view that amalgamation (of the RFC and the RNAS) was desirable and essential."[17] This open dissent shocked the Admiralty and did great damage to its cause, but Sueter had been working up to this ever since the change in direction brought about by the arrival of the Balfour-Jackson regime. He had, for example, probably written the memorandum on "The Formation of an Air Department" which Churchill sent to the Prime Minister (Asquith) in June 1915. "It looks to me," wrote Asquith's Private Secretary, "like a scheme for providing Winston with something to do. . . . The Naval Wing is a failure," he added, "because it has degenerated into a crowd of highly skilled but ill-disciplined privateersmen. What is wanted is to make the Naval Wing more 'naval,' not more 'aerial'."[18] Even more imprudently, Sueter was responsible for an article which appeared in the *Globe* newspaper on October 13, 1915, describing the RNAS as the Cinderella of the Navy and called for the formation of a Royal Air Service. Sueter's open disloyalty and private intrigue certainly "helped to create the Air Service from under the Admiralty's nose. Whatever our faults may have been, we air pioneers raised the Air Service on a higher plane than Admiralty squabbles. Some of us sacrificed our careers. . . ."[19]

The immediate results of all this seem to have been almost inevitable. Sueter was exiled to the Mediterranean and left the Admiralty in February 1917, just at the time when the fortunes of the RNAS seemed to be improving. This was largely brought about by the departure of the intractable Balfour-Jackson regime and the arrival of Admiral Jellicoe as First Sea Lord in December 1916. Jellicoe, one of the first officers to fly, had already won the sympathy of many airmen for his early and continued interest in naval air power. "When Admiral Jellicoe became First Sea Lord," said one, "there was a complete change in the attitude of the War Staff, and no more was heard of there being no time to consider air matters."[20]

Under Jellicoe's guidance the Admiralty became more amenable to argument. One of the first fruits of this was the appointment of Cdre Godfrey Paine as Fifth Sea Lord and Director of Air Services. The appointment of this "big fine-looking man . . . of Irish origin, and something of a character," widely known as an air enthusiast of some standing, would have blunted the attack of the Curzon Air Board had it been done a year earlier.[21] By now, however, the campaign for a united air service had gathered momentum, culminating in the Cowdray Air Board and Smuts Committee Report, and was unlikely to be diverted by such palliatives as this. The Jellicoe regime's more amenable demeanour seems to have been essentially a matter of negotiating style, for the Admiralty was still resolutely opposed to the idea of a united air service incorporating the RNAS.

But now Jellicoe's prestige and confidence were beginning to suffer as a consequence of the U-Boat campaign. At the same time the unexpected support for the notion of a separate and independent Air Service offered by the Navy's rising star, Admiral Beatty (C-in-C Grand Fleet), did much to reconcile the Navy to the loss of the RNAS. Beatty had already demonstrated an acute awareness of the potential of air power at sea, especially in his proposal for massed aerial torpedo attacks on the German High Seas Fleet. In retrospect, he plainly pinned too much faith on the importance which a new air service would attach to the meeting of naval needs, but he was sure that the RNAS so far had proved too parochial and too little exposed to outside air influences. Even the requirements of Fleet operation, that most specialised of maritime functions, "are not such that they cannot be acquired in a short time. They are part of the knowledge required by airmen generally, whether belong[ing] to the RFC or the RNAS."[22] These concessions, which were shortly to prove a grave embarrassment to the Admiralty and to Beatty personally, were explained by the C-in-C's anxiety to have a definite and settled policy on the functions of air power at sea. "I have at varying intervals for some time been clamouring," he wrote, "for a definite decision as to the functions of the Naval Air Service and have up to the present not received any reply that has provided the necessary definitions."[23] Such a policy had been produced neither in the wild and pioneering days nor in those of orthodoxy. Perhaps the new Air Service would do better? In effect, Beatty advocated the abandonment of the RNAS because he thought the Navy of the First World War had failed to evolve a satisfactory policy for it, a grave indictment of all those who had directed its affairs.

The RNAS was duly absorbed by the RAF in April 1918, but by this time Beatty had already had further thoughts on the means by which a policy for naval aviation might be produced. In November 1917, for instance, he recommended that "in order that development may proceed on sound lines it is desirable that control be centralised in the hands of a Flag Officer," who would command the air component of the Grand Fleet. Admiral R. F. Phillimore was duly appointed Admiral Commanding Aircraft in January 1918.[24] The Admiralty also urged that for the first time specific provision be made in the Naval Staff for an agency that would liaise with the new Air Ministry, supervise policy in the U-Boat war and co-ordinate air operations from East Coast air stations. Accordingly, Capt F. R. Scarlett was appointed Director of the Air Division (DAD) on January 14, 1918.[25] Although the prospect of imminent execution seems to have concentrated the Admiralty's mind wonderfully, this last-minute repentance came much too late to save the RNAS.

The birth of the RAF came at a time of grave crisis as the German Spring Offensive of 1918 got under way and the leaders of the new service squabbled amongst themselves and resigned. Naval voices were very soon raised against the wisdom of the past surrender and the present system. The Admiralty became very concerned when it realised the extent to which the higher councils of the new service were dominated by ex-RFC officers who had no naval experience. This led to the remarkable suggestion that the Navy should borrow Trenchard, who had recently resigned as Chief of the Air Staff, for a period of six months "so that the higher ranks of the Air Force may be advised of the special needs and considerations of the Navy."[26] The failure to meet the Navy's operational needs and requirements in men and aircraft, wrote Beatty on July 30, 1918, in terms now very different from what they were a year before, showed that "Under the new organisation . . . the essential requirements of the Fleet in aeroplane construction will only be met if urged with vigour by the Naval Air Division. A clear-cut policy must be defined, the arguments necessitating the urgent supply to meet the policy must be continually pressed, otherwise, through failure to present the facts to the Air Ministry, machines will be directed to less important uses and the main Fleet will suffer."[27] Rather belatedly, it would seem, Beatty had realised how unreasonable it was to suppose that the creation of a new service would somehow provide the Navy with a policy on how it should use air power at sea.

In fact the foundation of the RAF made this more difficult anyway, as the great majority of the pioneers of air power at sea naturally elected to transfer into the new service. The first list of permanent commissions in the RAF was published in August 1, 1919. The one conspicuous absence was Admiral Murray Sueter, who had fallen victim to the memory of past indiscretions. He wrote to the Admiralty three weeks after the establishment of the RAF to ask whether he was to be transferred. Pointing out that he had "started the Naval Air Service in

August 1909 when I was appointed Inspecting Captain of Airships," and stressing his probably unparalleled services to the cause of air power at sea, Sueter
asked to be at least lent to the RAF so that he could "help in developing the naval
side of the new service." But as his file in the Admiralty noted, "this officer is
not required by the Air Ministry, and since his years' service in the RNAS have
not qualified him for a naval appointment, it is difficult to foresee how he is to be
employed outside the Air Service."[28] In point of fact, though, both the Admiralty and the Air Ministry appear to have regarded him as too unruly a figure for
them to accomodate in an era of peace, and by so doing deprived naval aviation
of a major stimulant. As an MP, Sueter later launched some natural but bitter
attacks on the Admiralty's past and present attitudes to air power which certainly did not help the cause to which he had devoted so much of his energy in
the past.

A good many officers of the RNAS had serious qualms about entering a service which might be dominated by the "RFC element" and were in any case
reluctant to leave the Navy, but nearly all of them did so. Some, like Admirals
Mark Kerr (the first Flag Officer to qualify as a pilot) and Sir Godfrey Paine,
took high if temporary positions in the new service. Although most ex-RNAS
officers moved into the mainstream of the life of their new service, many naturally gravitated towards those parts of it which concentrated on the development
of maritime air power. In 1927 one ex-RNAS officer, Gp Capt H. M. Cave-
Brown-Cave, led four flying boats off on a 23,000-mile trip to Singapore and in
so doing demonstrated the abiding interest of such officers in the role of air
power at sea.

Although such efforts compensated for it a little, the sudden departure from
the Navy of virtually all its airmen was bound to slow up the development of
naval aviation. Only towards the end of the inter-war period did the new generation of naval flyers begin to reach and fill the senior positions abandoned by
their predecessors 15 years before. As late as 1932, for instance, while the US
Navy had 25 captains or admirals on the Active List who had qualified as pilots
or observers, the Royal Navy had only one. This meant that there were no
senior officers who could argue the FAA's case with the fervour and authority
that came from personal flying experience. The FAA had supporters in the
senior councils of the Navy, but no representatives.

Indeed, Trenchard and the Air Staff hoped that the Navy would rather look
to the RAF for advice and guidance on the development of maritime air power
rather than try to manufacture its own. This was the reason behind the creation
of the Air Division, manned by RAF officers, in the Naval Staff. By the spring
of 1919, however, the Air Ministry was already unhappy with the way this
system was working, believing that the location of this body, its lack of executive responsibilities, and, doubtless, the naval background of its officers all
meant that the Air Division "tended to become the critic of the Air Ministry."[29]

Instead, Trenchard proposed the establishment of a General Officer Commanding Naval Headquarters to act as the executive commander of all units working with the Navy and the Admiralty's immediate air advisor. This led in September 1919 to the creation of RAF Coastal Area under Air Cdre A. V. Vyvyan, an ex-RNAS officer. The new command was set up in a rather raffish hotel. For some weeks, officers of Coastal Area had to deal with telephone callers disappointed to find that the establishment that they sought to patronise was no more. The Air Staff were also unhappy with results of this experiment. Relations between the Admiralty and their ex-naval colleagues in Coastal Area seemed too cosy. The Air Staff objected to the Naval Staff consulting Coastal Area directly, as they did in 1920 on the matter of flying boat policy, and decided to terminate the "undesirable" system whereby "questions of future policy are referred for the opinion of officers at Coastal Area . . . not in a position to be acquainted with the views of the Air Staff or the possibilities of future development."[30]

Shortly afterwards, the headquarters of Coastal Area was shifted from London to Lee-on-Solent and the Admiralty was forbidden to send papers directly to them, thereby ending the close relationship between the Navy and the air command which it would have to work with in war.[31] Routine contacts were of course maintained, but the Air Staff became very agitated over the question of contact on matters of principle or policy. A little later, Coastal Area produced and circulated a consultation paper on the desirable attributes of a reconnaissance aircraft, only for the Deputy Chief of the Air Staff, Air Cdre J. M. Steele, to object strenuously. "I think it is a very extraordinary procedure, and a very undesirable one," wrote this ex-RNAS officer, "that Coastal Area should authorise a paper of this sort to be circulated and especially that they should call for the opinions of several naval officers."[32] The Air Ministry was plainly anxious about the development of close links between the Naval Staff and Coastal Area, since this might be thought eventually to threaten Ministry authority over it. By insisting that the two organisations maintain a proper distance, the Air Ministry effectively deprived the Navy of a source of advice on policy matters that would have done something to compensate the Admiralty for the loss of the officers giving that advice.

This was particularly unfortunate, as the Naval Staff of the immediate postwar period very soon demonstrated how unready they were to make important decisions about naval air policy. Admiral Beatty took over as First Sea Lord on November 1, 1919, and was soon "full of the chaotic state in which he finds things . . . decisions lacking, letters unanswered. . . .", and this certainly included air matters. In December 1919, for example, the Air Ministry produced its estimates, apparently without consulting the Admiralty, and Beatty went "in a high state of indignation" to see Trenchard about the matter. Trenchard told him that the Treasury had been pressing him for some time and that he had been unable to get the Admiralty to tell him what its aerial requirements were. Beatty "saw that he couldn't have done otherwise and told him he was quite right," doubtless realising that such embarassments would recur unless the gap in the Naval Staff left by the effective disappearance of the Air Division was somehow filled.[33] For the moment, Beatty asked Capt Barry Domvile of the Plans Division to assume responsibility for dealing with the Air Ministry on air matters. Although Domvile had been secretary of the 1913–14 Air Committee, he did not have the personal experience necessary to frame policy. This he had to try to do, however.[34]

This is not to say that there was no thinking in the Naval Staff about the future of air power at sea. In fact an ex-RNAS officer whom we have encountered before, Cdr H. A. Williamson, had been loaned to the Plans Division by the Air Ministry and had occupied himself by producing a very extensive manual on the subject which was widely read by many senior officers of the time.[35] These included Beatty and Admiral Madden, C-in-C of the Atlantic Fleet, whose own reflections on naval aviation were quite extensive, as has been shown. All these observations and tentative plans were however made by men who could not give their full attention to the matter. It was a time of great uncertainty and constant change as the manifold problems of emerging peace, economic near-collapse and social turbulence made themselves felt. At the time of the Armistice there had been 336 officers in the Naval Staff; within two years economic considerations had forced the authorised strength down to 87. "Any further reductions," it was roundly declared, "would be an act of inexcusable folly and a crime against posterity." Commanders in the Operations Division were reported to be working a 73-hour, seven-day week at this time.[36] Calm contemplation of the kind needed to lay secure foundations for post-war naval air policy could hardly be expected in this frantic atmosphere.

Unfortunately, the Air Ministry was in no better condition, especially as it was by no means sure that the RAF would prove to be more than a temporary wartime expedient anyway. For the present, savage demobilisation had reduced it to a dreadful state, and this had inevitably carried over into the air units working with the Fleet. Beatty recognised that there was little that the Air Council could do about this and was content to wait for better times. But many of his colleagues were not so patient, using present deficiencies to urge Beatty to begin a campaign for the Navy to repossess its own air wing. As early as the spring of 1919, for instance, Phillimore observed trenchantly that "Failure to fight this matter to the finish and to acquiesce in the present and indefensible and illogical policy because a too hasty surrender was made last year – presumably under political pressure – will, I am convinced be fraught with great danger to the efficiency of His Majesty's Navy."[37] In September 1921 Beatty finally agreed that it would be a "dereliction of duty" to continue to accept the existing system. Thus began a long period in which the question of who should control naval aviation attracted at least as much attention as did that of the uses to which it could be put.[38]

The tendency to concentrate on ownership rather than purposes was also a feature of the deliberations of the Post-war Questions Committee, set up in 1919 under Admiral Phillimore to "consider in the light of the experiences of the war the military uses and values of the different types of war vessel" and the likely roles of naval aviation.[39] In its "Interim Report on Air Organisation" the committee presented for the first time most of the arguments that the Admiralty was repeatedly to use throughout the inter-war period in its campaign against Dual Control. For the moment, however, the report was suppressed since it conflicted with Government policy[40]. More generally, the committee listened to a large range of opinions, varying from the assertion that battleships were now obsolete to the dismissal of the air menace as a complete chimaera. Hard evidence was in short supply and, perhaps not surprisingly, the committee concluded generally that the battleship was still the dominant factor in naval warfare, with air power important but ancillary.

The committee's ability to provide a vision of the way ahead was weakened by its unbalanced membership. Apart from the chairman himself and the secretary, neither aviation, the sciences nor naval construction were represented.[41] It was also extremely materialistic in its concerns. "Phillimore's Committee," wrote Capt H. W. Richmond, "is busy deciding a mass of unimportant matters, asking us questions about what the speed of a battleship should be, the calibre of anti-TB guns, of anti-aircraft guns, whether torpedo control can be simplified and such like stuff. If that is the line they are working on, they won't do much good."[42] Finally the very idea of an inquiry of this kind was not popular. Probably because they feared that an investigation of the conduct of the First World War might prove divisive, the Board had from the start been very reluctant to accept the First Lord's (Geddes) suggestion that one should be held. There was also a reluctance to provide the committee with the information it needed. When Phillimore asked the Director of Naval Construction (DNC) for guidance on likely developments in armour protection, the Controller wrote: "I have spoken about this in higher quarters and the president will be told on a suitable occasion to keep off matters such as this. My view is that your policy should be to furnish the committee with assistance on general lines but should certainly not help their efforts in matters of which they can know very little and can only be considered as amateurs."[43] When the report was finally issued, very little use seems to have been made of it.

A further opportunity for open-minded analysis of the future of naval war occurred with the establishment of the Naval Shipbuilding Sub-committee of the CID under the Keeper of the Privy Seal, Bonar Law, on December 7, 1920. The Bonar Law Inquiry, as it became known, listened to a variety of Navy and Air Force witnesses who came to some very contradictory views about the future primacy of the battleship and was forced to conclude with a divided report which left matters very much as they were. Bonar Law himself and Sir Eric Geddes (a former First Lord) seem to have been impressed by the air case, but Churchill and Long (two other ex-First Lords) were not.[44]

The value of this inquiry as a review of the future of naval warfare was much reduced by the fact that neither the Government nor the Admiralty saw it in this light. "The present inquiry," the Prime Minister (Lloyd George) told the CID, "amounted to the question of whether we should have an entirely new Navy at gigantic cost. . . ."[45] Hankey later noted in his diary: "The PM rather irritable. . . . He wants to be able to prove that the capital ship is doomed, which would be rather convenient politically, but I have assured him that he can't."[46] The Admiralty inevitably took its cue from this. Beatty "wanted arguments," wrote Richmond, "to show that the battleships were necessary. I thought he was going about investigation the wrong way round. One should not try to prove what needed proving in one's own mind, but to find out what was right. . . . The thing must be approached in a far more scientific manner."[47] Circumstances seemed to call for an energetic departmental defence of the battleship and of the Navy, and so the case was carefully prepared, witnesses fresh from the sea were primed in naval strategy by the Naval Staff, and displeasure fell on Richmond, who was the only active officer to break ranks and side with the "opposition".[48] Some key witnesses, like Admiral Sir Percy Scott, did not appear at all, viewing the invitation as "a clumsy attempt to muzzle me," and others did not do themselves justice.[49] Calm contemplation was not aided by the fact that a virulent debate was also being conducted in the correspondence columns of *The Times*, which helped further to inflame the atmosphere. In sum, the Admiralty, anxious anyway about the US naval construction programme, tended to associate its own well-being with the survival of the battleship and looked at the inquiry in rather the same "political" terms as did the Government.

The inquiry was less a forum for debate and analysis than a means of the efficient presentation of views already arrived at. "The important point," commented Capt Bellairs, "as to whether the present type of Dreadnought is to be the capital ship of the future, for our strategy requirements, is, I think, being lost sight of."[50] And so for various reasons neither of the major inquiries which the Admiralty conducted at the onset of the post-war period offered significant guidance for future naval policy in general, or air policy in particular. As a later Director of Naval Intelligence observed, "No body of officers [is] now free to make that close study of strategy without which sound war plans are an impossibility. . . . Everyone is now intent on trees in the forest and has little comprehension of the size and shape of the forest itself."[51]

The Navy was thus not well prepared as it moved into the 1920s, a decade which saw the FAA growing slowly in numbers of aircraft, carriers and personnel and in tactical experience, especially after the arrival of the *Eagle* in the Mediterranean in 1924. It was also a period of acute controversy with the Air Ministry over the threat of bomb-versus-battleship, the relative importance of the two services in the defence of Britain and, most contentiously of all, over the control of the FAA itself.

By early 1920 the Admiralty had already decided that the existing machinery for the formulation of naval air policy was inadequate and "tends to relegate air matters to a subordinate position in naval staff work, instead of that prominent position that their importance justifies,"[52] and so formed the Naval Air Section (NAS) of the Naval Staff in June of that year. Its first chief, and for some time its only member, was Cdr Richard Bell Davies, practically the only surviving pioneer naval aviator left in the Navy and recipient of a VC for rescuing under fire a companion shot down during the Dardanelles campaign. He had also been much involved in all naval air development since, notably the first deck-landing trials on the *Argus* in 1918. The section gradually expanded until by the mid-1920s it comprised seven officers dealing with an average of 415 papers a month. By the end of the decade it was a full-blown Naval Staff Division.[53]

Even so, the NAS clearly did not begin to approach the US Navy's Bureau of Aeronautics in terms of power and autonomy, as its terms of reference make clear. NAS was to "assist ACNS in his consideration of all air questions relating to naval warfare . . . co-ordination of all matters dealt with by the Naval staff . . . advise generally on the naval side of questions of fleet air warfare . . . [liase with] AOCA and various branches of the Air Staff . . . assist ACNS and Controller as necessary in regards to material questions affecting Fleet aircraft or aircraft carriers . . . provide information on air matters, other than intelligence, required by other divisions of the Naval Staff."[54] Although Bell Davies worked with his very capable ACNS, Chatfield, to produce several tentative outlines of possible air developments,[55] these were mainly concerned with practical ways and means rather than with analysis of the fleet's long-term tactical or strategic needs. As chief of the NAS, Bell Davies was obliged to concentrate on technical matters of detail and had little executive authority. "When I first joined the Admiralty," he wrote later, "Admiral Chatfield had told me that on all matters of any importance I was always to consult him verbally before adopting any policy or initiating any proposal and this I had always done."[56] In fact he had neither the seniority, not probably the temperament, to provide the kind of dynamic leadership that naval aviation was soon to enjoy in the United States.

The Admiralty had always thought it "essential that one of the members of the Board should control the FAA and represent it at Board meetings,"[57] and Chatfield was the first to assume this role early in 1920. Of all the seven officers to hold the post through the 1920s, only three seem to have left any particular mark on naval aviation: Chatfield himself (1920–2), Dreyer (1925–7) and Pound (1927–9). All three were gunners and all believed in the necessity of naval air power, though Pound was noticeably less fervent than the first two. Chatfield's attentions were much taken up with the dispute with the Air Ministry. Dreyer was concerned with this too and was involved in the Admiralty's ill-advised attempt to reopen the issue before the Colwyn Committee in 1925.[58] Otherwise he was responsible for the great increase in the Navy's catapult programme. Pound, as we have seen, was primarily responsible for the drastic cutback in the FAA's expansion programme in the late 1920s. He was also the last ACNS for a while to have a seat on the Board, and this inevitably put a further institutional distance between the Naval Air Division and the Navy's senior councils.

Both First Sea Lords of the period, Beatty and Madden, were sympathetic to the development of naval air power. The Naval Staff were favourably impressed by Beatty's personal grip of the subject when he first arrived at the Admiralty in November 1919. He also thought the issue of the control of naval aviation important enough to consider resigning over it. Of the two, Madden was probably the more far-sighted about the potential of air power at sea and was a significant source of tactical and strategic ideas during his time as C-in-C Atlantic Fleet. His views were described ten years later as "well-balanced, [as] he did not fail to appreciate that aeroplanes were destined to play an ever-increasing part in maritime warfare, but he knew that as yet none of the Navy's functions in war could be undertaken by aeroplanes."[59] Nonetheless, he assumed office at a time made difficult for the Navy by heavy pressure for economic retrenchment and disarmament, and his gifts did not include the ability to inspire the kind of awe so useful to his predecessor in the many Whitehall battles of the time. Whatever his intellectual gifts, Madden was less effective a protector of the FAA against the vicissitudes of the time.

In sum, none of the Navy's senior officers had the time to establish the place and purpose of air power in the Fleet to more than a superficial degree. The Naval Staff found it difficult to fill this gap completely because they too were under the same kind of pressure. In 1927 they described themselves as being "down to bedrock," having contracted from 336 to 59 officers, and finding it "very wearisome having to deal with repeated attacks on the composition of and numbers on the Naval Staff." It is entirely to the Admiralty's credit that these violent and incessant attacks in Press and Parliament, inspired by demands for spurious and ill-advised economy measures, did not do more damage to military efficiency. But they certainly made the business of strategic contemplation more difficult.[60]

Less easily defensible was the Admiralty's very evident desire to avoid "undue centralisation" and to diffuse responsibilities for the FAA amongst a large number of Staff Divisions and materiel departments. Responsibility for the evolution of policy was deliberately dispersed in a way which ultimately produced more drift than direction. The Admiralty also sought to do the same for the design and construction of aircraft. In 1923, before the Balfour Committee, the Admiralty's proposals for the management of aircraft construction would have reproduced the situation in the US before the creation of BuAer, when the Bureau of Steam

Engineering produced the engines, the Bureau of Construction the fuselages and other bureaux the rest of the components, a system which made the procurement programme a "shambles, devoid of centralised co-ordination and control."[61] The Balfour Committee found against the Admiralty, though, and responsibility for the construction and design of naval aircraft remained in theory centred on the Air Ministry. But as we have seen, this was not a very satisfactory solution either. In practice this responsibility also became diffused, even if in a way different from that intended by the Admiralty.

By 1930 it was widely agreed that the development of naval aviation had lost its momentum. Anxiety about this inspired the creation, on September 21, 1931, of a new post: Rear-Admiral, Aircraft Carriers (RAA). The Navy needed a senior officer who could concentrate his whole attention on the evolution of naval aviation – but there were complications. He would have to fly his flag afloat, as otherwise his functions would tend to conflict with the Naval Air Division and, more significantly, with Coastal Area and the Air Ministry. The appointment had great political significance. The Naval Assistant to the First Sea Lord argued that the post "needed adequate safeguard to prevent the Air Ministry from using it as a lever to obtain further control of the Fleet Air Arm." Madden himself, though, thought that it might be used in the reverse sense as "a means of increasing our grip on Naval Air."[62]

Eventually the appointment proceeded and Admiral R. G. H. Henderson was selected to act as "the recognised naval advisor to other fleets on all matters connected with the Fleet Air Arm." He was an inspired choice, and had made a high reputation for himself as "a brilliant officer, full of imagination, resource and initiative"[63] since the days when he had worked to reform the Admiralty's campaign against the U-Boats of the First World War. The selection of such a highly regarded officer indicates the perceived importance of the task with which he was entrusted. Henderson had commanded the *Furious* in 1926–8 and was known to be a staunch advocate of naval air power, and his appointment did a very great deal to raise both the morale and the performance of the FAA, particularly in the area of operating massed striking forces from carriers. He eventually moved on to become Third Sea Lord and Controller, being instrumental in the Armoured Carrier Programme. His early death in 1939, the result of overwork, was nothing short of a tragedy for the Royal Navy.

Henderson was succeeded as RAA in 1933 by Admiral the Hon Sir Alexander Ramsay, who later became Fifth Sea Lord and first Chief of the Naval Air Service in 1938–9. Although overshadowed by Henderson, Ramsay was also an air enthusiast in a quiet way. He was supported by a Naval Air Division which was also beginning to gather prestige, influence and a capacity to get things done. The tenure of Capt H. C. Rawlings as Director in 1932–4 was particularly important to this development, seeing the effective birth of the FAA expansion programme, good progress in naval air materiel and the gradual beginning of real thinking about naval air tactics. The momentum was increased by the arrival of the first generation of post-war flyers to take up their first Staff appointments at the Admiralty, increasing the general sense of purpose as they did so. In 1935 the Division welcomed Lord Louis Mountbatten, whose own abilities and valuable connections provided important support for the development of naval air power. Though by 1936 the number of officers in the NAD had grown to about 20, they found that they could not cope with the expanding demands on their time and Staff work was piling up. There had been no attempt, for example, to put on paper the accumulated experience and reflections of the observer branch, established in 1920. In effect, the "oral" and personal tradition was still far more prominent in the FAA than in other areas of naval activity.[64] But all the same, the Air Ministry was plainly very perturbed about all this and strongly criticised the "tendency . . . to develop, within the Admiralty itself, its own organisation [the Naval Air Division] for the administration of the FAA which, to a considerable extent, duplicates and impinges on work proper to the Air Ministry."[65]

The Naval Air Staff were also steadily increasing their technical expertise and ability to initiate technical developments. Rawlings, for example, was a personal friend of Richard Fairey and was largely responsible for the production of the remarkable Swordfish. Over a whole range of technical areas, FAA officers ashore and afloat were responsible for the bulk of the materiel advance, while a scattering of them took up appointments in the Air Ministry. The various technical liaison committees also increased in effectiveness.[66] Although the Admiralty was by 1937 willing to concede that ". . . the views of naval officers are generally sympathetically heard in regard to design," it still continued to think that "arrangements made in respect of types and general development have not come up to the standard of other naval weapons."[67]

Responsibility for the design and production of aircraft was, as we have seen, one of the many issues that increasingly divided the Air Ministry and the Admiralty as the 1930s progressed. The Naval Staff argued that "naval air work lies outside the natural sphere of interest of a Ministry engaged on a large scale with land-air developments,"and believed that the present system produced muddle and delay in the production of aircraft and of such diverse air materiel as wireless-telegraphy equipment for aircraft and bombsights for use against moving targets.[68] For political reasons the Admiralty did not wish to appear to want to take this function over, but it certainly wanted to be more extensively involved in it.

All this was part of the Admiralty's renewed campaign to regain complete control of the FAA, which finally ended in victory in July 1937. The Inskip Award brought great changes to the institutions of naval air. Although naval responsibility for aircraft design was neither claimed nor awarded, a Department of Air Materiel was nevertheless set up in January 1938 to superintend the procurement of all aerial equipment for the FAA and to build up expertise so that there need no longer be a "blind acceptance of Air Ministry advice about FAA aircraft,"[69] which was actually something of an exaggeration anyway. At the same time a Department of Air Personnel was established to handle the difficult personnel aspects of the transfer of the FAA to full Admiralty control.

The Naval Air Division continued to operate in three rooms behind the main entrance of the old Admiralty building, an ancient monument protected from excessive cleaning or heating by the Office of Works. Now freed from many of its earlier technical and personnel preoccupations, NAD was expected to be able to concentrate more on the tactical and operational side of naval air work. It was to comprise three sections dealing with operations, staff requirements, and weapons and training. Its main function was to advise ACNS (Air) and all other Naval Staff Divisions on the influence exerted on naval strategy and tactics by aircraft. Like all other Naval Staff Divisions, NAD had no executive authority of its own but was supposed to provide the air component of naval war plans and operations, although it was not responsible for plans and did not conduct operations. The efforts of the two new departments and the NAD were to be co-ordinated first by the ACNS (Air) and later by the Fifth Sea Lord and Chief of the Naval Air Service.

This all sat rather oddly with the rest of the Admiralty's organisation, cutting right across traditional distinctions between Staff Divisions and materiel departments. The three new members of the system also tended to poach in the territory of existing institutions. The difficulty of accommodating the institutions of the FAA in the existing bureaucracy goes some way to explaining the almost obsessive desire on the part of all concerned to avoid "anything that might conceivably grow into an Air Ministry within the Admiralty"[70] by diffusing its functions around the existing bureaucracy. Fortunately this proved too difficult. All this bureaucratic engineering was moreover only a small part of the administrative effort expended by the Admiralty in taking over and expanding the naval air service, finding and training the personnel required, administering the new air stations and generally communicating with the Air Ministry. Responsibility for much of this lay in the hands of Rear-Admiral Naval Air Stations (RANAS), who would fly his flag at Lee-on-Solent and was eventually expected to assume ultimate command of Lee, Ford, Worthy Down, Donibristle, Eastleigh, Arbroath and Yeovilton. It was entirely appropriate that the first RANAS should be Rear-Admiral Bell Davies, with whom the development of the institutions of naval air might be said to have started 18 years earlier.

Bureaucracy has not only to administer but also to plan the future. What the FAA needed during the inter-war period was an almost visionary grand design of the kind that inspired sections first of the US and then of the Japanese navies. In 1926, for instance, the US Congress produced a long-term plan which "cleared the way for a rational programme of aircraft procurement and . . . gave recognition in precise detail to the special place fleet aviation should occupy in the years ahead."[71] This was the product of an effective and vociferous naval air lobby in the USA which could speak for naval aviation and provide the inspiration and perspective so often lacking in the Royal Navy. In Britain no deep study of the future role of naval aviation was undertaken because no specific Naval Staff institution or officer was directly responsible for providing one. There was in consequence no "grand design" for the FAA to set against the political, technical and economic pressures which restricted its progress. More generally, there existed no naval air lobby to challenge the Royal Navy's habit of associating the battleship's well-being with its own. There were few to suggest that air power, in the guise of carrier aviation, might replace the battleship but confirm rather than extinguish the strategic importance of the Navy.

The institutional feebleness of the FAA shows up in striking contrast against the strength and vigour of the various US naval air agencies. American naval aviation's highest representative was the politically appointed Assistant Secretary for Naval Aeronautics, a post held for a while at the start of the period by David Ingalls, a naval flying ace of the First World War. Effective leadership, however, was provided by Rear-Admiral W. A. Moffett, Chief of the Bureau of Aeronautics (BuAer), "who has tackled the subject with almost fanatical zeal, supported by the whole nation from the President downwards."[72] Moffett's immense personal prestige led to his holding this office for no less than 12 years until his death in 1933. In 1929 Admiral C. F. Hughes, the Chief of Naval Operations, tried to block Moffett's third reappointment but was over-ridden by the specific order of President Hoover.[73]

BuAer, from its inception in August 1921, had far greater responsibility than the NAS or NAD for such matters as the design and construction of aircraft, the management of air personnel, the general development of aerial warfare at sea and even for the provision of funds for naval aviation.[74] Behind the campaign for the creation of BuAer lay the US Navy aviator's assumption that the general status of the arm depended on its administrative standing. This belief was well justified, for with Moffett and BuAer "flying stock went up in the Navy Department, with an Admiral to fight our battles we began to get things done. . . . Best of all, we had a well informed group of properly accredited officers to present our case to Congress when aviation matters came up."[75] Moffett's various errors of judgement – over such things as the continued value of airships and small rather than large carriers – paled beside the fact that in him and in BuAer US naval aviation had found its voice and inspiration.

In the Royal Navy, however, the naval air lobby was more muted and the general vision of the way ahead less clear. The absence of bureaucratic drive, and the sense of long-term purpose of the kind it produced in Japan and the USA, does much to explain the fatal indecisions and drift in the aircraft and carrier procurement and expansion programmes. As we shall see later, it also contributed to the Navy's failure to think scientifically about the attack and defence of major warships in the air age.

Perhaps most important of all, the institutions of Naval Air did not prove appropriate to the systematic and sustained analysis of the role and place of naval aviation in future warfare at sea. Study of this subject in the 1920s had been dominated by questions of ways and means, by such things as the number of aircraft that might be available or the expected carrying capacity of the Fleet. Only in the early 1930s did the Royal Navy begin to investigate in depth the possible role and purpose of the Fleet Air Arm as a whole. In a sense, it all started with a paper on cruiserborne aircraft issued for remarks and criticism by Capt Rawlings and the NAD in January 1934. Probably because it was written in rather more expansive terms than such papers usually were, it attracted a great deal of interest and showed that there was such a wide divergence of views about air power at sea that the Naval Staff decided to investigate the whole problem more exhaustively. The Naval Air, Plans, and Training and Staff Duties divisions therefore got together and eventually produced the first volume of a long manual entitled "Fleet Air Arm Tactics and Equipment" in March 1936. They believed that there was a need to settle policy on the functions of the FAA, as "the adoption of a definite policy is essential to development."[76] Volume I covered FAA functions in a Fleet action; Volume 2 was intended to deal with trade protection.

The manual then went around the rest of the Admiralty, provoking significant comment. Henderson (then Controller) was plainly unhappy with it, disagreeing with some of the views expressed, and was reluctant to issue it to the Fleet.[77] Chatfield agreed. He thought it looked as if the Naval Staff were seeking to tell C-in-Cs how to conduct their business. The function of the Naval Staff was to keep in touch with the provision of materiel, to review and co-ordinate opinion on how it should be used, and periodically to lay down a policy to be followed. "This policy, however," he added, "must be based on the opinions of those at sea and in command and must not be created by independent thought in the staff departments of the Admiralty."[78] He agreed that the manual could be issued to the Fleet for comment if it was reworded to remove the appearance of being laid-down policy.

The Naval Staff accordingly released Volume 1 in January 1937. It attracted a great deal of attention and comment from Flag Officers all around the world, a process which took the better part of a year and culminated in a large Fleet and Staff discussion on December 7, 1937, led by Admiral Backhouse (C-in-C Home Fleet) Rear-Admiral J. H. D. Cunningham (ACNS [Air]) and Rear-Admiral G. C. C. Royle (RAA). It was followed by another large Fleet discussion in the *Barham* at Dragomesti in the Aegean on January 28, 1938. It was evident from all this that there were many ideas and much interest in naval air power, but also a great diversity of views. Unfortunately, Staff shortages and general pressure of work meant that the manual was not revised in the light of the discussions. No Volume 2 on trade protection emerged, and no consequent decisons were made or further action taken, either by the Naval Staff or the Board.[79]

The current fight to regain control of the FAA and the enormously complicated task of absorbing it once victory had been achieved diverted a good deal of the Naval Staff's time and energy away from the task of considering how best to use naval aviation and what its materiel requirements would be. "So far," noted the ACNS, "the problem of air requirements in war appears to have been dealt with piecemeal." The fact that the FAA was to be greatly expanded made the question of considering its purposes even more urgent. "So long as we continue to have no fixed idea of what we want," he said, "it is unlikely that whatever money is available will be spent to the best advantage."[80]

Accordingly, a committee was set up under Rear-Admiral L. E. Holland to consider the Fleet's "Air Requirements in War". Its forthright and realistic report, submitted on December 20, 1938, outlined a proposed naval air policy through to 1942, giving the numbers of carriers and catapult ships and the types, roles and functions of aircraft, and discussing the tactical employment of naval aviation in support of the Main Fleet and in the protection of trade. The report formed the basis of the Admiralty's proposals to the Cabinet early in the following year. Although its conclusions were generally sensible, they reflected rather than moulded Fleet training and had little actual effect on it before war broke out. The report also at last offered firm guidance on the procurement of aircraft and carriers, ending the uncertainties which had pervaded the Admiralty's staff divisions and materiel departments for so long. But the tardy arrival of such laid-down policy showed that the existing system was only able to provide firm decisions under the urgent promptings of imminent war.

To a certain extent the institutional weakness of the FAA was a natural reflection of the relative novelty of the technology that took air power to sea. Military bureaucracies tend to be conservative,[81] as they reflect the status of established groups whose pre-eminence is based on the proven effectiveness of existing weaponry. The dominating power and prestige of the heavy-gun capital ship made the gunnery interest the strongest in the Navy of the time, and this is often held to be one of the main impediments to the growth of naval air power. "In 1938," one commentator notes, "most of the senior officers in the Navy were specialists in gunnery and didn't like aeroplanes. In their opinion aeroplanes were fit to tow targets for their ack-ack guns, and nothing more."[82] The gunnery interest, it is said, dominated the Navy's institutions and was therefore able to deprive naval aviation of the funds needed if it was to realise its full potential and ultimately take over as the decisive weapon of the Fleet. Precisely the same situation applied well into the 1930s in the US Navy, in which ". . . the clique centring around the Bureau of Ordnance . . . known as the 'Gun Club' . . . maintained practically a monopoly of the top posts, both in the Navy Department and at sea, to the exclusion of others including naval aviators.'[83] Using their institutional strength, battleship admirals were thus able to protect their established interests against the challenges of the new technology.

Although there is plainly much to be said for this view, there is still a danger of overstating the case. In the first place, as will be shown shortly, many of the activities of the air were thought to be positively helpful to the success of naval gunnery. "I think," Chatfield told the Bonar Law Inquiry in 1921, "the Air will be of much greater assistance to the capital ship than a danger, and the Navy looks to the aircraft as its ally."[84] In many cases it is unwise to think in terms of the gun versus the aircraft. By no means did the two always compete. For this reason, it is relatively easy to find gunnery officers arguing against what was supposed to be the party line. In fact it was the major gunnery reformers, "Jacky" Fisher, Sir Percy Scott and W. S. Sims USN, who were among the first to embrace the new technology. The vigorous campaign waged by Chatfield, Keyes, Dreyer and the rest for control of the FAA was much influenced by their genuine appreciation of the importance of naval aviation. When Bell Davies first joined the Naval Air Section he was afraid he might be swallowed up by the dynamic Dreyer and his Gunnery Division. "Look here, Bell Davies," Dreyer reassured him "don't imagine that I intend to put any spokes into the Naval Air wheel. It seems to me much more likely Naval Air will be able to put spokes into the Gunnery wheel before long."[85] While few gunnery specialists went to the lengths of Admiral A. L. St G. Lyster (another gunner and future Chief of the Naval Air Service) in his statement that "there is nothing the Air cannot do and nothing that can be done without the Air,"[86] it would still be wrong to suppose that the "gunnery interest" simply comprised officers who "didn't like aeroplanes".

The Navy's evident determination to keep the FAA and its institutions as an integral part of the Navy probably had at least as much an effect on the progress of the air weapon. In its campaign for control of the FAA, the Admiralty repeatedly made it plain that it did not seek the re-establishment of the RNAS, a "corps separate from the Royal Navy, possessing its own sources of supply, administration, recruitment. . . . On the contrary, the Naval Air Arm will be one with the Royal Navy in all the above important points . . . an integral part of the Navy as a whole."[87] The Admiralty's unhappy experience with Sueter and the RNAS in the First World War reinforced its dislike of allowing Naval Air to acquire too much autonomy. Private empires might develop, and these were dangerous as they encouraged their leaders to forget that they were an integral part of a greater whole. It was particularly important to head off this development, since "aircraft are not auxiliary vessels to the Fleet such as destroyers, submarines or minelayers. They are an essential part of it. . . ."[88] The diverse employment of air power was thought to be an inseparable, constant and almost indistinguishable part of the tactics of Fleet action. The institutions of Naval Air should therefore be built as closely as possible into the fabric of Admiralty organisation, so that the fullest integration could be achieved. This does much to explain the constant attempts to diffuse responsibility for the naval air arm around existing organisations.

The Admiralty had another political motive for integrating naval air power as fully as possible into the Navy. This was pointed out at the time when the appointment of Henderson as RAA and the operation of carriers in task forces was being considered. "The change in strategical and operational distribution of the aircraft carriers," it was argued, "might be construed as an admission that the FAA afloat constitutes a separate force with its own special problems which are more allied to problems of air warfare than those of sea warfare. This aspect might be developed by the Air Ministry. . . ."[89] In other words, the Admiralty had to integrate Naval Air in order to defend it against the Air Staff.

Dual Control weakened the institutions of Naval Air and the naval air lobby in many other ways too. It deprived the Navy of the services of those officers who would have represented it in the highest echelons of the hierarchy through most of the inter-war period. Since the Air Ministry provided the air materiel, there were no technical air departments in the Admiralty and this meant that the Naval Air Division had to involve itself in the "consideration of technical details to a far greater extent than is desirable or correct for a staff division."[90] Having so much technical responsibility, the Naval Air Staff had too little time for strategic contemplation. More directly still, the Air Staff opposed the expansion of the Admiralty's air institutions wherever they had the power to do so. Only in 1933, for example, would they agree to attach an RAF officer to the Naval Staff, an arrangement first requested by the Admiralty 14 years earlier.[91] It seems that if the weakness of its institutions, and the consequent muting of the naval air lobby, is to be seen as restraint on progress, then the Air Ministry must certainly share responsibility for it.

The Norwegian campaign and the first few years of the Second World War generally showed however that the Admiralty's repossession of the FAA certainly did not solve all the pre-war problems. For a start, the FAA suffered from the general weaknesses of the high command of the time, as did all other branches of the naval service. The nature of the high command, the relationship between the First Lord (Churchill) and the First Sea Lord (Pound), and the extent to which Churchill interfered in naval operations was and is a matter of high controversy. The two titans of modern naval history, Capt S. W. Roskill and Professor Arthur Marder, have argued extensively over the degree to which Churchill dominated the direction of naval affairs, the first emphasising Churchill's degree of command and the latter making it more of a team effort.[92] Whatever the rights and wrongs of this controversy, the Naval Staff of the time were certainly often anxious about the directions that came down to them and, incidentally, tended to attribute most of the responsibility for them to their forceful First Lord.

One member of the Naval Air Division afterwards wrote of the "Midnight Follies [which] consisted of midnight meetings between Churchill, Pound and Phillips (the Vice-Chief of the Naval Staff). These were once described to me as Churchill wide awake and domineering, Pound half asleep, and Tommy Phillips sitting like a naughty schoolboy in his chair. The results of these meetings would be some signal with time of origin after midnight, directing some action, without consultation with the staff officers concerned. . . . Winston was a great man, but was not sufficiently versed in detail of naval matters to intervene, and Pound and Phillips were not the men to stand up to him. . . . I once asked a friend from the Fleet what they did when some obviously bad order came out by signals, with a time of origin after midnight. He laughed and said: 'We always waited until morning for a cancellation.' It must be clear that, with such a situation, there was little faith in the High Command, either in the Admiralty or in the Fleet."[93]

Inevitably, a good many of these misguided directives concerned the FAA. "We always had one commander sleeping in the office [of the Naval Air Division] during the war, and he would sort the signals when they came in early in the morning, putting aside anything that seemed to require immediate action. He would include any of the signals from these meetings. Often, on arrival of our head, Capt Clem Moody, one of these would be thrust into his hand. He would say something like 'My God!' and rush out, and later a signal would go out cancelling the previous one." From the Naval Air Division's point of view, the Admiralty's handling of naval air power left a lot to be desired, both in terms of lost opportunities and foolhardy ventures of one kind or another. There was, for instance, a scheme in which Skuas based on Hatston would bomb Sola airfield at Stavanger. The military benefits of such an attack did not seem commensurate with the risks, since at this range the Skuas could only hope to return if their navigation was faultless, the weather co-operative, no delays occurred and they did not encounter enemy aircraft. The duty commander, G. A. Rotherham, desperately tried to get the raid cancelled even though it was due to leave the following morning. He saw Phillips twice in the early hours, was unable to raise any of his immediate superiors, and only finally succeeded in stopping the raid by calling in the Fifth Sea Lord, Admiral G. C. C. Royle, by open telephone in the middle of the night. The point of all this was not so much that a mere commander did eventually succeed in getting a very dubious operation called off, but that it should have been ordered in the first place.[94]

There were several other instances of this kind of thing in the Norwegian campaign. Professional opinion in the Naval Air Division was against the *Ark Royal's* being ordered to use Skuas rather than Swordfish against the *Scharnhorst* on June 13 – with every justification as it turned out. But it was the case of the

Glorious which really inflamed naval air opinion. "I had often heard mutinous remarks in the Operations Division," wrote Cdr Rotherham, ". . . but that night the conversation could only be called red mutiny. The operations room had a small bar for the comfort of the duty officer in peacetime, as this office was always manned. It had not been closed in war but was naturally little used; however that night it was in full use. We mourned our friends and we damned the crass inefficiency that had caused the loss of this fine old ship.'"[95] Such errors, including the earlier loss of the *Courageous*, all showed, said another contemporary member of the Naval Air Division, "what little influence the few professional naval aviators of the day had upon current operations."[96]

The difficulty lay in the fact that many of the particular men who composed the high command at this time either did not fully appreciate the impact of air power, or did not quite understand all the correct nuances of its use. Churchill's own grasp of this was sometimes brilliantly right (as in the case of his single-minded pursuit of a good carrier fighter) but occasionally erred on the side of impetuosity. His immediate professional advisers, Pound and Phillips, were well known for being over-sanguine about the capability of ships to deal with air attack, and occasionally wrongheaded in their view of how the FAA should be used. Forbes, the C-in-C Home Fleet, was not noted for any particular enthusiasm for or knowledge of the air, as several instances of the Norwegian campaign seem to indicate. Lord Cork, the 67-year-old local commander of the Narvik expedition, was however an air enthusiast of some standing. At one point during the campaign he went up in a Walrus and was very eager to find some Germans to attack. "Got any bombs, boy?" he asked the pilot. Discovering that the aircraft did indeed have one 50lb bomb aboard, he added: "Well then, dive-bomb Narvik!"[97] For all his enthusiasm, though, Lord Cork's anomalous position meant that he was not really in a position to influence the nature of naval air operations.

In fact the Norwegian campaign is noted for its general confusion of command. The relationship between Lord Cork and the local Army commander was very ambiguous and so was that between him and the C-in-C of the Home Fleet. Forbes' relationship with other of his subordinates, particularly Admirals Whitworth and Wells, was not always clear in practice. It was still less so with the Admiralty, which was apt to intervene more than was usual in such circumstances. Lastly, liaison between the Navy and Bomber and Coastal commands of the RAF was not very good. Reconnaissance reports often failed to get through or took too long to do so. Faulty staff work led to the non-appearance of the RAF fighter escort for the *Suffolk* during Operation Duck, and to the absence of effective support for the *Ark Royal's* attack on the *Scharnhorst* at Trondheim. The earlier presence of this ship and its sister, *Gneisenau*, in northern waters during the evacuation of northern Norway was not detected, at least partly because Coastal Command had made no special effort to find them as they had not been informed of this operation. Altogether, the general efficiency of the web of command and co-operation linking the various parties and forces left a very great deal to be desired. Naval air operations suffered in consequence, just as did most other aspects of this muddled campaign.

No particular effort seems to have been made to improve the command and control of naval air operations and policy for quite some time after the Norwegian campaign, doubtless a result of the protracted influence of the "old guard" over the Naval Air Service. A good late example of this was Pound's choice of his old friend, Dreyer, as Chief of the Naval Air Service in July 1942. As Capt Roskill says, this was certainly an extraordinary appointment and one that caused hostility in Parliament and the Press and much unrest within the FAA itself, especially as it lost its representation on the Board at the same time. Although Dreyer, a most inventive gunnery officer of an earlier generation, had been a deservedly influential figure in the development of naval aviation 20 years before, he was by now quite unfitted for such a task and his appointment led to a general malaise throughout the Naval Air Service. This reached such a pitch that Churchill was eventually obliged to step in to insist that he be replaced, which he duly was in January 1943.[98]

He was succeeded by a new and vigorous regime. On the Naval Staff side there was the effective partnership of Admirals Denis Boyd (Fifth Sea Lord, with a seat on the Board) and R. H. Portal (ACNS [Air]). Boyd, an impressive officer, had plenty of experience in carriers, while Portal was a fully qualified aviator and the first of the second generation to reach Flag rank. The materiel side was handled by another second-generation flyer, Capt (later Admiral) M. S. Slattery, soon to be made Chief of Naval Air Equipment. Slattery worked very closely with the Fifth Sea Lord but, being concerned with the production of materiel, came under the Controller in the Admiralty's organisational charts. All this did much to raise the morale and efficiency of the FAA and symbolised the way in which the higher direction of naval air affairs improved as the war went on. This doubtless would have taken place much earlier if the Navy had not lost its first generation of flyers to the RAF in 1918.

The Naval Air Staff dealt mainly with operations, training, policy and plans, and its representation increased in size as well as quality as the war proceeded. By 1945 there were under the Fifth Sea Lord (the forceful and experienced Admiral T. H. Troubridge) and ACNS (Air) (Admiral L. D. Mackintosh) two large staff divisions: the Naval Air Warfare and Flying Training Division and the Naval Air Organisation Division, both well sprinkled with naval flyers. The supervision and co-ordination of these divisions fell generally to the Fifth Sea Lord, while policy and organisation was more the province of the ACNS (Air). Hierarchy and ultimate responsibility were often left shrouded in decent obscurity. All this meant that the FAA was much better placed to get a fairer share of the Navy's resources. As though to symbolise the new distribution of power in the Admiralty, one of the FAA's most celebrated observers, Capt Gerald Langley, even became Director of the Gunnery Division!

The aero-technical side of the FAA needed influence and bureaucratic muscle just as much. Links with the aircraft industry had to be established, and the technical staff of the Air Ministry and the MAP had to be goaded into meeting the FAA's requirements. More used to working with the Air Staff, they were not always very sympathetic to the Navy's special needs. They resisted, for instance, the acquisition of the indispensable Grumman Avenger and Corsair on the grounds of an alleged danger of carbon monoxide contamination in their cockpits. They also opposed the introduction of the Seafire into the FAA, believing that its forward view was too poor and its undercarriage too weak for carrier operation. The answer to this problem was to evolve a special deck-landing technique, with the nose up rather than down, which halved the landing speed. Such solutions to obscure but important problems were more likely to be found if the organisation brought users and designers more closely together than they had been before the war.[99]

The need for influence was also apparent in the FAA's dealings with the US Navy and the British Aircraft Commission in Washington. It was very important that this rich supply of good aircraft, air equipment and carriers be tapped with the greatest efficiency. And so an Assistant Naval Attaché for Air was sent out, invested by this title with enough prestige to deal firmly with Air Staff and MAP officials in the Commission if the occasion warranted, as it sometimes did. He and his other FAA colleagues also needed a certain status if they were to be able to place their orders – many of which were alarmingly large, if provisional – to justify their judgements to the Admiralty and to establish good relations with the US Navy. In fact this was usually the least of their problems. Admiral J. H. Towers of BuAer became a good friend of the FAA team in Washington, in the end inviting them to move into the Navy Department's offices on Constitution Avenue.[100] Thereafter the best of relations were maintained between the two navies. The FAA's general success in the United States illustrates very well the necessity for the kind of expert personnel, good contacts and bureaucratic "pull" which the growth of its air experience had by now begun to produce.

In the early part of the Second World War, however, such influence was quite limited. The establishment of the MAP at first did not help, for, as the faltering Barracuda programme showed, lines of responsibility remained vague. "Except for the Fifth Sea Lord [Admiral Lyster], who is excellent but cannot be everywhere at once," one officer wrote in 1941, "the Naval Air Staff is quite incapable of coping with the Air Ministry and the MAP."[101] Even some time later Admiral Slattery had still to warn a newly joined lieutenant: "You will have to attend a number of inter-service meetings, some of them at a very high level, and you must bear one thing in mind. The RAF will send an Air Vice-

Marshal in a Daimler, the Army will send a Brigadier in a Rover and I shall send you on a bicycle."[102] One of the particular difficulties lay in the fact that the FAA's materiel requirements were too specialised for the more orthodox departments of the MAP and Admiralty to cope with. In 1944, for instance, it was even necessary to set up a special Naval Air Radio Department.

Gradually, though, the technical side of the FAA won adequate representation for itself. By the end of the war there were four materiel departments in the Admiralty and Admiral Slattery was acting as a kind of Deputy Controller of Aircraft Design at the MAP as well as Chief of Naval Air Equipment. Not surprisingly, perhaps, the Navy at last began to get the kind of aircraft it needed. All was not plain sailing, however, and the prevailing problem was always how to keep the policy and materiel sides of the FAA close enough without appearing to create an "Air Ministry" within the Admiralty. One suggestion made by Churchill towards the end of 1940 might have gone some way towards solving this problem. He said that looking after the Navy had taken up all his time as First Lord, leaving too little for him to master "the highly specialised technique of what is virtually another air force with some additional complications." Churchill recommended Alexander, his successor as First Lord, to think about setting up an experienced "political" figure to undertake specialised supervision of the FAA.[103]

Alexander appears to have taken no action on this and it is easy to see why. Even when it was no longer justifiable to fear that the Air Ministry would seek to regain control of the Naval Air Service, the Admiralty remained almost morbidly sensitive to the dangers of the appearance of autonomy. This showed itself even in a habitual dislike of the widespread use of the phrase "Fleet Air Arm," which is "apt to convey an impression that the Fleet Air Arm is not an integral part of the naval services."[104] This anxiety was unnecessary and unfortunate in that it led to an over-insistence on blending the administration of naval air power into that of the Navy as a whole. The matter was discussed by Slattery in the autumn of 1943. There was too little co-ordination in the running of naval aviation, he argued, and the Navy would be well advised to aim at producing a British equivalent of the Bureau of Aeronautics, which the US Navy had created as long ago as 1921. "Such a scheme," he wrote, "would allow the head of the FAA – at present called the Fifth Sea Lord – to get on with planning and the administration of the FAA without continued dependence upon and reference to the remainder of the Admiralty organisation."[105] Since the operational efficiency of British naval aviation depended in large measure on the competence of the bureaucracy handling and directing it, it is sad that political circumstances, and the prejudices they inspired, should have prevented the adoption of such a policy 20 years earlier.

CHAPTER SIX

DOCTRINES OF BATTLE

"The scale of air attack that would be developed against our military forces on shore and our naval forces off the Norwegian coast was grievously underestimated when the operations were undertaken. In the result, when the situation became desperate, we were committed and desperate measures had to be taken. . . ."

ADMIRAL SIR CHARLES FORBES
C-in-C Home Fleet, July 1940

Naval policy and operational doctrine at this time were dominated by the requirements of the decisive fleet action that the Royal Navy was determined to seek in war. It is thus necessary to give some impression of what the Navy thought this central battle would be like and to show how air power was expected to affect it. Although no such battle ever took place, and although the documentation is sparse, there still remain enough fragments of evidence to indicate how the Royal Navy saw the decisive battle which it expected, or at least hoped, to fight in a future war.

As the British Fleet steamed towards its intended victim, the first need was to locate it exactly, making reconnaissance necessary during the approach phase. Unless the weather was particularly foul, or it had been decided for some reason to rely on the shore-based aircraft of Coastal Command, the reconnaissance aircraft of the FAA would be the first into action. These aircraft might possibly be flown off one or more of the light cruisers spearad in a wide screen some 20 miles head of the Fleet, a disposition known as the "A-K line" from the lettered positions the cruisers were expected to adopt. Generally, though, reconnaissance operations would be mounted from one or more of the carriers steaming with the main body of the Fleet. If the Fleet was in the kind of cruising disposition illustrated overleaf, the reconnaissance aircraft would pass over the leading destroyers and the A-K line and, operating in a continual chain, would try to search an area up to 135 miles ahead of the Fleet and 50–100 miles on either side of its course. Once the enemy fleet was located, reconnaissance machines would report its movements as the two fleets converged, paying special attention to the

BATTLEFLEET IN TYPICAL CRUISING DISPOSITION, 1924

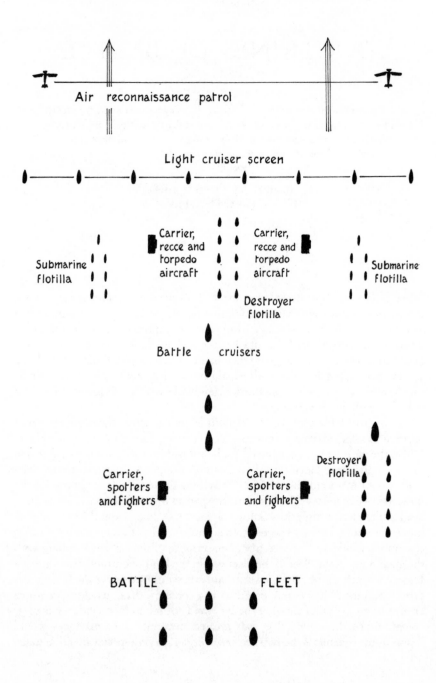

enemy's battleships and carriers and keeping a sharp lookout for any submarines that might be lurking in ambush or generally shadowing. Flying-boat exercises in 1933 had established that "shadowing submarines have little prospect of being able to maintain contact with forces escorted by A/S vessels and aircraft," and so looking for submarines was a most important subsidiary function of reconnaissance aircraft.[1]

The crucial importance of strategic and tactical reconnaissance had been clearly recognised during the First World War. Such work had been carried out during the Battle of Jutland in 1916, leading Admiral Jellicoe to submit three weeks later that ". . . the first requirement [is] for the Fleet to be provided with sufficient carriers and efficient seaplanes for scouting and spotting, manned by trained personnel." Accurate reconnaissance conferred the strategic and tactical initiative and it was generally agreed that a fleet without it could well be impotent against a fleet that was better equipped. "How can we hope to bring an enemy to action if they are well advised by their aircraft?" asked the C-inC Mediterranean, Admiral Sir John de Robeck, in 1921. "It would become a game of blind man's bluff where our Battlefleet plays the role of the blind man." A few years after this, the commanding officer of *Eagle* commented that "of all the uses to which aircraft can be put in a fleet, I think it is generally agreed that reconnaissance is the most important." By and large this was the general view for the rest of the inter-war period.[2]

However crucial to the outcome of the battle it might be, reconnaissance was a very difficult task. The most obvious problem was that of the weather. Frequently it was necessary for the airmen to concede that "owing to low clouds, air reconnaissance was not much use and . . . cruisers gained touch almost as soon as the aircraft did." Accurate oversea navigation, position-finding and reporting were all very difficult, too, and created enough uncertainties for cruisers often to have to be "spread to obtain more accurate information". It was also expected that enemy aircraft would force reconnaissance machines to "fight for their information". This led to the attractive notion of the fighter/reconnaissance aircraft, first exemplified by the Hawker Osprey of 1932. Led by such people as the then Cdr G. M. B. Langley, the FAA developed a special expertise in the extremely complex business of over-sea navigation and maritime search, and by the end of the inter-war period the A-K line had fallen into general disuse. In 1935 the FAA Committee was able to conclude, with much justification, that aerial reconnaissance was "the one field in which we can be reasonably certain we are ahead of any other air arm," adding rather typically, "and none of this is due to the RAF."[3]

This concluding remark was born of the current differences of opinion between the Admiralty and the Air Ministry about the vulnerability of surface ships to air attack. While the Navy tended to assess the impact of air power on naval operations in terms of the kind of battle being described here, the Air Staff used to think more of shore-based air power and its influences on maritime activities. In this regard, the Air Staff generally expressed confidence in their ability to find warships if they strayed into range. Indeed, when the problem of quantifying the ability to locate a maritime target for war-game rules first came up, the Air Staff made no distinction between finding a target on land and one at sea. In good weather aircraft would have a 100 per cent chance of locating it successfully, and a 50 per cent chance in bad weather.[4] The Naval Staff were not at all impressed by this. They pointed out that the Air Force's usual targets were geographically static and so the problem of reaching them was simply one of good navigation. Finding and recognising a target that moved about was a different matter altogether. Also, to be of any military significance, the target would have to be located early enough to allow an effective bombing attack to be organised, and this too would be more difficult than the Air Staff thought. Throughout the inter-war period the Admiralty consistently maintained that the Air Force seriously underrated the difficulties of reconnaissance at sea and overrated its ability to perform the task.

The Navy's scepticism was entirely justified by the RAF's maritime operations in the first winter of the war. The inability of untrained aircrew to tell the difference between merchant ships and warships led to over a dozen FAA officers being attached to various Bomber Command stations at the specific request of the Chief of the Air Staff, Air Chief Marshal Sir Charles Portal. Their function was to instruct Bomber Command crews in the mysteries of maritime operations and to tell them, in effect, what to bomb. The naval officers who went out on these missions were not impressed by what they saw. Whereas much naval thought and resource had gone, for instance, into the problem of "finding the wind" at sea (essential for accurate navigation and bombing) and had resulted in the perfection of sophisticated techniques (although experienced observers could estimate wind speed and direction for low flying simply by looking at the sea), no such progress seems to have been made by Bomber Command. "By Air Force methods, as taught to us by their armament officers," one such observer recalled, "you first did three bombing runs on the target from different directions, dropping a bomb each time, then you plotted the fall of these bombs, and thus deduced the direction and force of the wind that was affecting you. Only then were you possessed of sufficient knowledge to enable you to bomb accurately. An exercise which I would hate to practise in the presence of enemy fighters."[5]

This was an inevitable result of the low priority accorded to maritime targets by Bomber Command, whose attention naturally focused on the strategic bombing of cities. The fact remained, however, that the resources of Bomber Command would have to be called upon if shore-based airpower was to make any significant attack on the German Navy in harbour or at sea. Bomber Command's initial poverty in the techniques of oversea navigation is representative of the kind of practical difficulty which led the Naval Staff to be rather too sceptical about the ability of shore-based air power significantly to influence operations at sea. Exercises provided evidence both for scepticism and confidence about shore-based reconnaissance. In 1935 the Mediterranean Fleet was certainly impressed by examples of successful location and shadowing at night. Two years earlier, however, the Home Fleet had sailed 150 miles up the Channel on a perfect summer's day without being detected by Coastal Area. The Fleet, remarked the Air Officer Commanding, was sailing unexpectedly fast.[6] The matter was clearly not as simple as the partisans of both sides sometimes claimed.

If reconnaissance aircraft performed their task successfully their reports would soon give the Commander-in-Chief a picture of the enemy's strength, position and apparent intentions, which would in turn determine his next move. Almost certainly, the Fleet's air striking forces would be next into action.

Although the battle instructions on this point tended to vary over the inter-war period, the Commander-in-Chief would probably direct his strike aircraft to attack the enemy's battleships if he seemed to be trying to escape. A successful attack on the enemy battleline might cause enough damage, confusion and delay to allow the British Fleet to catch up and dispose of it by gunfire. "The torpedo machine is the only weapon we have," wrote Admiral Sir Roger Keyes in 1927, "which holds out the hope of fixing a retreating enemy, and as such may be all important in the British Fleet." An attack on the enemy fleet's flagship might impose "a sufficient reduction of speed . . . to make it certain that the enemy will be brought into action."[7]

If the enemy seemed willing to accept battle, however, it might be better for the air striking forces to concentrate their attacks on the enemy carriers, since crippling or sinking these ships would confer on the British the far-reaching advantages of air supremacy. "The fleet deprived of carriers," the Naval Staff stated in 1936, "will be unable to undertake any further major fleet operations in the face of an enemy who has carriers at his disposal."[8] The advantages of eliminating or at least reducing the enemy's ability to use his aircraft were significant, persuading many naval officers into equipping reconnaissance aircraft with bombs so that they could attack enemy carriers almost as soon as they found them, possibly doing significant damage to aircraft ranged on deck, or even to the flight decks themselves. From the very start of the battle the decisive advantage might be gained in this way.

The main air striking force, however, would be composed of torpedo aircraft, possibly reinforced by dive bombers and fighters. Two carriers could be expected to fly off some 50 aircraft at up to 100 miles' range. Flying in one formation so as to increase their mutual security against hostile fighters, these aircraft would make the fullest possible use of cloud cover, sun or heat haze in order to make an unseen approach. Depending on the weather, the tactical circumstances and their state of training, the torpedo aircraft would move into position either for a "formation" or the more demanding "individual scatter" attack. In the latter, the aircraft would approach their target together, suddenly break formation and dive independently to the attack, presenting the target with the problem of having to avoid torpedoes fired at it from several different directions at once.

The other option was some variant of the formation attack, in which groups of aircraft approached the ship in successive waves, making the best use of time and direction so that in avoiding one attack the ship made itself more vulnerable to the next. This method demanded less individual skill on the part of the pilot but made him more susceptible to AA gunfire. Whichever method was adopted, the aircraft would aim to fly on a parallel course to their target, turn towards it in a shallow dive and then dive steeply to the attack. Flattening out in the final approach, the aircraft would fly at anything between 30 and 100 feet above the sea, depending on their speed and the depth of the water, aiming to drop their torpedoes at about 1,000 yards, when the tops of the ship's funnels were roughly level with the horizon. Now much more manoeuvrable, the aircraft would then jink away through the AA fire and return to the carrier either independently or in company.[9]

The mechanics of such attacks had been thoroughly rehearsed in the inter-war years. Although torpedoes had been dropped even before the war, the first attack by wheeled torpdo aircraft against a moving target at sea had only taken place on September 7, 1920, when 12 Sopwith Cuckoos attacked the flagship of the Atlantic Fleet, *Queen Elizabeth*, hitting her at least four times. The absence of a good carrier aircraft, or indeed a good carrier, delayed progress for the next few years until the revolutionary Mediterranean cruise of the newly completed *Eagle* in 1924. The advent of this "comic looking ship" was to mark an important stage in the development of air power at sea when, on July 28 that year, "*Eagle* brought off an excellent torpedo-plane attack – I believe the first or second from a carrier – three hits out of five – then fighters arrived unexpectedly and strafed us – a most amazing spectacle – very enterprising to have 11 machines away together – We had the torpedo planes in sight for about 25 minutes before attack."[10]

The Air Ministry, however, had always had reservations about this form of attack, thinking that it made aircraft unnecessarily vulnerable to AA gunfire. As the inter-war priod proceeded, naval opinion also began to grow cooler towards the idea of torpedo attack, partly because of doubts about the physical effectiveness of torpedoes, even when they hit the target, but mainly because of a growing faith in AA defences. "We shall," wrote Chatfield, the First Sea Lord in 1936, "so completely equip the Fleet with anti-aircraft guns that I do not believe that it will be a profitable thing for aircraft to approach it." Some years earlier, Pound, in working out the Fleet's aircraft requirements, assumed that the serious damaging of three battleships was the minimum task that the FAA should be able to perform. This, he thought, would require a striking force of no less than 72 aircraft.[11]

Other factors, however, could be used to counterbalance the weaknesses which this scepticism reflected. Supposing, for example, the aircraft were able to attack ships when they were in harbour, unready to defend themselves and unable to dodge the torpedoes. Such a scheme had been at the back of Beatty's mind when he had asked for 120 Sopwith Cuckoos with which to attack the High Seas Fleet in its bases during the First World War.[12] The first such attack was in fact launched on the Second Battle Squadron as it lay at anchor at Portland in September 1919, when seven of the eight torpdoes dropped found their mark. The C-in-C Atlantic Fleet (Admiral Sir Charles Madden, a torpedo expert) was inspired by this to claim that "Even at its present state of development, the torpedo plane, owing to its speed, tactical handiness and range of vision, is the most dangerous form of torpedo attack upon heavy ships."[13] Ten years or so later, the Mediterranean Fleet under Admiral Chatfield devoted great efforts to investigating the dangers of such attacks on itself as it lay in harbour. The possibility of attacking the Italian Fleet in its harbour was investigated during the Abyssinian crisis of 1935–6, and just before the war the *Eagle* launched from extreme range a surprise dawn attack on British warships at Singapore. All these activities paved the way for the celebrated Taranto raid of November 1940, of which more later.

The potential of torpedo attack could also be increased if it was combined with some other kind of air attack. At first it was hoped that strafing attacks by fighters would distract the attention of the enemy fleet and so increase the chances of torpedo attack. High-level bombing was another possibility, though the Navy was generally deeply sceptical of this, having reservations about the accuracy of the bombing aircraft and about the limited damage that the bombs carried by seaborne aircraft could do against modern armoured battleships. In the early 1930s this problem was extensively investigated in the *Courageous*, with the conclusion that success could only be achieved either by tightly controlled formation bombing[14] or some form of dive bombing.

The Royal Navy "discovered" dive bombing when Lt Cdr St J. Prentice visited the United States in 1931 and quickly recognised its potential. But as we have seen, no adequate dive-bombing sight was forthcoming from the Air Ministry and this limited the possibilities. Even so, dive bombing was expected to prove a most useful way of backing up the probably deadlier attacks of torpedo aircraft.[15] One final way of improving the chances of an attack was by launching it at a time when the target's attention was focused on something else, as it would be immediately before, or even during, the battle.

Returning to the imaginary battle, once the Commander-in-Chief had fixed the enemy or neutralised the opposing air arm, he could still hope for

DESTRUCTION OF A BATTLELINE

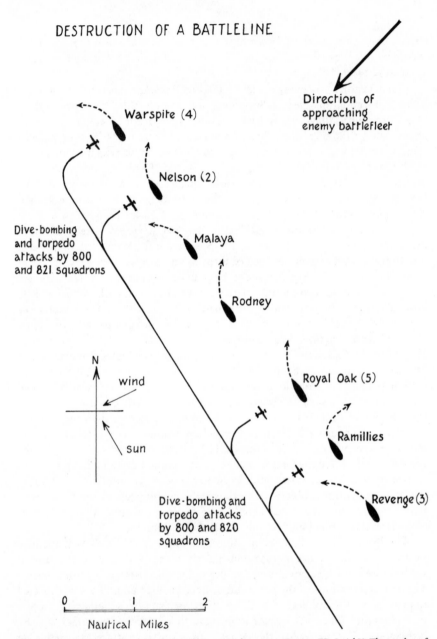

Direction of
approaching
enemy battlefleet

Warspite (4)

Nelson (2)

Dive-bombing
and torpedo
attacks by 800
and 821 squadrons

Malaya

Rodney

N

wind

sun

Royal Oak (5)

Ramillies

Dive-bombing and
torpedo attacks
by 800 and 820
squadrons

Revenge (3)

0   1   2

Nautical Miles

Sketch of the massed air strike on the Red Battlefleet, March 10, 1938. Exercise ZP, Serial V. The number of torpedo hits which each ship was judged to have taken is shown in brackets. Dotted lines show ship movements during the attack and final position.

useful advantage from any torpedo aircraft he had left. He could use them in fact to gain tactical objectives, as he would any other weapon of the Fleet, such as fleet submarines or destroyers. He might hope, for example, to reduce the enemy battleline to a shambles in the last moments before it was engaged by the heavy guns of his own battleships. Just such an attack was carried out in March 1938. The *Glorious* and *Courageous* launched a massed air attack with 78 aircraft during the combined exercise of that year. The *Glorious* launched a not very successful attack on the battlecruisers in the van of the "enemy" fleet, while the *Courageous* concentrated on the seven battleships astern. The enemy had deployed his battleships into two divisions in line-ahead, with the *Warspite* leading the *Nelson*, *Malaya* and *Rodney*, and the *Royal Oak* leading the *Ramillies* and *Revenge*. The twelve Swordfish in 821 Sqn flew parallel with the enemy line. Diving to attack the *Warspite*, they torpedoed her four times. The *Nelson*, the next in line, was hit twice as the aircraft carried out formation or wave attacks. Further down the line, dive bombers of 800 Sqn hit the second division 30 seconds before 15 Swordfish from 820 and 810 Sqns attacked the *Royal Oak* and the *Revenge*, securing five and three torpedo hits respectively. While many naval officers were, as we shall see shortly, rather too optimistic about the physical damage inflicted by such attacks, there was no doubt at all that they would have plunged the enemy battlefleet into gross disorder. In their efforts to dodge the torpedoes, the battleships had wrecked their own disposition and were therefore in the worst position to face the imminent destroyer attack. No ship of the first division, for example, was within 1,500 yards of another. In short, at the very moment when the enemy commander would have wanted the tightest discipline and order as he prepared for imminent action with a hostile battlefleet, aircraft had reduced his line to a state of chaos. Such an air attack could therefore easily prove decisive even if all the torpedoes missed.[16]

Recent developments in naval gunnery made confusion in the line particularly damaging to the efficiency of the Fleet. As Admiral Madden explained shortly after the First World War, "concentration of fire on one objective after another is the all important factor in a naval battle." But the increasing range of naval guns and the particular lethality of "plunging fire" meant that commanders could not achieve the concentration they wanted merely by positioning several ships against one, "as was done, for instance, in Nelson's time." Instead, it was a matter of fire control. Now the gunnery of the Fleet had to be treated as a whole and often directed from the "master ship" at targets invisible to the firing ship.[17] The disruption caused by torpedo attack would clearly make it more difficult for the commander to orchestrate the guns of his battlefleet as efficiently as victory would require.

The increasing range of the guns also meant that fire would be "indirect," with the fall of shot invisible from the bombarding ship. Thus some kind of "over the horizon" spotting was essential for battles, which could now "be fought and won without a view of the enemy being obtained from the capital ships of the Fleet."[18] In pre-war days the gunnery control officer's range of vision was extended to the maximum by placing him as high as possible in the ship, but the obvious need was for him or his representative to take to the air. The Dardanelles campaign had demonstrated the potential value of gunnery spotting when fire was indirect, and the same lesson was apparent from the invaluable aircraft spotting carried out in the extraordinarily difficult conditions of the Rufiji River Delta for the monitors *Severn* and *Mersey* against the German cruiser *Konigsberg* in 1915.[29]

Before the advent of radar-directed guns, in fact, the effect of air power on gunnery could easily be decisive. "Thoroughly efficient aerial observation," said Beatty in 1919, "is . . . vital to the future of ship's gunnery." A little later the US Navy came to the same conclusion.[20] Because naval gunnery could only realise its full potential with the aid of spotting aircraft, this function of the FAA was generally thought to be by far and away its most important once action had been joined.[21] A succession of spotters would then constantly take off and land on, flying near enough to the target ships to be able to spot the fall of shot, but not so near that they attracted the attention of AA fire or hostile fighters. They would also be constantly reporting the enemy's general movements, warning of impending torpedo attacks and generally ensuring that the commander had the fullest picture of the events that unfolded beneath them.

The complexity of the spotter's task had led in the 1920s to the production of aircraft like the slow, ungainly and ferociously ugly Blackburn Blackburn and the Avro Bison, which could carry a crew of up to four and provide them with a cabin with large windows, map tables and room to walk about. The operation of such large, difficult aircraft most certainly did "mark an epoch in the history of deck landing."[22] But fortunately for the development of British naval aviation, future three-seat spotters were less extravagant in their demands on the air resources of the Fleet.

Spotters were thought to be very vulnerable to marauding enemy fighters and so needed air protection. But long before they had begun their patrols, the Fleet's fighters would have taken to the air. In fact, fighters would have been active at every stage of the battle so far, especially if the approaching enemy fleet had its own aircraft and was also trying to carry out similar aerial functions. If so, then the first enemy aircraft on the scene would probably have been reconnaissance types. Ever since the First Sea Lord had suggested in December 1912 that an aeroplane could destroy a Parseval airship "by ripping her up with a fishing line and hooks,"[23] the Admiralty had been especially concerned with the problem of destroying the reconnaissance aircraft which could overturn the strategic purposes of the British Fleet by shadowing its movements. During the First World War German Zeppelins attempted to operate in this way. The Grand Fleet, crediting them with more efficiency than they deserved, devoted much energy and resource to the problem of destroying them.

As seaplanes were so encumbered by their floats that they could not achieve the necessary rate of climb to catch a fleeing Zeppelin, the requirements of this role did much to stimulate interest in wheeled aircraft, ships to operate them, and in the general development of air power at sea. The success of this policy was demonstrated when Flt Sub-Lt B. A. Smart flew a Sopwith Pup off the light cruiser *Yarmouth* and shot Zeppelin L23 into the sea on August 21, 1917. By the end of the war the Grand Fleet carried no fewer than 112 Sopwith Camels for this purpose.[24] The difficulties of this task increased during the inter-war period as shadowers became smaller, more elusive and better protected. Nevertheless, fighter aircraft were expected to drive away the enemy's reconnaissance aircraft at all stages of the approach to battle.

There was also a good deal of interest in fighters in the escort role, although the Air Staff were basically unsympathetic to this idea. They believed that the potential of fighters would be wasted in this role and preferred them to be out securing tactical command of the air in free-ranging offensive patrols.[25] Most naval officers were sceptical about this and were reluctant to let single-seat aircraft stray far from the Fleet. Instead they advocated two-seaters capable of long-range escort and support. Many hoped, for instance, that fighters would be able to help torpedo aircraft by strafing enemy destroyer screens and battleships to suppress AA gunfire. They might also be able to launch pre-emptive strikes on the crowded flight decks of the enemy's carriers, so blinding him to the deadly approach of the British Fleet.

There was much confusion about the last main function of the naval fighter: interception of hostile aircraft on their way to attack the Fleet. While it was generally agreed that fighters should try to shoot down enemy reconnaissance or spotting aircraft, there was much more ambivalence when it came to hostile torpedo or bombing aircraft. Nevertheless, fighters usually attempted to intercept incoming attackers, waves of them being put up when the tactical circumstances made an attack seem likely. Frequently, however, these interceptions proved too difficult. On April 10, 1938, for instance, strike aircraft from the *Courageous* launched a successful attack on the *Hood* even though the latter had a screen of 11 defensive fighters in the air at the time. In their 1935 summary of the current policy on fighters, the FAA Committee concluded that ". . . there are no clear ideas on the subject, and it is the exception rather than the rule for fighters to succeed in interfering with opposing aircraft in Fleet exercises." They thus believed that "Air opposition on passage is unlikely to develop at sea."[26]

The basic reason for this was very well known. "The speed of the planes is so good," remarked one early naval air enthusiast, Admiral Mark Kerr, that "many attacks will be brought off before the defending planes can get into the air and arrive at the position to attack the opponent's before the latter have time to fire their torpedoes."[27] While fighter endurance usually ruled out standing air patrols, it normally also proved impossible to get up an adequate air screen in the time available after being warned of an impending air attack. In 1924 Coastal Area considered this matter without coming to any very clear conclusions about it. One RAF officer's carefully considered solution was to deploy small and very fast fighter carriers 150–200 miles ahead of the A-K line. An intractable problem evidently required desperate solutions![28]

In many ways there was a parallel between the situations at sea and over land. The air defence of Great Britain posed very similar problems for the Air Ministry. Their preferred solution was to strike directly at the source of the enemy's air power: his aircraft industries and bases at home. In just the same way, air enthusiasts such as Admiral Mark Kerr argued that the first step would have to be to get command of the air, and "the most effective method of providing air superiority is that of sinking the enemy carrier before any or many of his aircraft have flown off."[29] This seemed a risky policy to many, however, and would obviously not solve the problem of how to defend the Fleet if it ventured within range of shore-based aircraft. The alternative – reliance on AA fire – was also the same at sea as it was on land.

The main reason for the remarkable inconsistency of the Royal Navy's attitude to air interception seems in fact to have been the link between it and changing evaluations of the efficiency of naval AA gunfire. In the early days this was generally admitted to be an inadequate defence. "It is to aircraft," wrote Admiral Chatfield in 1922, "that we must look for our chief defence against air attack, our AA armament filling in the loopholes in this armour."[30] Knowledge of such weaknesses led to an intensive campaign to improve naval AA. Even the Air Staff, normally highly sceptical of the efficiency of this method of defence, were forced to concede in the early 1930s that "the science of naval high-angle gunnery has made great strides in the past few years, and gunfire is undoubtedly a factor which must now be taken into account when considering the methods of attacking ships." As a result of this improvement, majority opinion held that "the gun is the principal means of defence against air attack."[31] The extent to which development was thought to have worked in favour of AA guns was strikingly demonstrated by Chatfield himself (now First Sea Lord) when he told Sir Thomas Inskip in 1937 that he believed that the presence of RAF fighters during a large German air attack on the British Fleet would be ". . . possibly as great an embarassment as assistance. If they attacked the enemy when the latter were within gun range of the Fleet, they would run the serious risk of being shot down by our own gunfire, as the Naval Staff do not believe that any C-in-C will hold his anti-aircraft fire and be content to rely solely for the security of his Fleet upon the unassessable outcome of a contest between fighters and bombers."[32]

To a certain extent, the stress on AA gunfire was something of a self-fulfilling prophecy, for it certainly contributed to the production of a long line of naval fighters whose relative inefficiency did much to justify the original assumption. Also, as the inter-war period progressed, the actual and desired ratio of fighters to other naval aircraft shifted to the latter's favour. In February 1934 it was decided that the ratio should go down from 2:3 to 1:2, and by 1939 the actual ratio was nearer 1:5.[33] "I intend," signalled the C-in-C Home Fleet (Forbes) during the Munich crisis, as though to set the seal on this misguided policy, "in view of the greater value of TSR aircraft than fighters in the present emergency, to disembark all fighters from HMS *Furious* and all except two Gladiators from HMS *Courageous*. . . ."[34] The culmination of all this was revealed three weeks after the outbreak of the Second World War when German aircraft attacked the *Ark Royal*. The carrier's Skua fighters were struck below with their tanks drained of petrol, and entire reliance was placed on the available AA gunnery.

But there were many who were disturbed at this trend. Doubts were expressed most forcibly by such air enthusiasts as Admiral Sir Reginald Henderson, who complained: "To my mind, the acceptance of the principle that AA gunfire is the primary defence of the Fleet against air attack is not justified by any data or experience. No realistic firing against aircraft has taken place since the last war, and . . . we are apt to overstate the capabilities of our weapons in peacetime . . . I think it would be better . . . to base our principles of defence on the definite known achievements of air fighting. . . ." Even Chatfield occasionally seemed less confident in private than he was in public. "The type of aircraft of which we cannot have too many in theory." he argued in 1934, "are fighters because they are defensive weapons which can seriously reduce the danger of our fleet of being unable to assert their gunnery superiority by reason of the enemy's attacking aircraft." A little earlier the then C-in-C Home Fleet (the future Lord Cork) had argued that "the best defence against hostile dive-bombing attacks is by means of our own fighter aircraft."[35]

This anxiety was reinforced by last-minute doubts about the efficiency of the AA gunnery actually mounted by the Fleet, and by certain developments in the science of air warfare. In 1938 one FAA crew were told to fly around the Fleet in Scottish waters completely as they wished. When they eventually returned to their carrier, they were astonished to discover that their route was exactly known. They had been plotted throughout by the cruiser *Sheffield* with the new RDF (or radar), a development which would obviously revolutionise air interception at sea. The potential of RDF in helping the Fleet prepare for attack was clearly revealed in the Combined Fleet Exercises of 1939,[36] but by this time the aircraft needed for air interception were no longer available. Just as war approached and new scientific developments seemed to make all things possible in air defence, the fighter component of the FAA was at its lowest ebb.

For all these reasons it was generally assumed that air interception would at best have been only partially successful and that a significant number of the enemy's seaborne (or perhaps shore-based) air striking forces would duly arrive over the Fleet. What in the opinion of the Navy would happen then? The aircraft would first of all have run the gauntlet of the Fleet's AA fire. Between the wars naval policy had settled on three kinds of AA armament. The 4in and 4.7in heavy AA guns were generally relied upon to deal with aircraft at high altitudes, but new ships such as the *King George V* class were fitted with 5.25in dual-purpose guns capable of dealing with aircraft and light surface craft. For aircraft flying at 1,000–3,000ft, the Navy relied on two-pounder pom-poms usually mounted in multiple batteries known as "Chicago pianos". Aircraft at close range would also be engaged by heavy machine guns, usually 0.5in weapons in multiple batteries.

The provision of these guns was also expected to be reasonably generous. The battleship *Rodney*, for example, had been refitted in 1937–8 and emerged with six 4.7in guns, three Multiple Pom-poms and four multiple 0.5in machine-gun batteries. She had also been fitted with an early form of RDF. The old battle-cruiser *Renown* had been practically reconstructed and was now equipped with ten 4.5in guns, four Multiple Pom-poms and 0.5in machine-gun batteries. The new *King George V* class was similarly equipped for close and medium range, plus eight 5.25in dual-purpose guns. To supplement all this, the Admiralty had been inspired by the Abyssinian crisis to convert several old C-class cruisers into AA ships, a device first suggested in 1923 by the perceptive Capt B. St G. Collard (later the chief victim of the *Royal Oak* affair). Collard said that since it was impossible to get all the necessary AA guns into the battleships themselves, "it may be possible to give such a powerful armament to the smaller cruisers as to enable them to produce an effective protective barrage through which the enemy aircraft will need to penetrate before they are able to bomb capital ships."[37]

This all seemed to offer reasonable protection against air attack, certainly by the standards of the other major navies, and was the basis for the Navy's quiet confidence in its ability to cope with such assaults. Because the technical nature of aircraft attacks on ships changed so much over the period and because the tactical conditions were capable of so many permutations, it was difficult to arrive at any precise measure of how effective AA armament was expected to be in battle. In 1927, for instance, the Naval Staff estimated for the sake of war-game rules that a force of 12 torpedo aircraft could expect the following casualties before and after their attacks (see table on page 151).[38]

In March 1938 the *Glorious* and *Courageous* launched a second massed air attack on the *Nelson*, *Rodney* and *Malaya* a week after the one already described. The two carriers put up 46 Swordfish and 11 fighters, launching successive wave attacks on the battle line. The *Nelson* was completely overwhelmed and would certainly have sunk after no fewer than 17 allowed torpedo hits, and the *Rodney*, *Malaya* and, by accident, *Royal Oak* were held to have been damaged. The Fleet had been given some 15 minutes' warning as the aircraft swept in

AIRCRAFT CASUALTIES DURING ATTACKS ON WARSHIPS*

Type of target	Target not in action against other ships		Target in action against other ships	
Four-ship squadron with Fleet	4	(1)	2	(0)
Single ship (screened)	2	(1)	1	(0)
Single ship (unscreened)	1	(1)	1	(1)

* Numbers in brackets refer to losses *after* attack

over the outlying screen and was able to concentrate fully on air defence as it had no other tactical distractions. Accordingly, it was estimated that 11 aircraft – nearly a quarter of the force – would have been shot down before they dropped their torpedoes. Twenty-seven aircraft had attacked the *Nelson*, and the C-in-C Home Fleet (Admiral Backhouse, shortly to become First Sea Lord) commented: "There is no doubt that the number of attackers was too great for the armament to have dealt with, even with the assistance of *Rodney* astern." He also pointed out that it would probably be unwise for a ship in such a position even to try to dodge the torpedoes as this would have made the gunners' task more difficult. Although an attack on the scale of that against the *Nelson* seemed impossible to defeat by the AA gunnery alone, the Navy plainly still expected to shoot down a high proportion of the aircraft sent against it.[39]

In his commentary on this attack, Backhouse stressed that it was extremely difficult to make accurate estimates of gunnery performance and aircraft casualties. Guesses had often to be made on the thinnest of evidence, and usually tended to overestimate the performance of AA defence. The effectiveness of torpedo attacks was frequently downgraded to an excessive degree. Sometimes, for example, it was assumed that if an aircraft could be seen clearly enough for the number painted on the side of its fuselage to be discernible from the target ship before it dropped its torpedo, then it certainly would have been shot down in war.

Many gunnery officers, however, recognised the need for some method of replacing such conjecture with fact. There was just too much guesswork in shooting at sleeves, smokebursts or "motorless gliders". One answer seemed to be a W/T-controlled target aeroplane of the kind first tried out in 1917. Although the resulting Fairey Queen Bee of 1932 was the world's first such target, development had been slow. It was in the hands of the Air Ministry, and the Air Staff were worried that, quite apart from the cost and many technical difficulties involved, success might spoil their chances of subsequently producing an offensive missile of the V1 type. Indeed, for a short while the Air Staff managed to get research on W/T targets officially banned for this reason.[40] In the event, the Queen Bees of the 1930s did not really solve the problem, firstly because they were expensive and so had to be rationed, and then because they simply produced more controversy about how representative of modern aircraft they were.

Despite these uncertainties, most senior officers grew much more confident in 1935 than they had been five or ten years earlier. As the very able Admiral W. W. Fisher (then C-in-C Mediterranean) argued in June 1936, great strides in gunnery materiel, much practice and the provision of air-defence officers in each ship had transformed the situation. Although it remained true that no fleet could withstand repeated air attacks of the kind to be expected if the fleet cruised for long periods within the reach of Italian air bases, for example, "the result of . . . intensive training was that instead of being extremely apprehensive of what might happen were the Fleet attacked in harbour or at sea, I became tolerably sure that the enemy, and not we, would suffer most."[41] In his speech on the Naval Estimates of 1937 the First Lord (Hoare) stated that battleships would certainly be attacked by air and might indeed be sunk, for "We have never claimed to make ships unsinkable." Nevertheless, the Fleet's own air power and its AA gunfire now combined "to make the Fleet in general and the battleships in particular the least attractive target for an enemy air force to attack."[42] Even the Air Staff, who usually took a jaundiced view of naval claims in this area, were willing to admit that a change had now taken place. "In view of the powerful defensive armament against air attack provided in modern battleships," they said in June 1937, "surprise . . . seems likely always to be the most important single factor affecting air attack on battleships."[43]

This general growth in confidence showed itself in and partly explained the declining attention paid to Fleet fighters. The protection of the Fleet against air attack actually required a balance to be struck between guns, avoidance and aircraft; the coming war would demonstrate that a good defensive system would need all three, properly co-ordinated. Experience was to show, however, that the Royal Navy had begun to get this balance seriously wrong by the end of the inter-war period. Misplaced confidence in AA also increasingly produced a tendency to under-rate the potential of air attacks on the Fleet. In 1931, for instance, Chatfield even seemed to suspect that air attack as a whole might prove a wasting asset. "My own recent experience of the Air Arm," he wrote, "makes me hesitate to subscribe to any policy that increased the strength of the air arm at the direct expense of less ambitious weapons. . . . The battle between the aircraft and the anti-aircraft gun is at present unsolved. My personal view trends strongly in the direction that attack of ships at sea by aircraft will be unremunerative in a few years."[44] Although this was actually going further than most would have done, it indicates that the Navy was more confident about its ability to cope with air attack than was to be justified by events.

One of the most obvious reasons why AA gunnery did not live up to expectations was the fact that most British ships were not equipped to the standard the Naval Staff thought necessary. When the Second War started, only four battleships and battlecruisers, the *Nelson*, *Rodney*, *Warspite* and *Renown*, had been rendered fit for modern conditions. A further two, the *Queen Elizabeth* and *Valiant*, were in the midst of reconstruction. The remaining nine were unmodernised and so known to be inadequately protected. This record contrasts unfavourably with that of the Japanese, who had improved all ten of their battleships, and the US Navy, which had refitted seven of its 15. The British ships had been kept in active commission instead, partly because of the run-down in the armaments industry, partly through fears of the expense and partly because of an understandable preference for new ships rather than refurbished old ones. The refit of the *Renown*, for instance, cost more than the building of a new ship would have done but still left her one of the weakest capital ships afloat. The new ships could not appear for several years, however, and in the meantime the Royal Navy had to make do with what it had.

As the scale and sophistication of air attack increased, there was also an unexpectedly urgent need for improved means of "fire distribution," the direction of which part of the AA armament of a ship or company of ships engaged which target. But with radar in its earliest infancy, it proved virtually impossible for ships to exchange information fast enough for there to be a useful "action plot" of the attack as it developed. For this reason AA defences were all too often overwhelmed by too many aircraft coming in from too many directions at once. In the heat and confusion of battle, therefore, many aircraft were not fired on at all.

Once a gun had been ordered to engage a particular target, there was a need for fire-control systems of a standard that was simply not available in the Royal Navy. In 1921 the Naval Anti-Aircraft Gunnery Committee (NAAGC) had recommended that the Navy proceed with the construction of a tachymetric fire-control system that would measure the bearing and speed of attacking aircraft. This system had been considered too complex and expensive for rough-and-tumble shipboard use, especially as the gun platform was bound to be unstable unless this was compensated for gyroscopically. Two stopgap systems (one known as the Standard Temporary System, the other simply as HX) were introduced from 1923, but most hopes were placed on the High Angle Control System Mk 1 (HACS I). With a built-in Vickers Predictor, HACS I was introduced in the 1930s and was expected to produce the same kind of fivefold improvement in accuracy as it had in land-based AA.[45] Such hopes were disappointed, however, and in December 1937 the Director of Naval Ordnance told a CID scientific sub-committee set up to consider the matter that land-based guns were three times as accurate as ship-based weapons.[46] This committee urged the Navy to proceed with the provision of good fire-control systems and a tachymetric sight as soon as possible.

By the end of the inter-war period the need for a tachymetric system had been generally recognised – especially in the lower echelons of the gunnery world – but by this stage there was very little chance of one being provided in time. There was also vigorous competition within the Navy and with the other services over this and other even more deserving research projects. Even some gunnery officers argued that production of a tachymetric fire-control system was much less urgent a requirement than, say, ensuring that all AA guns could elevate sufficiently or improving the lethality of the rather unreliable time/mechanical fuses used in AA shells until the US Navy produced proximity fuses. For reasons like this, said Chatfield in January 1938, "We are going through a most anxious time. Our battlefleet is composed largely of old ships, many of which fought at the Battle of Jutland. If we had to dispatch an adequate Fleet to the Far East to meet that of Japan, we would leave practically no modern ships at home to deal with the German and Italian fleets, which are composed of comparatively new ships. Moreover, our new ships, when completed, are now going to sea without their fire-control instruments owing to the heavy demands occasioned by the high priority of equipment given to the air-defence of Britain."[47] In the event, the first British fully tachymetric system did not materialise until after the war.

The situation was no better where close and medium-range fire was concerned. In this area the weapon from which all was expected was the Multiple Pom-pom, a gun advocated by the NAAGC in 1921 as a means of coping with aircraft that approached the ship closely but only for the briefest periods. This seemed to call for a gun capable of ". . . repeated rapid bursts of fire for one or two minutes . . . exactly as occurs in good grouse or partridge driving."[48] The resultant development of the Multiple Pom-pom through the 1920s was attended with much anxiety from those who doubted the wisdom of proceeding with a weapon in which accuracy and size of shell were sacrificed to such a degree in the interests of rapidity of fire. The Treasury also retarded its development and halved the number of guns to be produced.[49] The close-range weapons of the Fleet proved in the end to be woefully inadequate in action, lacking both accuracy and stopping power against modern aircraft, and being both expensive of ammunition and mechanically unreliable.

The Admiralty's plans to proceed with the construction of the *King George V* class of new battleships played a large part in the revival of the bomb-versus-battleship controversy of the early 1920s. One unlooked for benefit of this was the establishment in October 1936 of a CID committee of scientists under Major General Sir Hugh Elles, which came to be known as the "Sub-Committee on Bombing and AA Gunfire Experiments" or, more simply, the ABE Committee. Over the next three years its members worked hard to avoid what one member called "technocratic shenanigans" and to get to the truth of the matter.[50] They concluded that AA fire was not as reliable as the Navy generally thought, high-

lighting in particular the weaknesses in accuracy and stopping power noted earlier. Their investigations showed that neither the Admiralty nor the Air Ministry had properly analysed the problem of air attack and AA fire. "The data put
before us," they said in October 1937, "are insufficient to draw any reliable conclusions."[51] Because the two services had both failed to conduct scientifically organised trials, or even to collect and collate information in a properly ordered
way, it was necessary to undertake special trials before the ABE Committee
could come to any decision. This in itself was an indictment of the way in which
the two services had approached what was undoubtedly one of the major
defence issues of the period. The sudden apprehension about the validity of
long-held beliefs that this inquiry produced doubtless played a part in the Admiralty's last-minute efforts to improve the AA equipment, and to cast aside its
prejudices by ordering as many Swiss 20mm Oerlikon and Swedish Bofors
40mm guns as it could. As Capt Roskill says, it was a great pity for the Royal
Navy that this committee was not set up years earlier.[52]

However effective AA was thought to be, a proportion of attacking aircraft
would certainly get through to their targets. The accuracy and lethality of the
attacks launched by the surviving aircraft is therefore the last issue in the battle
which has been gradually developed in this chapter. As far as the Navy's own
torpedo bombers were concerned, this was not a matter of major controversy. In
most exercises torpedo aircraft hit their targets on one out of every two occasions. The Naval Staff proposed that as a rule of thumb this rate should again
be cut by rather more than half as an estimate of hits in the face of gunfire, at least
for the sake of war games. About one aircraft in six was expected to hit its target.
The lethality of torpedo attack had been much investigated in conflict and in
peacetime experiments. Again as a rule of thumb for Staff exercises, the following table was drawn up:

EFFECTS OF TORPEDOES ON SHIPS[53]

Number of hits	Percentage of speed and fighting power (FP) remaining				
	HMS *Nelson*	HMS *Repulse*			
	Mk VIII torpedo Speed and FP	Mk VIII torpedo		Mk X torpedo	
		Speed	FP	Speed	FP
1	95	95	100	95	100
2	90	90	100	85	100
3	85	85	100	75	95
4	80	80	100	60	90
5	75	70	95	40	75
6	65	55	90	20	50
7	50	40	75	—	—
8	35	20	50	—	—
9	15	—	—	—	—

There were extra complications to cover such eventualities as two hits in the same place, "vital hits" on propellers and so forth, or the varying effects of different types of torpedo. The Navy was generally much more perturbed about torpedoes fitted with magnetic pistols which exploded beneath the ship and so were expected to do twice as much damage as torpedoes exploding on contact. All this was a big improvement on the crude "one knot off for one hit, two for two and four for three" estimates of the mid–1920s.[54] Nevertheless, and even taking into account the fact that the *Rodney* was the Navy's most modern ship, these figures seem over-optimistic. Experience in the Second World War was to show that fewer torpedoes could do much more damage than this. Constructors and technical experts clearly overrated the efficiency of bulges and internal subdivision. On the other hand, it is also true that the Naval Staff much exaggerated torpedo-dropping accuracies.

The Navy's fear of deep explosions also explains the general apprehension about the so-called "B-bomb". The idea was that the aircraft would drop this special kind of bomb in the path of a warship so that it would float upwards to explode beneath the ship as it passed overhead. "Our new battleships," commented Chatfield anxiously in 1936, "will be 14in-gun ships; they will be very fast and very well armed, though the most vital part will be their bottom if a mine or bomb explodes under it. There seem to be no way to deal with it at present but we are working on it and may find a solution."[55] The Air Ministry was the driving force behind this development, and its interest in the proposal was a legacy of its earlier enthusiasm, generated by the US Navy's *Ostfriesland* tests of 1921, for the "water-hammer effect" of near-miss bombs exploding in the water alongside ships. Even the Air Staff agreed that the British *Gorgon* and *Monarch* trials of 1922–3 showed this danger to be largely illusory.[56] They remained interested in such projects, however, and the FAA Committee of 1935 conceded that the "credit for the inception of the type of bomb that will make this form of attack possible lies with the Air Ministry," adding drily, "it is the one major contribution to naval air work which has come from non-naval sources."[57] In point of fact, however, these bombs never became an operational reality, the technical problems proving too great.

As far as the more conventional forms of bombing were concerned, the Navy tended to be more sympathetic to the dive-bombing methods pioneered by the US Navy. The difficulty with high-level bombing was that great height was necessary to give bombs a reasonable chance of penetrating the armoured decks of modern warships. But the higher the aircraft flew, the lower its chances of hitting the ship in the first place. It was generally believed that the chances of naval bombing aircraft actually sinking capital ships were so slender that it would be better not to attempt it. Operating at lower heights, bombing aircraft would achieve greater accuracy and, very possibly, do useful damage against the superstructure and fighting positions of battleships, against cruisers and destroyers, and especially against carriers. It was generally agreed that bombers might do substantial tactical damage to the battlefleet, and that dive bombers would be particularly effective in this role.

As has been shown, the Air Staff remained cool about this particular method of attacking ships and were not very enthusiastic about torpedo-dropping either, telling the ABE Committee in 1937 that the vulnerability of the aircraft to AA fire, the inherent strength of the ship and the low payload of the torpedo meant that they "... always regarded this method of attacking warships as unsuitable for employment of aircraft."[58] Instead they preferred high-level bombing, more of the kind which they intended to carry out over land.

The existence and regular use of the remotely controlled target ships, the *Agamemnon* and *Centurion*, provided a good deal of raw information on bombing accuracy at various heights. There was certainly enough to show that the Course-setting and Fourth Vector bombsights, developed during the 1920s, were much improving accuracy. The following results from the *Centurion* bombing of 1933–4 give some idea of the correlation between height and accuracy, and also, incidentally, the particular advantage of dive bombing.

CENTURION BOMBING TRIALS 1933–4[59]

Method	Height (feet)	Bombs dropped	Hits	Hits (%)
Level	16,000	72	1	1.4
Level	14,000	260	4	1.5
Level	10,000	1,030	60	5.8
Level	7–9,000	460	58	12.5
Dive*	1,500	334	128	38

* 1933 figures only.

The ABE Committee was not at all impressed by these figures, pointing out that there were so many untested variables (such as weather conditions, skill of pilots and so on) that it was very difficult to know what could be made of them. The committee therefore ordered the inauguration of a further series of more scientific tests, though the war intervened before the work was completed. Perhaps for rather more partisan reasons, the Naval Staff were also unimpressed, arguing that pilots would certainly not be able to achieve such levels of accuracy in battle. Even if it did not shoot down aircraft, for instance, AA gunnery could be relied upon to break up formations and put bomb-aimers off their stroke. In this, of course, they were perfectly right.

But they were on much less secure ground when they considered the damage done by the few bombs that could be expected to hit. A whole series of experiments had demonstrated that battleships were indeed very difficult to sink. The Air Staff also never pretended to be able to dispose of battleships with the casual Olympian ease assumed by the more violent of their partisans. "Let me again restate," said Trenchard in 1925, "I do not claim to be able to sink a battleship."[60] At the Vulnerability of Capital Ships Committee (VCS) of 1936, it was the same story. The then Chief of the Air Staff (Air Marshal Sir Edward Ellington) was at pains to deny such claims. "I should like to say at the outset," said Air Marshal Sir Hugh Dowding, "that I agree broadly with the technical case as presented by the Admiralty." "The capital ship," added Air Marshal Sir John Salmond, another former Chief of the Air Staff, "is the one remaining surface craft which, if hit severely, will not sink. In my opinion it should have a useful life for some time to come in spite of the increasing range and power of the air arm."[61] What the Air Force did argue, however, was the much more important point that air power could, by damaging battleships, by sinking their escorts and by raiding their harbours, so reduce their freedom of action as to rob them of at least some of their tactical and strategic value. Experience in the early part of the war showed that the Admiralty did not take this particular aspect of the case as seriously as perhaps it should have done.

The nature of the problems they were confronting makes it very understandable that the Air and Naval staffs should take the positions they did. The Navy certainly devoted much effort to studying the role and vulnerability of the battleship in the air age. ". . . The fifteen years' exhaustive experiments that we have carried out since 1920," Chatfield told Churchill, "practically conceived and carried out . . . have given us ample facts on which to base estimates of the vulnerability of our battleships, not only to gunfire and torpedo attack but also to bomb attack."[62] The matter was analysed by a string of investigative committees and in large-scale experiments and trials. Practically every other year, major bombing trials were carried out against the *Agamemnon* and *Centurion*, often watched by trainloads of spectators brought down specially from the defence ministries in London. The physical effectiveness of the bomb against ships was investigated in the *Baden* trials of 1922 and the *Monarch* trials in 1923 and 1924. A large representation of a modern warship, known variously as the Chatham Float or "Job 74," was constructed and experimented upon throughout the period. In 1931 and 1932 there were the *Marlborough* trials, followed shortly after by another series against the *Bacchus*. Wholesale reviews of AA gunnery were conducted by the Naval Anti-Aircraft Gunnery Committee of 1921 and 1931, supported by innumerable trials and routine Fleet firings against

Queen Bees, and most thoroughly analysed by the ABE Committee of 1936–9. The more general aspects of the issue were studied in the Postwar Questions Committee of 1920–1, the Bonar Law Inquiry of 1921 and the VCS Committee of 1936. The closest attention was also paid to the unfortunately ambiguous lessons of the Spanish Civil War. Whatever else may be said about the Navy's attitude to the air threat to surface warships, they certainly cannot be accused of ignoring it.

Despite all this, however, the conclusions remained tentative, and it was inevitable that they should. For one thing, these trials usually only investigated one variable in the equation, whereas the real issue was the way in which one variable affected another. How, for instance, would AA gunfire affect the accuracy of bomb aiming? While the ABE Committee tried to put the two variables together and came to the conclusion that for every dive bomber shot down there would be one hit against a cruiser or two on a carrier, it was impossible to try this out in practice, short of introducing live firing into the RAF's bombing trials. It was almost as difficult to combine the variables of bomb accuracy and lethality, as the US *Ostfriesland* trials demonstrated. Conducted more in the spirit of a gladiatorial contest than of pure scientific inquiry, these trials actually proved nothing at all apart from showing that if an old, leaking and defenceless battleship is bombed for long enough, it will eventually sink. The British *Bacchus* trials, in which the RAF live bombed an old cruiser filled with wood to keep it floating, was more imaginative, though its lessons too were ultimately ambiguous.

The whole question was rendered more difficult by the fact that it especially concerned the future relationship of bomb and battleship, involving estimates of the relative value of weapons not yet in existence. It was difficult, for instance, to get reliable estimates of future bombing accuracy from early trials in which pilots had to be guided to their target by the primitive expedient of tugs on a piece of string tied to their ankles! For this reason, estimates tended to be more articles of faith than of scientific judgement. The Navy generally believed that science inevitably produced antidotes to its own advances and that the defence would therefore at least keep pace with the attack. The Air Staff disagreed: "What I do feel about it," the Chief of the Air Staff told the VCS Committee, "is there is more room for development in aircraft than there is either in the gun or in the battleship. . . . Therefore I should think the time will come when the battleship as we know it will probably be out of date, but that is not the same thing as saying it is out of date today. I think there has been a tendency when talking especially of anti-aircraft fire and protection of battleships to deal with the battlefleet of the future against the bomb and aeroplane of today. Sufficient weight has not been given to the progress likely to be made both in aircraft and in their use."[63] The one thing that these competing visions of the future had in common was the fact that neither could possibly be proved in the present.

Since the issue was inevitably characterised by such a high level of uncertainty, the investigations tended to confirm more opinions than they changed. Since it was also at heart a matter of conjecture, and evidence was of what Beatty called the "may-be type,"[64] it was entirely natural that the Navy should give the benefit of the doubt to the battleship – a weapons system of great and long-established value – especially as many naval officers considered that their own service interests were ultimately at stake. "In view of the wildly differing estimates of the future of submarines and aircraft and the nebulous data upon which hopes are based," the Admiralty were not likely to acquiesce in "a policy which will substitute such shadows" for the solid reality of a Navy based on the battleship.[65]

The conclusion of all these investigations was that the battleship and the battleline would come through an air attack, unless it was mounted in overwhelming numbers, in a state which would allow it to continue to exert decisive influence on subsequent naval operations. It was not omnipotent and in some circumstances it could certainly be sunk or disabled by aircraft, but it still remained the piece on the chessboard which dominated the game. "Properly supported by other weapons, it is the final arbiter at sea: to lose it is to lose the game."[66] It was described by another participant in the debate as "the citadel of all effective sea power, a citadel from which all other classes of vessel derive their power to range the seas steadily and consistently."[67] Accordingly, the last act in the archetypal naval battle considered in this chapter would be an awesome and bloody affair commanded by the heavy guns of the Fleet.

There is no doubt that the Royal Navy generally expected "that a decision at sea would only be achieved through two fleets of capital ships cannonading each other, probably on parallel courses and at long range."[68] The Navy was sure that there would be a central decisive battle in a future naval war and thought that this encounter would be dominated by gunnery. "While all weapons will bear their part in the defeat of the enemy," the Naval Staff wrote in 1934, "British tactics aim primarily at so placing the Battlefleet in action that gunnery superiority is assured and the destruction of the enemy is thereby achieved."[69]

Some senior officers were inclined to put too low a value on the contribution that air power could make to their final battle, either because they made insufficient allowance for the limitations of the materiel with which the FAA operated in the 1920s and early 1930s or because they overestimated the defensive capacity of the Fleet. One Deputy Chief of the Naval Staff, for example, shocked the Air Staff in 1934 by appearing to argue that "our main policy would be to destroy Japanese aircraft carriers and other aircraft-carrying ships by means of attack delivered by fighting ships, rather than by means of air attack on these vessels." In other words, he thought that the proper reply to a large increase in the Japanese fleet air arm would be to build more "fighting ships". "I cannot believe," commented one RAF officer, "that it really represents advanced naval thought."[70]

The *Glorious* entering Malta's Grand Harbour, 1932. (Capt French)

The bridge of the *Glorious*. The black sector at top right was used to display the time the photograph was taken. (Capt French)

The Navy's three most modern carriers operate together for the first time: the *Courageous, Furious* and *Glorious* at sea in the Western Mediterranean during the Combined Fleet exercises of March 1933. (Capt French)

The same three carriers at Malta. *Courageous*, bottom centre with the lift lowered, flew the flag of Admiral Henderson, who did much to develop the concept of carrier strike forces. (Capt French)

The period just before the war was one of intensive training on the *Furious*. Here a pair of Swordfish practice deck landing. Note homing beacon and attendant destroyer. (Capt French)

Overleaf Most naval officers imagined that the culmination of the central battle would be a dramatic and savage encounter between two fleets of capital ships. Here the *Nelson, Rodney, Royal Sovereign* and the rest of the 2nd Battle Squadron are shown in battle formation, firing at a distant target. (Albert Sebille, *Illustrated London News*)

The *Furious* in the last of her many guises. After her final (1938) reconstruction the lower flying-off deck was no longer used for this purpose. (Capt French)

The *Ark Royal*, the Navy's most modern carrier at the outbreak of war, sinks slowly after being torpedoed by U81 in November 1941. (*Illustrated London News*)

The *Illustrious*, the first of the celebrated armoured carriers. *Illustrious* won the Battle of Taranto, survived enormous damage and participated in the final naval/air battles of the Pacific campaign. (Imperial War Museum)

When war came, air power was shown to be a decisive factor in operations at sea. **Opposite top** A contemporary attempt to plot the 88 bombs which fell on or near the cruiser *Suffolk* during Operation Duck in April 1940. **Opposite bottom** The *Suffolk* at Scapa Flow after the operation, with her quarterdeck awash. (Admiral Torlesse)

Carriers first demonstrated their worth during the Norway campaign of 1940. **Top** Difficult conditions on the *Furious* off northern Norway. (Capt French) **Above** A Swordfish lands on the *Argus*. (Capt Fancourt)

Naval air power was also based ashore during the Norway campaign, particularly at Hatston in the Orkneys.
Top Blackburn Skua fighter/dive bombers. **Above** Swordfish. (Capt Fancourt)

Carriers operating together off Norway. **Above** The *Glorious* steaming alongside the *Furious*, with the destroyer *Diana* in attendance. **Below** The *Glorious* parts company with the *Furious*. Three weeks later the *Glorious* was sunk by German battlecruisers. (Capt French)

Above Admiral Sir Dudley Pound, First Sea Lord 1939–43. (Fox Photos) **Below** Admiral Sir Ernle Chatfield, First Sea Lord 1933–8, who superintended the Admiralty's successful campaign to regain control over the FAA. (*Illustrated London News*)

Two advocates of naval air power. **Left** Admiral Sir Charles Kennedy-Purvis as captain of the *Glorious* in 1932. He later became Deputy First Sea Lord, 1942–6. (Capt French) **Below** Admiral Sir Thomas Troubridge, captain of the *Furious* in the Norway campaign and Fifth Sea Lord 1945–6. The aircraft in the background is a Fairey Fulmar two-seat fighter. (Capt Gowlland)

The aircraft of two navies compared. **Above** A line of Swordfish biplanes on one side of the deck and modern folding-wing Grumman F4F Wildcat single-seat fighters on the other. (Capt Fancourt). **Below** A Sea Gladiator makes a difficult landing on the carrier USS *Wasp*.

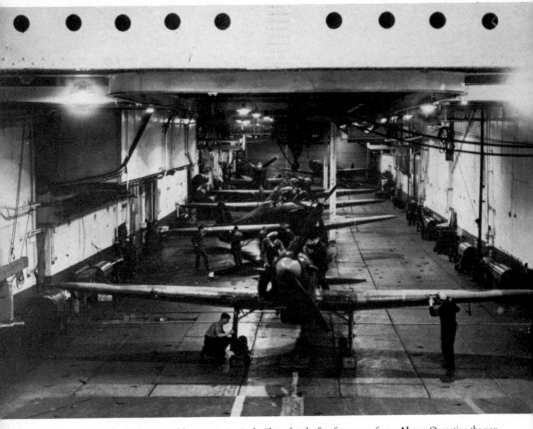

Modern fighter aircraft began to arrive in the Fleet after the first few years of war. **Above** Operating the non-folding Sea Hurricane was difficult in narrow carrier hangars. **Below** Like the Hurricane, the Seafire was an adaptation of a modern high-performance land fighter. (Capt Fancourt)

A Sea Hurricane being refuelled. (Capt Fancourt)

The Fairey Barracuda, used variously for torpedo bombing, dive bombing and reconnaissance. Although the Barracuda was eventually quite successful, its arrival in the Fleet was much delayed. (Capt Fancourt)

The *Unicorn*, the FAA depot ship, at Trincomalee. Ceylon, 1944. (Capt Fancourt)

Grumman Avenger with aircrew. (Capt Gowlland)

Nor did it.

The Royal Navy's caution and scepticism about the role of air power at sea has in fact sometimes been exaggerated. One recent authority, for example, maintains that "conservative battleship admirals thus returned to the old pre-war anti-intellectualism, their naval colleges and Fleet manoeuvres looking to another Jutland and virtually ignoring the promise of the aeroplane and sub-marine.''[71] The reference to Jutland is especially significant, for the Royal Navy is frequently said to have had a near-fixation on the implications of an engage-ment in a past war which hindered its preparations for the battles of the future.

But the fact that the Navy expected the decisive battle of the future to be dominated by the heavy guns should not be taken to mean that its senior officers simply anticipated "another Jutland". On the contrary, a future clash between rival battlefleets was expected to be significantly different from those even of the recent past, principally because of the anticipated influence of air power at sea. As we have seen, naval opinion on how exactly air power was to be used was uncertain and fluctuated as time went by. In the discussions on the Naval Staff's manual, *Fleet Air Arm Tactics and Equipment*, for instance, there was revealed a wide diversity of opinion on the relative value of reconnaissance, fighting, spot-ting, dive bombing and torpedo attack, and much discussion of the technical ways and means by which these functions might be carried out. But there was general agreement tht air power would inevitably play some of these battle roles. "It is difficult," wrote the C-in-C Home Fleet in 1933, "to conceive of any naval operation in war where there will not be a call for aircraft.''[72]

In many circumstances, moreover, the influence of air power could easily prove decisive. Such a case was put forward by Admiral Sir Charles Madden, the then C-in-C Atlantic Fleet and future First Sea Lord (1927–30), in conver-sation with Air Cdre R. Brooke Popham in the autumn of 1920. "As no doubt you know," the Air Commodore subsequently reported, "he is extremely keen on all air problems. He told me that it was his considered opinion that the re-sults of a naval battle in the future depended on the air and the side that had aerial supremacy would win a naval fight provided the ships were anywhere near equal." Madden particularly stressed the help aircraft would be to Fleet gunnery and "went on to say that in seven years' time according to the present building programme the British Fleet would be inferior to the Japanese or to the American fleets. In view of the financial position of the country he saw no possibility of our building programme being increased and the only chance he saw of keeping naval supremacy was to be supreme in the air. He also added that, given air supremacy, he would be quite willing with a British Fleet to take twice the strength of any other fleet.''[73]

While the role of air power might be considered ancillary, it was vital all the same. How, for instance, could the Royal Navy cope with the new fast and powerful ships of the German Navy, unless through the FAA? "Of our six capital ships," said Pound (the First Sea Lord) in 1939, "only the *Hood, Renown* and *Repulse* have sufficient speed to catch the German ships. Our battleships would have to co-operate with aircraft carriers in hopes that the enemy's speed could be reduced as a result of torpedo aircraft attack and the raiders then brought to action by the battleship."[74]

In this conception both the aircraft and the gun were therefore generally considered a vital part of the armament of the modern Fleet. It is difficult, however, to gauge contemporary opinion as to where exactly the balance between the two should be struck, except by investigating how they were actually employed. Although most of the exercise reports of the period have unfortunately been destroyed, enough survive for us to be able to pick out the main features of the development of naval aviation through the inter-war period and to see the place it was expected to take in a future war at sea.

The first few years after the First World War was generally quiet, although the striking function of naval air power was greatly developed in this period. The tempo of fighter, torpedo and reconnaissance work with the Fleet greatly increased in 1924 with the arrival of the *Eagle* in the Mediterranean Fleet. The following year saw assembled in the Bay of Palma a "noble array" of the battleships and cruisers of the Combined Fleets, and for the first time there were three carriers present, the *Eagle, Hermes* and *Argus*. Thereafter carriers worked together quite regularly.

On July 27, 1928, for instance, the *Eagle* and *Courageous* were on opposite sides in a Mediterranean Fleet exercise. The first phase of the Fleet action was a struggle for command of the air. Aircraft from the *Courageous* "took off at dawn, the two fighter flights escorting the squadron of Darts to make a torpedo attack on the 'enemy' battlefleet. It was our duty to make a circle round the Darts with one flight of fighters while the other flight flew on ahead to make an attack on the *Eagle* and damage her flying deck before her aircraft could take off. When our flight arrived over the *Eagle* we found her with all aircraft lined up on deck just about to turn into the wind, so that they could take off, and therefore presenting a most vulnerable target to our bombs and machine-guns. We made an initial dive on our target in formation, then split up for individual dives in a converging bomb attack, after which we would zoom up away from the ship in all directions, rejoining in formation when well out of range of the anti-aircraft defences on board.

"Needless to say, the *Eagle's* machines would not take this lying down. . . . Taking off, they sent their fighters after us to give battle. . . . For the next few minutes the sky was thick with small aircraft buzzing round each other like flies in a most realistic dogfight. . . . Meanwhile, our torpedo flights would be rapidly approaching the battlefleet, escorted by the other fighter flights. Another dogfight would ensue as the opposing fighter flight attempted to close in on the torpedo planes, in order to shoot them down before they could make their dive to drop torpedoes. . . . Then . . . the torpedo planes would dive from the direction of the sun until they were within twenty or thirty feet of the surface of the water. Swiftly skimming along at the same level, they would release their torpedoes when in the correct position. Directly they had done so, they would reel round and, still out of sight of the ships on which they had made their attack, they would fly low over the sea until out of range of gunfire. Finally, back into formation, they would return to their ship and land on.'[75]

There were further developments in the Combined Fleet Exercises of the following year. The highlight of these was the particularly interesting Exercise MZ. It aimed to reproduce "the North Sea situation during the war staged in the Mediterranean actually upside down. . . ." The Mediterranean (or Red) Fleet represented the British Grand Fleet "and have to protect convoys along the African Coast and up the Sardinian coast and troops convoys from the Bonifacio Straits to Toulon. The Atlantic Fleet [Blue] is in the position of the German Fleet, [and] we do not know if they are out for blood or merely for a tip-and-run raid on a convoy. . . ." At the end of this series of exercises there was a "very interesting" Fleet discussion in the Coal Shed on the South Mole at Gibraltar. It transpired that the battle had become a general chase and the British Fleet had won, although they partly came to grief in the night, with several friendly cruisers engaging one another and "the British 4th Destroyer Flotilla discharging all its torpedoes against our battlefleet." Both C-in-Cs spoke and Admiral Sir Frederick Field "as usual was extremely good."'[76]

Even leaving aside the night action, it would be misleading to describe this series of exercises simply as explorations of the past. During daylight hours at least, every phase of operations was influenced by the activities of the airmen. Dawn patrols went out from all the carriers to locate and shadow the enemy fleet, on one occasion being ordered out to a search depth of 145 miles. There were numerous attacks by Dart torpedo aircraft on enemy battleships, and bombing and fighter attacks on hostile carriers, some of which were as fiercely resisted as those of the previous year. A flight of Flycatchers from the *Furious* attacked the *Courageous* but ". . . were attacked by our own fighter patrol, a fine dogfight resulting."[77] There was bombing practice against the target ship *Centurion* and a mass spotting exercise conducted in the expected presence of hostile fighters for the guns of all the assembled battleships.

In short, the Combined Fleet Exercises of 1929 show that by this time the Royal Navy was well disposed towards and well experienced in all the various battle functions of air power. The FAA's role, to use the common tag of the time, was to "Find, Fix and Fight" (the "three Fs") in a way which would transform a Fleet action. Progress in all these aspects of the development and use of air power for the battlefleet continued during the 1930s, especially in the Mediterranean Fleet under Admirals Chatfield and W. W. Fisher, and particularly during and after the Abyssinian crisis. By the late 1930s, therefore, much had been achieved.

The 1929 Combined Fleet Exercises were perhaps also significant in a more specific way, for they saw the beginnings of the idea of the carrier task group. On March 26, 1929, the *Courageous, Furious* and *Eagle* (with the *Argus* in attendance) were placed under the command of Capt A. Lambert and practised transferring their aircraft from one carrier to another. This followed an exercise two days earlier in which the first three carriers (and the *Vindictive*) launched a search and then a massed air strike of 40 torpedo aircraft and fighters against the combined Battlefleet and the *Argus*. In fact the result was not altogether happy. It took an hour for the air striking force to be gathered and the actual attack was not very successful. "On only one occasion," the Naval Staff commented afterwards on this episode, "has any officer been called upon to operate more than two carriers, whereas in war it is more than probable that at least four and possibly more aircraft carriers will be required to be handled as a unit."[78] The Navy's slow carrier construction programme, though, meant that in this respect theory would outrun practice for some time. Nevertheless, during the early 1930s much progress was made in operating carriers as a tactical unit and in assembling "massed air strike forces," especially under the tutelage of the Rear-Admiral (Carriers), Admiral Henderson.

But even if they were operated as a unit, British carriers were thoroughly integrated into the Battlefleet. Countless exercises demonstrated, and subsequent war experience amply confirmed, that carriers were vulnerable ships needing protection from all manner of perils and not least from the dangers of surface attack. In the exercises of March 1925, for instance, the cruiser "*Curacao* cruised to windward of the *Eagle* waiting for her to turn into the wind and fly off planes. When the *Eagle* did so, she was entirely unsupported and was put out of action in seventeen minutes." Carriers needed surface escorts, not only to guard them against the kind of ambush which befell the *Glorious* off Norway and so nearly struck Task Group 77.4 off Sumar on October 25, 1944, but also to act as an anti-submarine screen, for carriers were also regularly sunk by submarines in exercises and in war.[79] The most obvious threat, however, was air attack launched from enemy carriers. The results of carrier-versus-carrier strikes were often decisive to the outcome of the subsequent battle, and so cruisers had often to be detached to act as AA escorts. "Whilst appreciating to the full the value of an aircraft carrier for reconnaissance and air attack," commented one senior officer in 1938, "this exercise brings home the heavy liability and encumbrance a carrier may become."[80] All this, of course, was seen to confirm the wisdom of the Armoured Carrier Programme.

The Royal Navy's conception of the role of naval aviation in a Fleet action does not seem to have been materially different from that of the US and Japanese navies. "The strategic concept of the Japanese Navy," wrote one of their first aviators afterwards, "was undoubtedly based upon the doctrine of annihilating the enemy in decisive battle, with battleships the backbone of the Japanese Fleet." At least until the "Second Shanghai Incident" of 1937, the main functions of the Japanese naval air force were orthodox operations in support of the battleline.[81] Even after the Third Replacement Programme of that year, this remained the dominant conception, as is perhaps demonstrated by the construction of the super-battleships *Yamato* and *Musashi*.

The US Navy also conducted its operations along much the same lines. In Fleet Problem XX of February 1939, for instance, there was a sequence of aerial events very similar to that developed earlier in this chapter. The US Navy's major exercises invariably concluded, as did their British equivalents, with a traditional setpiece engagement between two hostile forces of battleships.[82] The US and Japanese navies seem to have been more confident than the British about the possibilities of air interception, but this was one of the few differences in conception about the role of naval air power in a Fleet action. They appear, however, to have had higher expectations about the effectiveness of these roles. In US and Japanese practice, massed air strikes usually involved more aircraft and did more damage, and the preliminary carrier-versus-carrier phase of the action was therefore inevitably longer. This difference was however largely a reflection of the relative size and performance of the air materiel deployed by the three navies.

The US and Japanese navies were further ahead, however, in their conception of the way in which carriers could be used for detached and semi-independent operations. In 1937 the Japanese carriers *Ryujo*, *Hosho* and *Kaga*, and naval air stations in Formosa and Kyushu, became heavily involved in operations around Shanghai in the Sino-Japanese War. The Japanese Navy learned the necessity of having long-range fighter escorts and high-performance aircraft and was made aware of the potentialities of carrier aviation in helping to project naval power ashore. The Japanese also needed to whittle away the superiority of the US Navy before they dared engage it in decisive action, and the China war reinforced the notion that naval aviation might be a means to this end. So it was that Yamamato was inspired to form the carrier task forces that would later cross the Pacific to attack the US Battlefleet at Pearl Harbour. Strategic necessities thus pushed the Japanese into a clear lead in the development of independent naval air action.

The US Navy's main strategic preoccupation was the defence of vulnerable points (such as the Panama Canal and Pearl Harbour) against sudden naval attack, complicated by all the problems of a westward advance of the US Pacific Fleet to Hawaii and beyond. This, too, increased the need for carriers on detached and independent operations. In 1932, for instance, the *Saratoga* and *Lexington* launched a massed air attack on Pearl Harbour to test the island's defences. In 1929, in similar style, the *Saratoga* launched its celebrated 83-aircraft strike from 150 miles against the Panama Canal. Although a bold, imaginative and significant operation, it also demonstrated how vulnerable carriers could be. The exposed position of the *Saratoga* led to her being claimed as sunk on three occasions that morning, by submarine, by the *Lexington* and, finally, by a squadron of battleships. Isolated deployment of this kind was plainly very dangerous, making senior US Navy admirals cautious about the implications of the whole exercise. "The launching of 83 planes from the *Saratoga*'s deck on the morning of January 26," commented Admiral W. A. Wiley (C-in-C US Fleet), "is and will remain an epic in the history of aviation. No single air operation ever conducted from a floating base speaks so eloquently for the advanced state of development of aviation as an integral part of the Fleet."[83] The chief organiser of the attack, Cdr Eugene E. Wilson, left the US Navy shortly afterwards and later wrote: "Our own high rankers, while appreciating the tactical skill Bull Reeves had shown, had entirely missed the point of his accomplishment."[84] This doubtless explains why the US Navy did not in the event develop carrier task forces in the 1930s. As late as 1942 the US Navy "still held that carriers should act independently, to evade the enemy, and that even as many as two carriers in company represented a great risk."[85] The Japanese, however, and possibly even the British, appear to have been more prepared to operate their carriers in company.

In their various operations off Russia, China and Palestine British carriers also occasionally broke loose from the Battlefleet to project their power ashore in semi-independent operations. In the Combined Staff exercises held every year at the Army Staff College at Camberley, the possibilities of an attack on Singapore by Japanese carriers were explored regularly from the defender's point of view.[86] If there had been a war against the Soviet Union in the late 1920s, the combined staffs assumed that British carriers would operate on the China Station, in the Black Sea, the White Sea and the Baltic and that there would have to be a strike on the Soviet Fleet in a special operation involving aircraft, mines and motorboats on the lines of the 1919 attack on Kronstadt.[87] Had there been a war with Italy over the Abyssinian crisis of 1935–6, "it was the intention to use the carriers for attacks on Italian bases, not to retain them for future reconnaissance or for achieving air superiority." The latter, on account of "Italy's geographic position and her large number of shore-based aircraft, would not have been obtainable, except locally or temporarily except by surprise."[88] Admiral Ramsay (the RAA) planned to use his carriers for bombing attacks on Port Augusta and Catania air base and to launch a general assault on the Italian fleet base at Taranto with bombs and torpedoes.[89] While the British did not expect their naval aircraft to take on shore-based air power in quite the manner the US and Japanese navies did, and their operations were not on the same scale either in conception or performance, the difference between them was still a matter of degree rather than of kind.

All in all, there is no doubt that by 1939 the US and Japanese navies had moved ahead in the development and tactical employment of naval air power with the Fleet and in independent operation. This is certainly so when measured in terms of the offensive and defensive power of the naval aircraft employed. While all three navies remained generally faithful to the continued primacy of the heavy gun, there were more who doubted this order of priorities in the US and Japanese navies than there were in the British. Royal Navy opinion, while much more advanced than that in all the other European navies, was unsettled and shifting, making a sensible and steady programme of aircraft and carrier procurement more difficult. In some particulars – such as the anticipated role and importance of fighter aircraft – British "sea opinion" had gone grievously astray in 1939. Nevertheless, it is plainly going much too far to accuse the Royal Navy either of "ignoring the promise of the aeroplane" or of being solely concerned to refight the Battle of Jutland.

This survey of the Royal Navy's doctrine of battle and general view of how its air power should be best used cannot end without some consideration of two related matters: the use of maritime air power for trade protection and in support of amphibious operations. As far as trade protection was concerned, the experience of the First World War had demonstrated the value of aircraft in the campaign against the U-Boats. Probably the RNAS's chief contribution to this battle was the maintenance of extensive patrols by land-based aircraft, perhaps best epitomised by the celebrated Felixstowe "Spider's Web" based on the North Hinder Lightship. By the end of the war the RAF was maintaining a daily average of 190 aeroplanes, 300 seaplanes and flying boats and 75 airships for the purpose. Every month, as a rule, British aircraft made 28 sightings, 19 attacks and flew 14,000 hours, a record not exceeded until mid–1943.[90] It is now clear that these aircraft sank few if any submarines, but they nonetheless had a vital harassing and deterrent role. Their beneficial influence was more strikingly demonstrated when they were attached to specific convoys. Ships in convoys provided with some air escort stood a much higher chance of reaching port unscathed than did those without, and this was quickly realised at the time.

Despite all this and the fact that the Admiralty consistently maintained throughout the inter-war period that the defence of the maritime communications of the Empire was the main justification for its existence, the Navy was very ill-prepared for the task of defending trade against submarines in 1939. Not all of the reasons can be easily attributed to the financial stringencies of the times. Capt Roskill writes of the "personal antipathy of many senior officers to convoy, which they regarded as a defensive measure and so one to be avoided by a service whose greatness (allegedly) lay in its readiness to assume the offensive in all and every circumstance."[91] A dislike of the humdrum business of trade protection certainly played a part in the inattention paid to its requirements. The Air Staff shared this lack of interest, as indicated by their attitude to the provision of aircraft for trade-protection duties. The proper function of aircraft lay in the direct assault of the enemy's homeland and if air resources were diverted to maritime purposes "beyond the essential minimum required for fleet action purposes, the permanent subtractions from our total air striking power which will result will vitally endanger the security of . . . Great Britain and ultimately the whole Empire.'"[92] In any case, they believed that the air menace to trade was much more serious and that the way to deal with it was by destroying the industries producing the aircraft and bombs which such a campaign would require.

It was also generally believed that developments such as Asdic had largely solved the submarine problem and that consequently, the main threat to shipping was once more posed by the surface ship. Air resources should therefore be devoted to the battlefleet, whose activities (whether as a united force or one split into trade-protection detachments) were the most effective counter to this threat. The British were by no means alone in this view. As late as July 1940, for example, the Chief of Operations of the German Navy argued that since the submarine had reached the limit of its potential," the main protagonist in the war against the enemy's ocean communications is the battleship itself.'"[93] Sizeable parts of the German Navy were concerned to launch such forays as those of the *Graf Spee, Bismarck, Scharnhorst* and *Gneisenau*, while comparable Royal Navy formations were tasked with defeating them. In fact, even if the submarine did not turn out to be defeated after all, First World War experience suggested that the battlefleet would probably still dominate the scene by providing the cover without which auxiliary and escort forces could not be expected to operate. Either way, success in trade protection seemed to depend on the British Main Fleet's successfully destroying or neutralising its opponent, and it therefore is not surprising that air resources should have been concentrated on the battlefleet. It has to be said, moreover, that with all their faults British anti-submarine doctrine and trade-protection policy were far in advance of those of either the Japanese or American navies.

By and large, the Navy of the inter-war period also did not devote much time and effort to the examination of the role that naval air power might play in amphibious operations. Although there were quite a few minor exercises, particularly on the Mediterranean and West Indies Stations, amphibious and combined operations involving carriers did not take place very often. Whenever naval aircraft were required ashore, as they were during the Russian and Turkish civil wars, in China and Palestine, they usually operated independently, either as seaplanes or by using existing air bases if they were conveniently available. Some of the techniques were explored in the annual Joint Staff Exercises at Camberley, which regularly investigated ways of mounting and repelling a Japanese naval assault on Singapore. But these were only paper exercises, and the mechanics of amphibious operations were generally neglected during the inter-war period.

One reason for the relatively low priority accorded to the study of such operations was the general conviction that it would be costly for carrier-based aircraft to attempt to engage land air forces and bases. The extent of Japanese air losses in their early raids on the Chinese mainland (before the advent of their new fighters) was particularly taken to heart.[94] Nevertheless, exercises of this kind were occasionally tried. In March 1935, for example, the Home Fleet with *Courageous* and *Furious* steamed up the Channel, evaded reconnaissance patrols and launched an hour of attacks on several air bases in the Solent area as they went past, destroying in the process a large part of the air striking force being marshalled against them.[95] Whether the Navy could afford to take such risks depended on the general strategic situation, particularly the existing balance between the British and enemy battlefleets. Just as with the protection of trade, it was generally thought that command of the sea had first to be achieved in a decisive Fleet action before such diversions of naval strength could be justified. In 1934, for instance, the Joint Staffs considered the possibility of British carriers attacking targets on the Japanese mainland but felt that "the carriers would themselves run a considerable risk of damage, and it is doubtful if the results to be expected from carrierborne attack against Japanese air bases would justify risking the irreplaceable carriers before a decision had been reached between the main Fleets."[96] So, for reasons of doctrine and philosophy, the aerial requirements of this central and all-important battle for the command of the sea naturally took precedence over those of such subsidiary activities as the defence of trade or the support of military operations ashore.

Though the US Navy had the same articles of faith, strategic realities intervened to modify their application. The Americans were faced from the start with a strategic necessity for a general advance into the Western Pacific in the face of hostile air power operating from Guam, the Carolines and the Marshalls. "The US Fleet," a recent study shows, "would have to mount sufficient strength in the air to overwhelm the enemy's combined fleet and shore-based air force. Hence the necessity for large numbers of US Naval aircraft and the carriers from which to fly them"[97] From the start, in other words, the US Navy sought to provide itself with the kind of naval air force that would allow it to take on an enemy's naval air force and shore-based aircraft simultaneously, rather than in sequence, as implied by British practice. The war was to show that this alternative and more ambitious solution to the strategic problems confronting both navies was the better one.

We have already seen that the Royal Navy has been much criticised for its conception of the main battle and of the balance that it consequently thought should be struck between the gun and the aeroplane. It is also possible to argue that the very idea of a major Fleet action was wrong. There was, writes Professor Marder, an "excessive emphasis in pre-war training on a fleet action." Capt Roskill also writes persuasively of the influence that the Navy's overconcentration on the concept of the battlefleet and the decisive battle had on its ability to protect maritime communications and support amphibious operations.[98]

In the case of the Royal Navy, the traditional assumptions of naval strategy were not modified to the extent they were in the US and Japanese navies. The British usually assumed, except possibly in the case of Italy, that their probable adversaries would be fighting the same kind of war as them. They rejected the notion that, by making the decisive battle the focus of their concern, they were merely preparing for the last war. Admiral L. E. Holland (then ACNS and eventually to be lost in the *Hood*), for instance, certainly believed that this concentration on the Fleet action was the right policy to follow in preparing for a war with Japan. "It is generally accepted," he said, "that in the case of a war against Japan the same processes which brought about main battle in the past will be again at work and the final round will be fought between the main fleets." He agreed that this was not quite so true where Germany was concerned and that, at least for a time, "main battle between concentrations of capital ships" would yield to detached operations on the trade routes as the main feature of the war at sea. Even here, though, "the pressure brought by sea power will eventually be challenged in main battle," once the German Navy grew big enough to contemplate it, perhaps by the mid–1940s.[99]

This was a natural and really not unreasonble assumption. Even Grand Admiral Raeder admitted that he was breaking all the rules by attempting to invade Norway without securing command of the sea in a decisive battle. It followed that the aerial needs of the Battlefleet should take precedence over all others, and in the circumstances of the time this tended to mean that the particular requirements of trade protection and amphibious operations would be neglected. But this reflected more the way the Admiralty thought about the general nature of warfare at sea than it did a particular neglect of maritime air power.

Certainly, at the time of the 1937–8 discussions about *Fleet Air Arm Tactics and Equipment* there were many who voiced fears that an excessive concentration on this stereotyped form of battle on the high seas would blind the Navy to the requirements of those occasions when the FAA would be acting independently, possibly attacking the enemy's shore bases, harbours, dockyards and so forth. "The memorandum," wrote Admiral Sir Roger Backhouse, present C-in-C Home Fleet and the next First Sea Lord, "may be said to visualise, almost exclusively, action between two battlefleets both accompanied by carriers. This condition is only applicable at present in a Far Eastern war. It assumes, also, that both fleets intend to fight – so that what might be described as an unorthodox form of battle results. While it is appreciated fully that these conditions must be given great weight, functions of the Fleet Air Arm in a war much nearer home must be considered also."[100]

The manual being discussed was actually only the first volume of the intended treatise on the functions of air power at sea. It dealt largely with Main Fleet operations and it was hoped that a second volume on the role of air power in the protection of trade would follow later. In fact, though, it never did, and its non-appearance – through lack of time and resources – aptly symbolised the Admiralty's order of operational priorities in the inter-war period.

CHAPTER SEVEN

THE TEST OF WAR

". . . in the Fleet Air Arm the Navy has its most devastating weapon."

ADMIRAL OF THE FLEET
VISCOUNT CUNNINGHAM OF HYNDHOPE

The first year of the Second World War showed up some of the dangers of the Admiralty's concentration on the aerial requirements of the main, decisive battle. The Navy was soon surprised and dismayed by the extent to which aircraft were needed for amphibious operations or naval operations within reach of enemy shore-based air power. The Norwegian campaign was after all, as Admiral Wells said, "the first time in history that carrierborne aircraft have been employed in prolonged operations of this nature." There is no doubt that air power made all the difference to the outcome of the land battle. When it was available, as it was for the Allied landings at Bjerkvik on May 13, 1940, it could provide fighter cover and close support for troops at their most vulnerable moment, when they first went ashore. The same benefits continued to be conferred when the troops fought their way inland, and FAA aircraft had a disproportionately good effect on the soldiers' morale wherever they appeared. Conversely, their absence depressed the troops greatly. "Our men," reported General Auchinleck, "seemed distressingly young, not so much in years as in self-reliance and manliness generally."[1] For this reason it was courting disaster, he thought, to commit troops to a campaign with inadequate air support. Hostile air power was damaging enough against men in action, but in some ways it was even more dangerous in the rear areas, where it could, and in Norway invariably did, interrupt communications, disrupt supplies and hinder mobility.

Air power was therefore fundamental to victory in the land battle, and since the RAF could not provide this support initially, and found it difficult to get ashore subsequently, the FAA had to assume the bulk of the burden. This unexpected commitment quickly revealed the qualities required if the FAA was to be involved in similar operations later on. Norway showed that carrier-based aircraft needed to be capable of taking on their shore-based counterparts, that their flyers had to be skilled in Army co-operation, and that the Fleet had to be able to mount sustained and gruelling air operations for long periods of time. All this came as something of an unwelcome shock to a Navy which had grown used to devoting only a small proportion of its aerial resources to such subsidiary tasks.

These lessons were reinforced by the extremely disappointing outcome of the British and Free French assault on Dakar in September 1940. Operation Menace, as it was called, was spoiled by hasty and muddled planning, indifferent performance and bad luck. "Finally," commented the Vichy Flag Officer at Dakar, "the English aviation proved a heavy failure, not a single bomb or torpedo has hit a military objective."[2] Air cover was provided by the *Ark Royal*, but her Skuas were outclassed by the French Morane 406 and Curtiss Hawk 75A fighters and none of her feverishly improvised attacks on French ships and shore installations succeeded in their general objective. It was altogether a most lamentable performance.

Once the Germans had overrun most of Continental Europe and the Japanese had entrenched themselves in a series of defended islands and bases across the Pacific, it was obvious that amphibious operations would assume a much greater importance in the conduct of the war than had been envisaged before 1939. Consequently, much effort and resource were devoted to their preparation. One of the first fruits of this was the successful attack on Madagascar in May 1942.

Two new Armoured Fleet carriers, the *Illustrious* and *Indomitable*, participated under the command of Admiral Denis Boyd. A few air combats and a strike on Antsirane, the main air base on the island, by Grumman Martlets and Fairey Albacores virtually eliminated French air resistance. The FAA provided tactical reconnaissance and air strikes, sometimes a few hundred yards ahead of the troops as they advanced ashore. Finally, several French warships and submarines were sunk by bomb and torpedo, and within a few days French resistance crumbled. It was, wrote Churchill, "a model for amphibious descents."[3]

One of the most significant things about the whole operation was its demonstration that it was possible to move a large invasion force over 8,000 miles in absolute secrecy and stage a surprise attack. "In all these operations," said USN Fleet Admiral Chester Nimitz later, "the employment of air-sea forces demonstrated the ability of the Navy to concentrate aircraft strength at any desired point in such number as to overwhelm the defence at the point of contact. These operations demonstrate the ability of naval carrier-based aviation to make use of the principles of mobility and concentration to a degree possessed by no other force."[4] A sequence of such operations followed over the next three years. They saw a gradual increase in the size and effectiveness of naval air support and culminated in the savage and gruelling operations against the Japanese home islands in 1945.

For this campaign the British Pacific Fleet comprised two fast battleships, usually four armoured Fleet carriers, supported by destroyers, cruisers and a large Fleet train, and sustained with much difficulty from a base 4,000 miles away. Shore-based air power was taken on and defeated, but at a heavy cost in life and materiel. Japanese air bases were attacked day after day, and large numbers of aircraft were shot down and ships sunk on both sides. "The Third Fleet's operations off Japan in July and August 1945," it has fairly been said, "were the most polished professional aerial performances of the war at sea. This was the consummation of the carrier art. The great fleet turned and wheeled as one, concentrating to strike, dispersing to fuel, shuttling up and down the coast of Japan at will, advancing and retreating as one great supple weapon."5 With command of the sea now safely assured, navies could project their power ashore with decisive, war-winning effect. By dint of great concentration, the Royal Navy had been finally able to deploy in the British Pacific Fleet a weapon that compared well with its American counterparts in terms of quality and so was able to share in this virtuoso demonstration of the naval art. Nevertheless, the enormous disparity in industrial and military resources meant that it was by now very much the junior partner in terms of scale.

Maritime aircraft also proved much more important than expected in the protection of trade. In the inter-war period the Naval Staff had underrated the threat of the U-Boat to maritime communications, largely because it had over-rated the tactical effectiveness of Asdic. Accordingly, the Royal Navy's conception of the use of maritime air power in the defence of trade had mainly been restricted to the provision of seaplanes for detached cruisers hunting for surface raiders, and to a desire to maintain large shore-based aircraft for maritime patrol. It rapidly became clear, however, that many of these assumptions were wrong and that air power had a much more vital role to play in the defence of trade.

In the first place, and as the Air Staff had long prophesied, air power itself had become a major threat to maritime communications, and shipping had either to be re-routed or protected against it, especially in the narrow seas. On many occasions in the North Atlantic and Arctic Oceans and in the Mediterranean, only the FAA could provide the necessary cover against hostile aircraft. In August 1942, for instance, there took place Operation Pedestal, the passage of the last of the celebrated Malta convoys. So great was German and Italian air and maritime strength in the central Mediterranean that a mere fourteen cargo ships required a close and distant escort of 44 British warships, including three carriers. Although it was a costly exercise carried out with inadequate aircraft, the FAA proved capable of maintaining a moving screen of defensive fighters that largely prevented enemy aircraft from doing the convoy decisive damage. But the carriers had eventually to turn back and this was when most of the losses occurred. Even carriers were vulnerable against such odds, and had to be deployed with caution.

German aircraft made themselves felt against the Atlantic convoys too, especially in the shape of the Focke-Wulf 200 Condor, which either attacked merchant shipping directly or provided the information which U-Boat Command needed to direct its operations against convoys. Since fleet carriers could not be used for these more humdrum convoys, the failure to provide trade-protection carriers in the inter-war period meant that the British had to resort to a series of expedients. These started with the Fighter Catapult Ships of December 1940, whose task essentially was to drive away the shadower in a manner reminiscent of the anti-Zeppelin operations of the Grand Fleet in the First World War. From this time on, the interception of enemy reconnaissance and attack aircraft became a main preoccupation of the aerial component of convoy escort forces.

FAA aircraft were used offensively as well. They attacked German and Italian trade and military communications, particularly in the Mediterranean during the North African campaign, and then German shipping in the Channel and Scandinavian waters. Some of these were large and important enterprises, and the last of the FAA's operations in European waters was in fact a strike on Kilbotn in May 1945 which sank the U711 and harassed German shipping. Generally, though, the ability to provide aircraft to defend as well as to attack maritime communications meant that the submarine remained the main threat to British trade and military supply.

Aircraft proved even more important in the defeat of the submarine in the Second World War than they did in the First. One obvious reason for this was the increased lethality of air attack. The development of new aerial weapons, increasing aircraft range and improved operational techniques rendered A/S air patrols much more directly dangerous to submarines than had been the case with the largely scarecrow efforts of the First World War. In 1941 only just over two per cent of aircraft attacks on submarines resulted in a kill, compared with 60 per cent by 1945. Aircraft destroyed just under half of the 784 U-Boats lost in the Second World War, the great majority of these going to the aircraft of Coastal Command. A total of 29 U-Boats, with a further five French and Italian submarines, were sunk by the FAA, either alone or in conjunction with surface ships. Perhaps more important, all A/S aircraft played a vital role in harassing U-Boats and disrupting or deterring their individual and collective attacks. Indeed, the Operational Research section of Coastal Command estimated that one shore-based aircraft should on average save some 16 merchant ships in its operational life.[6]

The deficiencies of the RAF in shore-based maritime aircraft at the beginning of the war, and the dramatic improvement which followed their steady increase in range, number and effectiveness, were precisely mirrored in the FAA. When the war began the Royal Navy had no trade-protection carriers, effective A/S aircraft or weapons. Worse still, it also seemed doctrinally deficient. The carrier *Courageous* was the chief casualty in this relearning process, falling victim to the mistaken notion that the best way of safeguarding trade was to hunt down the

U-Boats in offensive patrols. The *Courageous* was sunk by U-29 on September 14, 1939, with heavy loss of life while several of her destroyer escort were away chasing Asdic echoes. The same fate very nearly befell the *Ark Royal*. The loss of two of its precious carriers in the first few weeks of war would have been a crippling blow for the FAA.

Although doctrinal deficiencies were remedied with commendable speed, materiel shortcomings proved much harder to rectify. The FAA had neither the weapons nor the aircraft for the task. Two Skuas attacking a U-Boat early in the war were blown into the water by the explosion of their own bombs and their crews had to be rescued by their intended victim. Apart from the U-64 destroyed by the *Warspite*'s Swordfish at Narvik, the FAA accounted for only one submarine in the first 18 months of the war. The real problems, though, were the FAA's limited range and numbers. Much of the answer was provided by the world's first escort carrier, the *Audacity*, whose success in four Gibraltar convoys in the last quarter of 1941 inspired the FAA into a belated programme of escort carrier construction. The next such carrier, *Activity*, did not arrive until September 1942, although the US-built *Archer* began operations in March 1942. As experience in the use of escort carriers increased and as co-ordination with Coastal Command improved, the contribution of air power to the defence of maritime communications became very clear.

Its importance in a war in which the Allies were held together by a crisscrossing network of convoys bearing food, military supplies and personnel was fundamental. By the end of the war, and in striking contrast to the modest anticipations of the Naval Staff in the inter-war period, the direct defence of maritime communications absorbed a very large proportion of the Royal Navy's effort and resources, both in terms of ships and aircraft. In 1944, for instance, much of the FAA afloat was deployed in the 43 British escort carriers on active service. Of the 176 operations in which they participated, all but 23 were concerned with some aspect of the use and defence of maritime communications.

But if the war showed up the unwisdom of neglecting the aerial requirements of trade protection and amphibious operations, what light did it shed on the Fleet's pre-war doctrine of the main battle and its readiness to fight it? If we take the FAA's battle tasks in the same order as they were presented earlier, the Norwegian campaign showed the importance and the general lack of good air reconnaissance. Its failure led to a disastrous dispersion of British naval forces at critical times. Thus, during the final evacuation, some of Forbes' forces were distracted away to the east by a report that German ships were on their way to Iceland, and this played a part in the loss of the *Glorious* shortly afterwards. Except for the Narvik Invasion Group, German naval units, and especially the *Scharnhorst* and the *Gneisenau*, seemed able to roam about the North Sea as they pleased. "It is most galling," wrote Forbes afterwards, "that the enemy should know just where our ships . . . are, whereas we generally learn where his major forces are when they sink one or more of our ships.'[7] The resources of the FAA in this area were not always used to their best advantage, as with the *Furious* in the first few days of the campaign and the *Glorious* in the last. Coastal Command was however ultimately responsible for reconnaissance in the North Sea, especially when the carriers were fully engaged in taxing operations ashore, and its general failure in this direction must mainly be attributed to the Air Ministry's neglect of shore-based maritime air power before the war. So weak was the RAF in this regard that a party reconnoitring for possible airfields arrived at Bodo on May 4 in two flying boats chartered from Imperial Airways.

The Royal Navy had long recognised that effective reconnaissance was fundamental to the success of its operations, and was probably more skilled in this than was any other navy or maritime air force. The negative report sent back by the FAA *Maryland* from Hatston which inaugurated the pursuit and eventual destruction of the *Bismarck* is a classic example of the importance of this role, and of the FAA's expertise in carrying it out. Nevertheless, not all naval commanders were so fortunately placed. Desperately short of shore and sea-based aircraft for this purpose, and strategically hampered in consequence, Admiral Cunningham endlessly appealed for reinforcements. "For weeks on end," he wrote in April 1941, "I have had no knowledge of the whereabouts of the Italian Fleet.'[8] This deficiency was almost exclusively a function of the low numbers of FAA and RAF aircrew and aircraft.

Having found the enemy, the FAA's next task was expected to be to "fix" him by crippling his major units, unless of course there were enemy carriers present. In the Norwegian campaign the FAA undertook just the kind of strike role it had expected, though always with painfully inadequate materiel and all too often in a hastily improvised manner. Things went well when the equipment was adequate and the conditions co-operative, as in the *Konigsberg* attack, although this was the exception rather than the rule. There were other disappointments against the French and Italian fleets later that year, largely as a result of the inadequate numbers, aircraft and training of a force in the middle of a hasty expansion. Because of all this, the margins were too narrow for decisive air attack except in the most favourable of circumstances. Torpedo attack at sea soon proved to be a function of mass, not of individual precision and heroism. But when the *Bismarck* operation began, one of the only two carriers available, the *Ark Royal*, was 1,500 miles away ferrying aircraft to Malta. The other, the *Victorious*, had a total striking force of a mere nine Swordfish. "It was incredible," commented one German observer with understandable hyperbole, "to see such obsolete-looking planes having the nerve to attack a fire-spitting mountain like the *Bismarck*.'[9] No such attack, however, bravely conducted, could hope to dispose easily of modern capital ships or to usurp the function of the heavy gun in accomplishing their final destruction. In battles like those off Calabria, Cape Spartivento and Matapan, and the pursuit of the *Bismarck*, the FAA eventually succeeded in fixing the fleeing enemy in just the way that had been rehearsed so many times before the war.

Spotting was generally expected to be the next FAA function in the sequence. All its skills, virtues and benefits were demonstrated during the Norwegian campaign by the flight of the *Warspite*'s Swordfish seaplane at the Second Battle of Narvik, just as they had been by the Seafox launched from the cruiser *Ajax* during the Battle of the River Plate several months earlier. Some of the difficulties, however, were made evident during the *Suffolk*'s bombardment of Sola airfield. Spotting and close reconnaissance were also carried out at Calabria and Matapan, but generally this role declined in importance because the kind of battle it was intended to serve happened so very rarely. In many shore bombardments, however, it was frequently vital, especially in the Mediterranean.

The Norwegian campaign also showed the great importance of winning command of the air over the battle area. Bomber Command did all in its power to help by attacking German airfields. In the third week of April alone Bomber Command launched 200 sorties against airfields in Denmark and Norway, only to be largely defeated by the intractability of the target, the difficult country and its own general unpreparedness. Bomber Command's use of the 1912 Baedeker guide to Scandinavia during these frantic weeks shows the extent of the difficulties the RAF was facing in this area. The RAF had also to be very careful not to cause civilian casualties or damage non-military property. Their inevitable failure put the onus for contesting German air supremacy on the FAA, and the deficiencies of pre-war fighter policy were revealed all too clearly when the FAA tried to carry out this function. The Fleet obviously needed high-performance aircraft capable of intercepting incoming hostile strike aircraft and of escorting outgoing friendly ones.

In the last stages of the action off Calabria there were heavy and continuous raids on the British Fleet by shore-based aircraft. The British had no fighters and so were forced to defend themselves merely by AA gunnery and evasive manoeuvre, just as they had had to do a few months earlier off Norway. On countless occasions in the Mediterranean later on a few fighters made all the difference. But they were often not available either to reinforce success, as in the air strikes of May 26, 1941, against Scarpanto airfield during the air/sea battle of Crete, or to prevent the losses which characterised the rest of the battle. Although much was frequently achieved with very little, the lack of modern fighters was the FAA's gravest weakness throughout the war. The deficiency was not properly made up until its final stages, and only then largely by the wholesale adoption of American aircraft.

At Matapan naval aviation served the heavy guns of the Fleet in just the way that had been foreseen in the inter-war period. The FAA also showed, however, that it was capable of fighting the naval battles of the future as well as those of the past, battles in which the carrier rather than the battleship assumed the central role, however temporarily. There had been some early indications that this might be so in the *Hermes'* attack on the French battleship *Richelieu* and the *Ark Royal's* on the *Dunkerque* in the summer of 1940, but the most dramatic evidence that "in the Fleet Air Arm the Navy has its most devastating weapon"[10] came on the night of November 11, 1940, at the Italian Fleet base at Taranto. A force of 21 Swordfish from the *Illustrious* sank three Italian battleships and transformed the strategic situation in the Mediterranean. "As an example of economy of force," said Admiral Cunningham, "it is probably unparalleled." Although there was something of a repeat performance against the *Tirpitz* in 1944, such encounters were rare in European waters, partly because the targets were so few and far between and partly because once located they proved surprisingly difficult to sink, certainly with the small forces that the FAA had to send against them.

In fact battleships confounded most pre-war estimates by proving extremely resistant to bomb and torpedo, even when unprotected by fighter aircraft. The *Bismarck*, for example, occupied the attention of eight British battleships or battlecruisers, two carriers, 11 cruisers, 21 destroyers and 300 sorties by aircraft. A total of 60 torpedoes were launched at her and she was bombarded for several hours by the heavy guns of the British battlefleet. Finally she had to be scuttled. "There could hardly be any better proof of the modern battleship's staying power."[11] Leaving aside the question of the provision of air cover, as the war progressed the battleship developed a surprising ability to defend itself with the advent of such things as proximity fuses for AA shells and the radar direction of AA guns. Thus by 1945 the new British battleship *Vanguard* was claimed to be able to engage 14 separate aerial targets simultaneously, by day or night. Extensive trials in the late 1940s (particularly against the *Nelson*) also revealed the continued constructional resilience of the modern battleship.[12]

For such reasons the kind of battle for which the battleship was primarily designed did not prove as irrelevant as most pre-war air enthusiasts had envisaged. The presence and effectiveness of one side's heavy units frequently dominated the other's plans and dispositions, as the close attention paid to the movement of the handful of German battleships and battlecruisers clearly indicated. Even when not in play, heavy-gun capital ships were frequently able to determine the game, especially in the earlier part of the war.

In fact, though, the battlefleet was often in play in more or less the way envisaged in pre-war exercises. Just such an action occurred off Calabria on July 9, 1940. Admiral Cunningham wrote afterwards: "First we had the contact of long-range reconnaissance aircraft; then the exact position of the enemy relative to our own Fleet by the FAA aircraft from the carrier, and the informative and accurate reports of their trained observers. Next the carrier's striking force of torpedo bombers went in to attack, though on this occasion, through no fault of their own, they were not successful. Meanwhile the cruisers, spread on a line of bearing, pushed in to locate the enemy's battlefleet, and finally the heavy ships themselves came into action." It all bore an almost uncanny resemblance to pre-war Fleet exercises and table battles at the Tactical School at Portsmouth.[13] Although air power affected its every turn, this was still a naval battle of the traditional sort, even to the extent of the "Enemy battlefleet in sight" signal from the cruiser *Neptune*.

Nor was this the only example of its kind. The battles of Capes Spartivento and Matapan and the destruction of the *Bismarck* and *Scharnhorst* all demonstrated some of the facets and required many of the skills of all the battlefleet exercises of the inter-war period. A recent study shows also that the Pacific war also cannot simply be regarded as a carrier campaign. There were five carrier battles but 22 other major naval surface actions, of which the US won eleven, the Japanese ten and the last was a draw.[14] As late as June 17, 1944, there appears in Admiral Spruance's orders for the battle of the Philippines little that would have seemed remarkable ten or fifteen years earlier. "Our air," wrote Spruance, "will first knock out enemy's CVs [carriers] as operating carriers, then will attack enemy battleships and cruisers, to slow or disable them. Task Group 58.7 [Admiral Lee's battleline] will destroy the enemy fleet by fleet action if [the] enemy elects to fight or by sinking slowed or crippled ships if [the] enemy retreats."[15]

All this helps to explain the Admiralty's continued anxieties about the battleship construction programme. In 1939 there were twelve battleships (two *Nelsons*, five *Queen Elizabeths* and five *Royal Sovereigns*) and three battlecruisers (the *Hood*, *Repulse* and *Renown*) in commission, and five more *King George Vs* under construction. Shortly before the war the Admiralty had been authorised to proceed with the construction of the *Lion*, *Temeraire*, *Conqueror* and *Thunderer*, four modern 16in capital ships designed from the start to be the equal of the best foreign construction. "In normal circumstances" the Admiralty would have sought authorisation for another two such ships in 1940–1.

All these orderly proposals came to nothing when war broke out. "It is far more important," the First Lord (Churchill) shrewdly observed, "to have some ships to fight with . . . than to squander effort upon remote construction which has no relation to our dangers."[16] Accordingly, and after some agonising, the first two *Lions* were suspended and the last two postponed to save resources and dockyard capacity. In compensation, the Admiralty planned to build the *Vanguard*, making use of some spare 15in gun mountings of the *Royal Sovereign* class as a means of getting another battleship with a minimum of time and effort.

The Admiralty were very perturbed about the consequences of all these delays and cancellations. "Our capital ship position," said the new First Lord (Alexander) in September 1940, "is tighter today than it ever has been since the war started. We have literally no margin whatever and everywhere we are below the strength really necessary."[17] A little earlier in the year, tight margins had been successfully used by the Naval Staff to ward off Churchill's proposals for specially armoured battleships that would be of use in his wistful plans for some enterprise in the Baltic. The battleship position between the protagonists, they claimed, would not allow the withdrawal from service of the *Royal Sovereigns* for the time this conversion would take.[18] Nevertheless, first priority in 1941 had to be accorded to the repair of ships damaged in war (a number much inflated by enemy air activity) and to the building of the escorts and merchant ships required in the battle of the Atlantic. Carriers and battleships would have to wait. The Admiralty, though, still wanted to start the *Lions* and to hasten along the last two of the *King George Vs*. In a disastrous few weeks at the end of the year their aspirations were reinforced by the sinking of the *Barham* by U331, the disabling of the *Queen Elizabeth* and *Valiant* by Italian frogmen at Alexandria, and, perhaps paradoxically, by the loss of the *Prince of Wales* and *Repulse* to Japanese air power.

Nevertheless, the Naval Staff were not wholly committed to the completion of the *Vanguard*, whose keel had been laid in April 1941 but whose schedules had already been delayed by the general manning crisis and even more urgent constructional priorities. In 1942, in fact, the possibility of turning her into an aircraft carrier was investigated. "Their proposal," said Churchill, "gave me a bit of a shock, in view of the strong desire you expressed to see that this powerful battleship be commissioned as early as possible." Later he professed himself to be "greatly concerned at the way she has been cast aside."[19] The idea was found impractical and the *Vanguard* slowly proceeded, but even Cunningham, when First Sea Lord, considered her "a waste of labour and money".[20]

In 1942–3 the emphasis was on carrier construction. "As our need for aircraft carriers is relatively much greater," said Alexander of the 1943 programme, "I do not include any battleships in this programme as they can only be built at the expense of Fleet carriers."[21] But this in no way implied that the Admiralty had broken faith with the battleship. The relative need for them had merely declined with the arrival of the *Anson* and the *Howe* and the effective destruction or neutralisation of the French, German and Italian battlefleets.

This impression is reinforced by the Admiralty's plans for a post-war Fleet, which first saw the light of day in early 1944. The Naval Staff told Churchill that they "should ultimately need 12 capital ships if our postwar navy is to be a well-balanced one," but that on the basis of present plans the Navy would be three short by 1950, even assuming that no more were sunk. They therefore urged that the *Lions* be resuscitated. Cunningham weighed in with a reasoned memorandum about the future nature of war at sea. "Sea power," he wrote, "exercised by a proper proportion of surface forces, carrierborne and shore-based air forces is the means by which sea communications are controlled." The battleship and the carrier were complementary and the battleship remained "the basis of the strength of the Fleet . . . [and] . . . a heavier broadside than the enemy is still a very telling weapon in a naval action."[22] Churchill appeared convinced and overruled the objections of Lord Cherwell, his scientific adviser. "The sovereignty of the battleship," he said, "was still maintained." Accordingly, the *Lion* and *Temeraire* were duly authorised to proceed. Intended to complete in 1952, they had made very little progress by the end of the war, apparently more through lack of resources than of conviction.[23]

The Admiralty based its proposal on the assumption that new inventions had not rendered the battleship obsolete. "On the contrary," said Alexander in January 1944, "the U-Boat danger to battleships has been largely mastered and the air menace to them is under much better control than ever before."[24] In company with many others, Lord Cherwell strongly disagreed with this proposal and with its implications for future naval construction. In July 1944 he accordingly wrote a paper for Churchill in which he attempted to prove, as far as ships and aircraft were concerned, that technology was increasing the powers of attack at the expense of those of defence. "I fear," he concluded, "the battleship will not survive in the evolutionary race with aircraft."[25] Much of the experience of war seemed to indicate that he was right.

The Norwegian campaign offered the first pointers in this direction, in fact, especially by demonstrating the inadequacies of contemporary AA gunnery. Admittedly the conditions in narrow, steep-sided fjords were all in the attacker's favour during this campaign, but even on the high seas AA gunnery was not as effective as most naval officers had expected. In general terms, British AA gunnery proved not to have the necessary accuracy, volume or stopping power. Ships tended in desperation to blaze away with everything they had, using up their ammunition at such a rate that the First Sea Lord (Pound) began to protest. Anxious at the rapid depreciation of alarmingly limited stocks of AA ammunition, he signalled to Forbes: "Although I am unwilling to suggest restriction in the use of any anti-aircraft gun, it is obvious that expenditure of this nature at the recent high rates must be curtailed."[26] As the war progressed, air power showed a disagreeable ability to build up attacks which overwhelmed by sheer weight of numbers. The super-battleship *Yamato*, for instance, was sunk by a continuous attack by no fewer than 400 aircraft. Even the best fire-control and distribution systems could not cope with such an assault.

The lethality of aircraft attacks increased, too, from an initial level that was surprisingly low. Coastal and Bomber commands' repeated and frequently valiant efforts to attack German warships at sea and in harbour showed that these operations were very costly and generally much much more difficult than pre-war air enthusiasts had argued. The Luftwaffe's early efforts in the North Sea were no better, but the task of *Fliegerkorps X* in Norway was easier because their targets were nearer, less well defended and operating in very restricted waters. Even so, only the AA cruiser *Curlew*, two destroyers and a sloop were lost to air attack throughout the two-month campaign. Thereafter the rate increased.

British losses in the Battle of Crete in May 1941 were equivalent to those of a moderately sized fleet action. Soon, too, there were developments such as the gliding and guided bombs of the kind which sank the battleship *Roma* in the autumn of 1943, and the heavyweight, free-falling Tallboy which disposed of the *Tirpitz*. By the end of the war air power was responsible for a third of the losses of British warships of destroyer size and over, a rate much exceeding that due to surface action.

Air power also damaged a good many ships, often in a way which effectively neutralised them. In the Norwegian campaign, for example, there was steady and debilitating attrition: two battleships, one carrier, seven cruisers (two seriously), five destroyers and two sloops were damaged by air attack. But the influence of air power on naval operations cannot simply be measured in terms of the actual losses and physical damage it inflicted. Even the most routine and humdrum of naval tasks could test fortitude to the utmost when they had to be conducted under constant threat of air attack. Of his experiences during the evacuation from Dunkirk, one young RNVR officer wrote: "Continuous bombardment seriously interrupts all forms of work and makes contact and communication very difficult. Psychologically it is most serious as noise gradually paralyses the mind and instils a sense of defeat as it begins to seem impossible to strike back. It produces a bad nervous state if continued all night so that the victim seems to hear in the most ordinary sound the whistle of a bomb, in the slap of a bow-wave the noise of a machine-gun fire and in the roar of the wind down the ventilators the approach of bombers."[27] Operations in such conditions, especially if they went on for long periods, put a terrific strain on ships' companies and inevitably affected efficiency.

Air power also had a great effect on the dispositions of fleets. In the Norwegian campaign it was found to be unwise to put AA cruisers in fjords, where their radar was inoperative, even if it did give comfort to the troops ashore. Radar came into its own later, and with the *Ark Royal's* experiments with the *Sheffield's* RDF, the first steps along the path towards the sophisticated fighter-direction facilities of later years were quickly taken. There was the growth of the idea, also, that the defence of a fleet against air attack required ships to be skilfully placed and manoeuvred together, sheltering under an umbrella of defensive fighters and AA gunnery. At Crete and elsewhere it was shown that the lone wolf was much more vulnerable than the pack. In many ways the smallest ships were most at risk, and this often had significant effects on the traditional checks and balances of naval operations. In Norway the vulnerability of A/S trawlers to aircraft, for example, made their larger consorts more open to U-Boat attack, or would have done had the German torpedoes not proved so defective.

The vulnerability of surface craft, large and small, to air attack increased the need for air cover to the extent that it became a prerequisite of naval operations

within reach of land. Without it the utility of warships and their freedom to manoeuvre were drastically curtailed. Evidently shaken by the battle of Bergen on
April 9, 1940, for instance, Forbes retreated to the safer waters of the north. Operation Hammer, the direct assault on Trondheim, was also called off largely for
the same reason. On such occasions, and they occurred with increasing frequency, sea power was obliged to yield to air power. The Norwegian campaign
did not however show that sea power was less potent than it used to be; merely
that in the future it would need to take new forms. By the end of April, for
example, a new form of fleet had begun to evolve naturally and without conscious direction in the waters off Norway. There Admiral Forbes had – in the
Ark Royal and *Glorious*, the battleship *Valiant*, the cruiser *Berwick* and 12 destroyers – a forerunner of the later carrier task force. "It was a beautifully
balanced squadron," commented one participant, "with its two big carriers, the
heavy guns of the battleship, and the speed and eight-inch guns of the cruiser
fully screened against submarines."[28] The Norwegian campaign was the first
naval operation to be significantly affected by air power, and it was clear that
things would not be the same again.

It was increasingly a question of striking a balance between gun and aircraft,
for both were essential. The battleship continued to exert a decisive influence
over the outcome of the war at sea, even, for instance, in such unlikely episodes
as the Battle of Crete. This encounter took place within easy reach of the Italian
battlefleet, but only after a series of skirmishes and near-disasters for the Italians
had persuaded them into a policy of obsessive caution. Conditioned to a state of
strategic inferiority, they failed to make the intervention during these desperate
days which might well have proved most dangerous for the British. There were
enough instances of this to lend much weight to Chatfield's subsequent claim
that ". . . if we had failed to rebuild our capital ships, we should have lost the
war."[29]

Nevertheless, the absence of a carrier began increasingly to appear more
decisive than the presence of a battleship. A carrier might have made all the
difference to the excursions of the *Bismarck* and the *Tirpitz*, or for that matter
to that of the *Prince of Wales* and the *Repulse*. If Admiral Phillips had been
escorted in his fateful foray into the Gulf of Siam in December 1941 by the
carrier *Indomitable*, he might well have been protected against the unco-
ordinated and unescorted stream of Japanese aircraft sent against him. The
Indomitable might even have been able to find and fix the Japanese naval forces
to the north, so presenting Phillips with the surface action he so clearly
wanted.

For such reasons there slowly began to evolve a new style of naval warfare
in which the carrier began slowly to usurp the title of "capital ship" from the
battleship, particularly after the battle of Midway in 1942. In a justly celebrated line, Samuel Morison described the battleship encounter in October

1944 between Admirals Nishimura and Oldendorf as "firing a funeral salute to a finished era of naval warfare. One can imagine the ghosts of the great admirals from Raleigh to Jellicoe standing to attention as the battle line went into oblivion."[30] The circumstances and even, to an extent, the outcome of that encounter were determined by the positions and activities of both sides' carrier forces elsewhere in the area. By 1944, therefore, the carriers had clearly moved to the centre of the stage, a development seen earlier by some than others. Admiral C. E. Kennedy-Purvis, the Deputy First Sea Lord, was one of the first. "I personally," he wrote in September 1942, "hold the view that the time is coming when the aircraft carrier force will form the core of the Navy."[31]

This process was however slow and steady enough to make it understandable that the Navy, both before and during the early part of the war, should think that the balance between the gun and aircraft had shifted neither so substantially nor so soon as to justify a drastic reallocation of resources. Since this partly explains the continued deficiencies of the FAA during the Second World War, it was something of a self-fulfilling prophecy.

This survey of the Second World War leaves two dominant impressions: first, that the FAA and the general impact of air power at sea was of great and rapidly growing importance to the conduct of naval operations; second, that the FAA achieved an astonishing amount with astonishingly little. The most enduring of the FAA's deficiencies was the continual shortage of men, aircraft and carriers in nearly all of the Navy's operations. This made it difficult for commanders to assemble the large numbers that complete success usually required. When the *Eagle* entered the Mediterranean in 1940, for instance, she carried a mere 18 Swordfish. To protect the Mediterranean Fleet against the Italian Air Force she carried three Sea Gladiators flown by volunteer Swordfish pilots. The problem was aggravated by the poor quality of her aircraft. With such forces it is perhaps not surprising that encounters like that off Calabria should have proved so disappointing to the British.

The continued existence of these deficiencies was made embarassingly clear when Admiral Nagumo's carrier task force came into the Indian Ocean in April 1942. It was essentially five carriers against two, and 360 excellent aircraft against 78 indifferent machines. "FAA aircraft," wrote Admiral Layton, "are proving more of an embarassment than a help when landed. They cannot operate by day in the presence of Japanese fighters and only tend to congest aerodromes."[32] This imbalance of forces obliged the aggressively minded Admiral Sir John Somerville to proceed around the Indian Ocean in a very gingerly way. There was some thought of his making use of the FAA's particular expertise in night operations but, fortunately for the British, neither side found the other. The losses of the Indian Ocean raid (the empty carrier *Hermes*, the cruisers *Dorsetshire* and *Cornwall*, and several other smaller vessels) were severe enough but seem in retrospect a relatively light penalty for the inferiorities that this raid revealed.

Two years later, after the FAA's raid on the *Tirpitz*, the Rear-Admiral, Escort Carriers, wrote: "It was a grand sight with the sun just risen to see this well-balanced striking force of about 20 Barracudas and 45 fighters departing at very low level between the two forces of surface ships and good to know that a similar-sized force would be leaving again in about an hour's time. . . . It . . . made one wonder what might have been if the Fleet Air Arm had been adequately supplied with aircraft in the early days of the war."[33] To complete this portrait of the Royal Navy and its attitudes to air power, we must finally turn to the fundamental question of why the FAA so often had to make do with so little.

CHAPTER EIGHT

ULTIMATE CAUSES

"Nothing we can do in the air is going to alarm Germany, who is steadily increasing her lead in that element. The war will not be won in the air and if we have to fight Germany again, blockade must be our principal weapon. . . . So long as we retain naval supremacy we cannot be defeated in war. . . .

The importance of naval supremacy for the British Empire has in no way been diminished by the invention of flying or by any other developments in scientific warfare. If Great Britain suffered defeat at sea, the finest air force in the world could not save her or the Empire from complete destruction nor would any hostile air force be necessary in order to bring such destruction about."

RT HON ALFRED DUFF COOPER
First Lord of the Admiralty, March 13, 1938

By 1939 the Royal Navy had yielded the race to develop air power at sea to the US and Japanese navies. Where they both deployed over 600 front-line aircraft at sea, the British could only manage some 230. Such low numbers encouraged the development of relatively inefficient multi-purpose aircraft, weakened the performance of the FAA over the whole range of its activities, and made it particularly difficult for naval aviation to make that quantum jump from being a supportive, ancillary weapon of the Fleet to being a dominant and even decisive one. This would also require high-quality aircraft, not the "disgraceful obsolete material which has hitherto been flung to them," in Churchill's words of March 1940.[1] On virtually every indicator of performance, British naval aircraft of this time were behind their US and Japanese contemporaries. The FAA's personnel were highly trained and deeply expert but dangerously few in number. Finally, while the British had more carriers built and building than any other navy, many of them were the obsolete results of early pioneering days.

All this made it inevitable that the Royal Navy should consider its air arm to be an indispensible but essentially ancillary adjunct to the Fleet, both in its pursuit of the all-important central battle and in the direct defence of maritime communications. "The work of the Fleet's aircraft," said the Admiralty in April 1936, "is second only in importance to the fighting of its guns."² For the Royal Navy the notion that air power could win battles on the high seas by independent endeavour was very strange, though it was generally agreed that few such battles could be won without it. All other navies thought the same, but there were in the US and Japanese navies larger and more influential minorities who suspected that aircraft might one day replace the heavy gun as the primary weapon of the Fleet.

Responsibility for this generally unsatisfactory state of affairs is sometimes attributed to the pigheaded conservatism of an Admiralty obsessed by the power of the battleship. "I also came to realise," wrote Liddell Hart, "that to most admirals the respective value of battleship and aircraft was not basically a technological issue, but more in the nature of a spiritual issue. They cherished the battlefleet with a religious fervour, as an article of faith defying all scientific examination. . . . A battleship has long been to an Admiral what a cathedral is to a bishop."³ Because they had such instincts, the argument goes, generations of battleship admirals starved the FAA of the allocations of resources it needed to survive and prosper, and so failed to realise the extent to which the advent of air power could affect naval operations.

It would be idle to pretend that the Royal Navy did not have its share of battleship diehards, of whom Admiral Sir Tom Phillips, the chief victim of the battle of the Gulf of Siam, is the most celebrated example. But as a general explanation of the FAA's deficiencies in 1939 this kind of proposition is over simple and unconvincing. Arguments which lay the blame for particular deficiencies generally at the door of the "mere fighting blockheads" at the top of the hierarchy have the merit of simplicity but little else. They certainly do not explain the paradox of a Navy which went to war with good carriers but bad aircraft.

It is also not sufficient to say merely that the Admiralty was obsessed with battleships, even if indeed it was. It is necessary to know why. Conservatism of this kind, if it exists, is as least as much a symptom of malaise as it is a cause, because in such circumstances there is necessarily a vicious circle at work. The FAA was deprived of resources for a variety of reasons which certainly included a degree of scepticism in the upper reaches of the Navy. The lack of resources in turn produced an indifferent performance which confirmed and reinforced original doubts. But there were always other elements in the process.

The tendency to underrate the performance and the potential of air power at sea, and in consequence to deny it the resources which it needed, has also to be seen as the product of a whole series of misjudgements about minor matters. Many of these related to technical issues and were made by experts for technical reasons. The violent dispute between Tennyson d'Eyncourt (the DNC) and H. E. Wimperis (the Air Ministry's Chief Scientist) over the affect of near-miss bombs, and the contemporary deliberations of the Institute of Naval Architects, show that the battleship's friends could be just as "scientific" as its enemies.[4] Moreover, the abolition of arrester wires and the introduction of multi-purpose aircraft, which seem in retrospect to have been mistaken policies generally impeding the development of British naval aviation, were both the result of the agitations of the airmen themselves. In these cases, at least, scepticism about the potential of air power at sea was clearly the result of deficiencies and errors of policy and not the cause of them.

This scepticism was reinforced by other things. "The basic reason for the Admiralty . . . failings," writes Admiral Sir Caspar John, "was the emasculation of the Navy on April 1, 1918, when the bulk of its air knowledge went to the RAF, and took all too long to replace. . . . In my opinion all the failings in World War II stemmed from that one cause."[5] Deprived of its leadership at the top, naval aviation for many years lacked the bureaucratic muscle needed to push for the kind of progress and expansion that would have made the sceptical think again. Progress was rapid when the new generation began to reappear at the end of the inter-war period, but not rapid enough to make up for the deficiencies of the past until well on into the Second World War.

The progress and standing of air power in the Royal Navy was also much impeded by the effects of the economic climate. In the inter-war period the requirement for cutbacks in expenditure came together with optimistic assessments of future international developments to produce the Ten Years Rule, which instructed the services to base their planning on the assumption that there would be peace for the next ten years. First appearing in August 1919, it was specifically applied to Japan in 1925, became formally self-perpetuating in June 1928 and was finally cancelled only in 1933.[6] Connected with the notion of ten years of peace was a sequence of naval disarmament negotiations set in motion by the Washington Treaty of 1922. Since the international scene therefore seemed to suggest a diminished need for armaments, it clearly strengthened the hands of those who sought to control or reduce the amount of money spent on defence.

This all inevitably hindered the development of the FAA. As far as the expansion of the FAA's aircraft strength was concerned, the tone was set by the Geddes Committee report of 1922, which suggested that the Navy could make do with 24 aircraft rather than the 78 then deployed.[7] Although the total slowly grew through the 1920s, the Ten Years Rule restricted expansion, particularly in the period 1928–31. In the 1930s expansion was impeded first by the existence of a single aircraft quota in disarmament negotiations and then by the Air Ministry's prior claims on defence resources in its preparation for war against Germany.

The carrier construction programme suffered similarly. In the early 1920s economic considerations played a part first in the decision to complete all of the four older carriers and then in their late arrival and overlong retention. The

Naval Staff's carrier replacement programme of 1925 had virtually collapsed by 1930 at least partly for the same reason. In the following decade it was further unsettled by the publicly expressed doubts of the Air Staff and the inevitable uncertainties generated by the various naval disarmament negotiations then in train. Even during rearmament, the financial rationing of 1938 prevented the Admiralty from going wholeheartedly for its New Standard Carrier Fleet. Limited resources and the competing demands of other defence requirements also impeded the carrier construction programme once the war began.

There were other reasons for delay in the aircraft and carrier construction programme, most notably the Naval Staff's preference for a "wait and see" policy. Nevertheless, the effects of economic stringency on the FAA were particularly severe, as the development of air power at sea was at a critical stage, needing to prove itself but as yet lacking the materiel to do so. There was severe pressure on the size and quality of the Naval Staff and this inevitably weakened the leadership and employment of the FAA. Uncertainties and scepticism were prolonged by cutbacks in research and development. AA ammunition was strictly rationed, for example. This made trials and practices particularly artificial and so allowed the overlong survivial of old-fashioned attitudes about AA gunnery, fighter protection and aircraft attack. This worked to the inevitable benefit of weapons like the battleship, whose value was already established, rather then to the unproved aerial alternatives. The shortage of money therefore strengthened the Navy's tendency to play it safe.

The FAA was neither fish nor fowl, rather like Coastal Command, and so in straitened times was not the main focus of concern either of the Air Ministry or of the Admiralty. In fact, the FAA was vulnerable not only because it was in a curious sort of no-man's-land between two dimensions of war but also because it was the area in which rivalry and friction was at its greatest. Deeply concerned about their own well.being and genuinely doubtful of the relative value of sea-borne aircraft, senior officers of the Air Staff were apt to divert the scrutiny of the economisers away from the Air Force proper and onto the FAA. In March 1931, for instance, Air Marshal Sir John Salmond, the Chief of the Air Staff, was summoned before the May Committee to give some account of himself and his service. He later wrote that he had spent 90 minutes justifying the RAF's existence and prospects, and then, entirely typically, ". . . pointed out the . . . possibility of immense savings on the Coast Defence Programme and in the Fleet Air Arm."[8]

The Treasury usually found the Air Staff's arguments convincing and frequently used them against the FAA's expansion programme. For example, Sir Warren Fisher, the long-serving Permanent Secretary of the Treasury, accepted the argument that the FAA should be part of the RAF and often used Trenchard (then a retired Chief of the Air Staff) as an unofficial defence adviser. Moreover, when the time for rearmament came, the Treasury was important in seeing that responsibility for the country's main defence, and the share of resources which went with it, was handed not to the Navy but to the Air Force. For some years then there was a kind of tacit alliance between the Treasury and the Air Ministry against the Navy in general and the FAA in particular.[9]

This all had a markedly adverse effect on aircraft production and operational deployment both before and during the war. Even once the spectre of a single aircraft quota had receded, the finite capacity of British industry meant that there were only so many bites to the apple. The more the Navy was allowed, the less there would be available for the RAF. Aircraft production for the RAF always fell far short of its targets in any case, and this greatly aggravated the problem.

Controversy remained even after the aircraft had been produced, for there was continued dispute about how they might best be employed. In early 1942, for instance, the Chief of the Air Staff wrote that "one of the ways in which we could best help the Russians would be to weaken the German fighter force and so reduce the adequacy of the air support given to the German armies. If by our operations in the West we can succeed in further weakening the German air force or at least further preventing its recovery, the chance of the enemy launching a successful offensive against Russia . . . will be reduced." For this reason, daylight "circus" operations were carried out over France "with the object of inducing German fighters to accept combat with out fighters."[10] Just such a sweep was carried out on January 10, 1941, by over 100 British fighters which saw nothing and achieved nothing. On the same day the carrier *Illustrious*, defended by only a handful of outmoded fighters, was pulverised in the Mediterranean by *Fliegerkorps X*. Did not such events, argued the Admiralty, justify a reallocation of fighter resources? The Admiralty appealed in similar manner for modern aircraft like the Avro Lancaster for Coastal Command. "If I could get," wrote Pound in April 1942, "the number of bombers we lose in a few days [over Germany] we could make a great start."[11] In both instances, though, maritime air power conflicted with the apparent demands of continental war, and lost.

The problem was aggravated by the fact that, for most of the inter-war period, responsibility for the FAA was shared between the Admiralty and the Air Ministry under the terms of the Trenchard-Keyes agreement of 1924. ". . . The *fons et origo* of our deficiencies," wrote Admiral Richmond (no great friend of successive Boards of Admiralty) in 1942, "lies in the separation of the Naval Air Service from the Navy and not in a lack of appreciation on the part of the Navy of the possibilities and future of aircraft in war at sea."[12] Dual Control had many bad effects on the development of the FAA and it is easy to see why naval officers tended to blame it for most of the deficiencies. It created problems in the attraction, training and retention of personnel. It hindered efficient aircraft design. It weakened the institutions of Naval Air and it meant that too much time and effort were devoted to the tactics of wresting the FAA back from the

Air Ministry, rather than to the study of how it might be used in war. Even with the best will in the world, administration between two departments would in any case have been more difficult and lengthy. When those departments were locked in a bitter conflict of principle, the resolution of the most inconsequential of issues could easily require Herculean efforts. This is why the Navy never accepted the permanency of Dual Control.

Behind this controversy over practical ways and means there lay a broader doctrinal, even philosophical, dispute over the nature of air and sea power and their relative importance in national and imperial defence. The potential antagonism of the two dimensions of war had been clear from the start. With something less than perfect tact, for instance, Alexander Graham Bell in 1916 told the National Convention of the US Naval League that "we . . . look forward with certainty to the time that is coming, and indeed is almost now at hand, when sea power and land power are secondary to air power, and that the nation which gains control of the air will practically control the world."[13] The thrust of this apocalyptic vision was that air power would be the decisive form of warfare in the future. Such views were precisely mirrored in Britain. "We are inclined to think," said Churchill in 1921, "that the growth of an independent Air Force will in the future take place largely at the expense of the two older services and that important economies will be secured thereby."[14]

From the start the fortunes of the RAF were hitched to the star of the bomber offensive, and the Air Staff laid great stress on the decisive future role of strategic bombing. Trenchard and the Air Staff were in fact never so thoroughgoing about the potentialities of strategic bombing as to deny the older services a vital role in the next war, but they responded sympathetically to those who argued that they should take first place in the nation's defence. "The Air Ministry," they said in 1936, "are primarily concerned with the maintenance of the object which is invariably the prosecution of the offensive, the only means by which the ultimate victory is possible. Time and again, the Admiralty have shown their inability to appreciate the first principle of air warfare. . . . All naval strategy is primarily defensively designed towards the maintenance of the fleet-in-being, whereas we aim to strike directly at the source of all enemy air power to accomplish the object by achieving the offensive aim."[15] This piece of strategic gibberish accompanied a rejection of naval complaints about the absence of A/S and reconnaissance patrol aircraft in the Mediterranean during the Abyssinian crisis, and so must have been doubly offensive to the Admiralty.

The aspect of the air case which had the most impact on the public mind, and was therefore the most important politically, was the reflection that a hostile air force would certainly be using similar endeavours against Britain. This summoned up horrifying visions of future conflict. "It is quite possible," said Sir Archibald Sinclair, a future Secretary of State for Air, "for our industries to be entirely deranged, our great cities to be shattered by incendiary and high-explosive bombs, out people demoralised by incessant bombardments and the terrors of gas, and reduced to the verge of starvation by the destruction of communications, our Government paralysed, and all this while the Navy still holds command of the seas, and yet incapable of firing a shot in out defence."[16]

The Admiralty, needless to say, was not impressed by this and continued to see itself as "the only true first line of defence for the Empire". The alternative verities of the Admiralty's time-honoured doctrine were well rehearsed in the autumn of 1929 by no less a figure than the Prime Minister, Ramsay MacDonald. "In our case," he said, "our navy is the very life of our nation. We are a small island. For good or for ill, the lines of our Empire have been thrown all over the face of the earth. We have to import out food. A month's blockade, effectively carried out, would starve us all in the event of any conflict. Britain's navy is Britain itself and the sea is our security and our safety."[17] To the Navy, the defence of maritime communications and the supply of food and military materiel which they represented was the fundamental prerequisite of all subsequent forms of defence and offence.

In the 1920s, however, the Air Staff went further. They argued not only that strategic bombing was the decisive form of future war, but also that air forces could take over many of the functions of the older services and perform them at a fraction of the cost. They claimed to be able, through a policy of "air control," to police disaffected parts of the Empire more cheaply and more efficiently then could the Army (a claim described by the CIGS, Field Marshal Sir Henry Wilson, as one of "hot air, aeroplanes and Arabs"). They also claimed that they could supervise such enclosed waters as the Persian Gulf, play a major role in the defeat of seaborne assaults on Britain or its imperial possessions, and do much to protect British trade and menace that of any enemy. "The Air Ministry," observed one member of the Admiralty Board in 1921, "are evidently out for a big thing – we can shut up shop if they carry out all their ideas."[18]

This notion of "substitution," as it generally became known, was much connected with the bomb-versus-battleship controversy of the time. The views of the Air Staff on this were much less extreme than many of their partisans believed. Their case, put briefly, was that battleships and other surface craft were now so vulnerable to the attacks of aircraft that the ability of navies to execute their traditional functions was, or would soon be, gravely compromised. The Navy naturally rejected this notion but in terms also much less dogmatic than is sometimes supposed. Chatfield was at pains to show that the Navy did not claim that battleships, even modern ones, could not be sunk by aircraft. "The sailor does not pretend," he said, "and never has, that any ship can be built that is not vulnerable. If ships were not vulnerable there would never be any naval victories. We do not say we are never going to be hit by aircraft, because we know we shall be hit, but we must try to hit the enemy's battleships with our aircraft more frequently and more efficiently than they hit ours."[19] In short, surface warships, and by extension the navies they represented, would still perform vital roles in future war, and aircraft could not usurp them. The bomb-versus-battleship controversy appeared in many other guises too. The prolonged inter-service squabble over the relative importance of guns and aircraft in the defence of Singapore against Japanese naval attack, for example, was clearly another battle in the same war.

Because naval officers tended to use the terms "battleship" and "capital ship" as though they invariably meant the same thing (which they did not, as other kinds of ship could be the "capital," or most important, ship at any particular time), the prestige of the Navy became more bound up with the continued dominance of the battleship than logic properly warranted. This made the prosperity of the first seem to depend on the second. "If we were to do away with the capital ship," said Madden, meaning the battleship, "then we should be doing away with the naval power of this country."[20] Dispassionate evaluation of the relative utility of aircraft and battleships in sea warfare became more difficult, blinding the Navy to the possibility that the carrier might be the capital ship of the future. From this perspective naval officers who pressed the claims of naval aviation too far could be thought to be as disloyal as they were mistaken.

The progress of the FAA was even more directly involved in the doctrinal divide over the principle of the "unity of the air". The Air Staff so adhered to this principle as to propose that the Navy's carriers need only to be complemented with half their aircraft, with the remainder being drafted in as necessary.[21] Their fervour in espousing the principle of the indivisibility of the air had much to do with the assumption that the prosperity and even survival of the RAF depended on it. In 1919, for instance, Trenchard wrote to Beatty that the return of naval aviation to the Admiralty would be dangerous, especially as "in view of the large number of Naval and Army officers and Members of Parliament who consider that the Air Force should be broken up, endless discussion would ensue with Cabinet, Parliament and Press and this would result in a delay of the formation of the basis of the Air Service which it is so essential to start at once."[22] Once the growth of the Luftwaffe made the RAF's own survival secure, the Air Staff grew noticeably less attached to this particular tenet.

The Admiralty, of course, would have none of this. "The air side," claimed Chatfield, "is an integral part of our naval operation . . . not something which is just added on like the submarine, but something which an integral part of the Navy itself, closely woven into the naval fabric. Whether our air weapon is present or not will make the whole difference to the nature of the fighting of the Fleet and our strategical dispositions. That is a fact which will increase more and more year by year."[23] It followed from this that full efficiency would only be possible if the Admiralty had full authority over the FAA.

Much the same could be said about Coastal Command. Throughout the inter-war period many naval officers cast covetous eyes on this organisation, which they considered largely as an inadequately nourished descendant of the RNAS. There was ambivalence in the Admiralty of the 1930s about whether it should be reclaimed along with the FAA. Such a policy might possibly weaken the Admiralty's case for the FAA, and would certainly cause manpower and financial difficulties.[24] Generally, though, senior officers were disappointed not to be awarded Coastal Command by Sir Thomas Inskip in 1937 and believed that the issue would inevitably re-emerge later on.

The controversy duly resurfaced in 1940. In December Lord Beaverbrook commented that "the condition of Coastal Command is a grave reflection on the Air Ministry, which starves it of equipment and has not given it the right type of aircraft." Evidently to the surprise of the Admiralty, Beaverbrook went on to suggest that Coastal Command be handed over to the Navy. This was going too far for Churchill, who argued that it "would be disastrous to tear a large fragment from the Royal Air Force. This is not the time for an inter-service controversy."[25] After some months of further discussion, a compromise was reached in April 1941 whereby the Admiralty assumed operational control over Coastal Command but left all other aspects of the service to the Air Ministry. Relations between the Navy and Coastal Command subsequently became very cordial and were generally a model of their kind.

When one service claimed dominion over all military activities in the air and another did over those at sea, there was bound to be a problem in drawing up lines of demarcation between these overlapping dimensions of war. Doctrinal dispute over matters of high principle then became unavoidable. It also proved extremely important, because it had direct and practical effects on the development of forces like the FAA and Coastal Command which straddled the two dimensions. This effect was almost invariably harmful and does much to explain the deficiencies of the two forces at the outbreak of war.

The philosophical controversy had a more general significance, mirroring fundamental differences in the way that Britain's strategic problems were perceived and dealt with. Obscure debates, such as that over the bomb and the battleship, were significant not just for their immediate practical consequences, but also because they were the chief expression of the struggle for priority between the Air Force and the Navy in the defence of Britain and her Empire. The allocation of defence resources depended directly on the outcome of the struggle. So too did the efficiency of the FAA depend upon the relationship of the Navy to the Air Force.

The problem was exacerbated by the fact that prevailing weaknesses in the British economy meant that there were not many defence resources available anyway.[26] The weaknesses in the visible trade balance that were evident from the 1870s onwards became even more apparent when the world economic situation reduced the country's trade in invisibles. In 1932 Britain began to live on her capital. Although the actual effects of the First World War might be a matter of some controversy still, they certainly meant that Britain went into the 1920s saddled with a huge National Debt whose servicing gobbled up a disconcerting proportion of the Government's revenues. In 1931, for example, it was reported that all the proceeds of income tax and 45 per cent of death duties would be taken up simply to service the National Debt. All this was aggravated by the periodic recession of the inter-war years and particularly by the world economic crisis of 1929–33, which contributed greatly to the collapse of the unmodernised staple industries of the Victorian period – iron, steel, coal, textiles – and to the slow growth of the industries of the future.

This resulted in a good deal of social distress and a natural concentration on the economic and social issues which were "the meat of politics in the twenty years between the wars".[27] In this context, defence issues could not regain the importance they had held before the First World War. More ominously still, Britain began to slip behind the other major powers. In 1927, when the volume of world trade reached an index figure of 118 (taking 1913 as 100), British exports had slumped to 73. Comparisons with Germany were particularly worrying. In the years 1935–9 Germany produced an average of 20.4 million metric tons of steel a year against Britain's total of 11.8 million tons. In 1936 Germany was reported to be 80 per cent self-sufficient in food and animal fodder and 40 per cent self-sufficient in motor fuel. In 1939 Britain's output of machine tools was less than a fifth of Germany's. And so it went on. In February 1940 the Treasury calculated that Britain's overseas assets and gold reserves would last another two years if carefully husbanded. Six months later, with the Continent lost and the Battle of Britain beginning, the Chancellor of the Exchequer forecast that Britain's gold and dollar reserves would be totally exhausted by Christmas.[28]

In this bleak environment long-term economic survival, let alone prosperity, could not be assumed but would have to be achieved by conscious endeavour. The economic wisdom of these pre-Keynesian days was that Government expenditure should not exceed Government revenue and that Britain should balance her books. Her export trade should be improved, and the first step here was, wrote Hankey in his National Paper of July 1919, that "nonproductive employment of manpower . . . [be] . . . reduced within the narrower limits consistent with national safety."[29] Defence spending was considered as coming within this category because it seemed to siphon resources off from vital exporting and manufacturing industries. It would therefore have to be curtailed.

Even if some of its economic assumptions now seemed somewhat oversimple, the Treasury's thinking on these matters was by no means wholly negative. There was, according to the Treasury, an overriding need for long-term financial stability if the country was to survive the undoubted perils of the future. A sound economy was Britain's "Fourth Arm of Defence" and should not be undermined by excessive military spending in the short term. This proposition underlay the savage restrictions of the 1920s and early 1930s and the disappointingly slow rate of rearmament from 1933 onwards. It was important, the Treasury inspired the Cabinet to say in February 1936, that rearmament should not interfere with the normal course of civil trade and industry.

Until revoked in March 1938 this restrictive proviso much hampered Britain's attempt to catch up with Germany's military expansion. Nevertheless, it is important to remember that the Government at this time was trying to face up to not just one but a host of perils. In a little over two years' time, a Treasury memorandum would show Britain to be on the edge of bankruptcy. This possibility was in its own way as much a threat to British security as the ambiguous policies and programmes of Hitler's Germany.[30]

However well.intentioned it may have been, retrenchment in defence expenditure had a savage effect on all aspects of British military readiness, particularly perhaps on that of the Army. Although the Navy took the largest share of the country's defence resources, it also felt itself neglected from the very start of the inter-war period. "The politician has his knife into the Navy," wrote Beatty, "and his Navy is going to suffer. The effects of which are going to be very far reaching unless we can bring him to understand that the decline of his Navy means the decline of his Empire."[31] The celebrated Geddes Axe (which removed a third of the captains from the Active List, for instance) was followed by a decade of merciless economising which brought the Navy to a very low ebb by the early 1930s.

This applied not only to such obvious indications of naval strength as the number and quality of men and ships, but also to the health of a naval armaments industry which had atrophied to an alarming degree. There were, for instance, serious deficiencies in the country's capacity to provide AA guns and fire-control systems. Soon after the war, the Admiralty warned the Cabinet how necessary it was to give naval shipbuilders a measure of security by providing them with regular orders. This had not happened and so skilled workpeople had drifted away and the plant had not been modernised to the necessary extent. So when, for instance, the Navy's revolutionary armoured carriers were built, some of them had to be clad in armour plate provided by Czechoslovakia.[32]

The FAA suffered from all of these trials and tribulations as well. In fact, in many ways it was in an even worse position because it suffered the consequences of the RAF's troubles as well as of those of the Navy. The British aircraft industry had suffered along with the shipbuilders. Whereas Britain had produced 30,000 aircraft in 1918, it only managed 503 in 1924. There was only a trickle of orders, skilled draughtsmen and workmen left the industry, firms closed down and Britain stayed in the era of the slow wood-and-fabric biplane while her competitors moved into that of the all-metal monoplane. No new squadrons were added to the RAF during 1931–34, and when the air rearmament programme finally began there were no modern bomber designs to hand. Accordingly, progress reports of the 1936–8 period were a demoralising catalogue of collapsing schedules and missed targets. "The more I hear of the air situation," wrote Tom Jones, Baldwin's Private Secretary, in 1938, "the more appalled and depressed I am."[33] Even the celebrated Spitfire and Hurricane had foreign instruments, foreign guns, and engines and airframes made with foreign machine tools.[34]

As the inter-war period proceeded, the strategic predicament that Britain found herself in became increasingly apparent. If Japan, Germany and Italy joined in alliance against Britain and France, warned a COS sub-committee in 1938, ". . . . the British Empire would be threatened simultaneously in Western Europe, in the Mediterranean and in the Far East, by an immense aggregate of armed strength and would be faced with the gravest danger. . . . It is not possible to envisage without the deepest misgiving, the military implications of a situation arising in which the British Empire becomes engaged in war with Germany, Italy and Japan and with France as our only major ally."[35] The problem was that Britain simply did not have the resources to meet the commitments presented by this scale of threat. "In my view," wrote Chamberlain in 1936, "we had not the manpower to produce the necessary munitions for ourselves and, perhaps if the US stood out, for our Allies, to man the enlarged Navy, the new Air Force, and a million-man Army."[36]

In some ways the problem was worse for Britain than it was for most of the other major belligerents. At the Washington Naval Treaty negotiations and subsequently, for example, the Admiralty had frequently argued that Britain's needs for naval power were greater than they were even for Japan and the USA because of the far-flung nature of her Empire, and because of the possibility of a naval threat nearer home. Neither Japan nor the USA were in this position and nor were Britain's European adversaries. In just the same way, as the Air Staff pointed out, "the USA has no problem of defence against air attack by land-based air forces,"[37] and this applied to Japan too. Accordingly, these two countries could afford to devote their air resources to maritime purposes to a much higher extent than could the British, who had also to consider air menaces nearer home. Britain's European adversaries, however, were able to concentrate virtually the whole of their air efforts into the development of metropolitan air power. In this situation it was entirely natural that the Air Staff should so strongly resist attempts to siphon their air resources off into the FAA, Coastal Command and the aerial requirements of imperial defence.

By preparing for the one kind of naval or air threat, therefore, it seemed as though the British would necessarily increase their vulnerability to the other. Rather the same thing could be said of most other aspects of British defence. Her economic limits required Britain to concentrate her efforts, but her strategic circumstances seemed to make this virtually impossible. Admiral Backhouse, the First Sea Lord, appreciated the dilemma. "The trouble is," he said in November 1938, "that we are now trying to take on more than we are really able to . . . and we simply cannot produce more than we are doing."[38] By the late 1930s Britain seemed to have three options, all of them unpleasant.

The first was stoutly argued in the spring of 1938 by the First Lord (Duff Cooper), who objected to the system of defence rationing insisted on by the Treasury. The country's defence needs must come first. "What these adequate defences are is certainly more easily ascertainable than are the country's financial resources. The danger of underrating the former seems to me to be greater than the danger of overrating the latter, since the one may lead to defeat in war and complete destruction whereas the other can only lead to severe embarrassment, heavy taxation, lowering of the standard of living and reduction of the social services." The country should decide first on its defence needs and then look at its means of meeting them. If these were found to be absolutely irreconcilable, then either her social system or Britain's foreign policy would have to be changed.[39] In the event, this path of "victory at all costs" was the one Britain chose, but only very late in the day and under the threat of imminent defeat. The result was victory in war, near-bankruptcy and the collapse of her Empire.

The second alternative was for Britain to concentrate her defence resources on the Japanese threat, a concentration urged most strongly by individual politicians such as Sir John Simon and Ramsay MacDonald and, above all, by the Admiralty, which had from the start of the inter-war period largely based its claims for primacy in national defence on the apparent Japanese menace to the Empire and to British trade. This association of interest was only broken in the spring of 1939, and then by no means cleanly.[40] The question was put squarely by Lord Swinton in October 1937: "Are we to put Germany or the Far East first? I assume finance precludes our taking both in our stride. No doubt production does too. It is for the Cabinet to [say] where the greatest danger lies and where we should concentrate. This, of course, directly affects both the Admiralty and the Air Ministry. If we have to make provision in the Far East, that means a great increase in the Fleet. It also means aircraft, which can only be provided in the fairly near future to the detriment of our home position." In response, the Navy case was put by Sir Thomas Inskip: "If our Fleet were defeated or unable to keep our communications open, we could not long survive. If, on the other hand, our air striking force were inferior, we should suffer more than the enemy at home . . . but the result might not at once be critical. . . . My point is that we may be forced to consider a smaller air striking force."[41]

Such arguments resulted in the Navy's having the biggest slice of the country's defence resources through most of the inter-war period, although that slice was still insufficient for the Navy's needs. During the war the controversy appeared in such guises as the debate over the relative priority to be accorded to the strategic bombing campaign and the defence of maritime communications, and the share of the nation's air and other resources that these campaigns should be allocated.

The third strategic alternative was to concentrate on the requirements of a war against Germany. British public and political opinion was generally hostile to the idea of sending a field force to the continent of Europe. "We should not lose sight of the fact," said Chamberlain, "that the political temper of people in this country is strongly opposed to continental adventures. . . ."[42] For this reason the European orientation tended to work predominantly in favour of the RAF. Chamberlain himself, the country's two top Civil Servants, Sir Warren Fisher (of the Treasury) and Sir Robert Vansittart (of the Foreign Office), and the Air Ministry were amongst the influential groups in Government circles which argued that Germany's apparent capacity to deliver a "knockout blow" with a bombing campaign against British cities was the prime and most urgent threat. At first the response to this was thought to be the creation of a deterrent bombing force; later it was partially replaced (rather against the wishes of the Air Staff) by reliance on a home defence system of AA batteries and fighter squadrons equipped with the best of modern aircraft. Either way, the Air Force was the prime beneficiary of this strategic concern, and the other two services were inevitably the losers.

In a way, geography made this threatened reorientation of defence priorities possible from the very beginning, when Blériot flew across the Channel in 1910. In 1923 the Cabinet accepted that the country needed an air force "adequately to protect us from air attack by the strongest air force within striking distance of this country."[43] When German rearmament translated this vague anxiety into increasing dread, the importance of the RAF in national defence began to rise. In February 1934 the special Defence Requirements Committee (DRC) based its recommendations for rearmament on the assumption that while Japan was the immediate menace, a rearmed Germany, fully mobilised in the air, would be the dominant threat by 1942. Japan, in any case, would not attack unless a war with Germany afforded her the opportunity. If Germany was deterred, therefore, then so would be the Japanese. The DRC's recommendations were cut back for the sake of economy but in a way which increased the relative advantage of the RAF, a process which did not please the Admiralty. Britain could not be rendered "safe and secure," claimed Chatfield, "by the unilateral rearmament of one service only."[44] All the same, the shift in emphasis continued, spurred on by mounting alarm at German air efforts and fear at the apparent inadequacy of the British response. By 1939 the Navy had fallen in the space of two years from top to bottom in spending priority.[35] A year later, as the German Army advanced across France and the Luftwaffe threat moved nearer, this change of emphasis seemed eminently justified. "The crux of the matter," the Chiefs of Staff reported in May 1940, "is air superiority."[46] After that, over half Britain's war production was devoted to the RAF.

Although access to US naval and military production partly made up for it, this change in defence priorities undoubtedly worked to the disadvantage of the Royal Navy. The effects were especially bad for the development of maritime air power, since this was where the conflict of interest between the Admiralty and the Air Ministry was at its greatest before and during the rearmament programme. Both in times of famine and of feast, the FAA was a special victim of the struggle for priority and resources between the two services with which it was connected.

The real point about this struggle for priority was that both the Admiralty and the Air Ministry (and come to that the War Office too) were basically right. Britain needed air power, sea power and land power to survive and win, but lacked the resources for all three. Conflict was inevitable, and occurred in all the other belligerent states too, but in Britain's case the gap between resources and commitments was particularly severe. It was a constant theme all through the period. "The whole question of the Navy, Army and Air in relation to one another," wrote Churchill, even as Germany collapsed into defeat, "will of course be one of the larger problems which will have to be settled after the war by any Government that is responsible."[47] In short, the vicissitudes of maritime air power, and the FAA in particular, are best seen not as the outcome of pig-headedness in the Naval or Air Staffs, but as a consequence and clear illustration of Britain's whole predicament in defence after the First World War.

A NOTE ON SOURCES

In the main, the material in this book is derived from three sources: official records, interviews and private papers, and the published literature.

The official records are those of the Admiralty (Adm Group of Papers), Air Ministry (Air), the Cabinet Office (Cab) and the Prime Minister's own papers (Prem). Unless otherwise stated, they are all to be found at the Public Record Office (PRO), Kew. All quotations from official documents are Crown copyright and are reproduced by courtesy of The Controller, HM Stationery Office. Actual quotations come from internal departmental minutes or memoranda, either of the Air Ministry or the Admiralty, unless the references say otherwise.

Private papers and personal reminiscences have also proved very useful in supplementing these official departmental papers. Much of this material came from the Navy and Air Force officers whose help I gratefully acknowledged in the preface. I have also made use of the collections of private papers at the National Maritime Museum (NMM) and at the Archive Centre of Churchill College Cambridge (CCC). I am grateful to the trustees of the NMM for permission to quote from the various papers held there, and to Lord Keyes for his permission to use the Keyes papers at CCC.

Finally, I have availed myself of the published literature. In the references I have used a short form in which the author's surname is followed by the year of publication in brackets and the page number(s). Full details of the books cited can be found in the select bibliography.

Chapter 1
NORWAY 1940
1 Raeder, report to Fuehrer, 9 Mar 1940, Fuehrer Naval Conferences.
2 Quoted in Roskill (1954) p 189; see also Moulton (1966) and Derry (1952) for the campaign as a whole; main documentary sources are the Home Fleet War Histories, mainly Adm 199/393, /473–480 and /485–490.
3 Troubridge, report of proceedings, *Furious*, 30 Apr 1940, Adm 199/479; correspondence and interviews with Capt G. A. French and Cdr C. A. Jenkins, 1977–8.
4 Vian (1960) p 36.
5 Details in Adm 199/479.
6 Quoted in Dickens (1974) p 109.
7 Quoted, ibid, p 148–9; interview with Lt Cdr F. C. Rice, 1977.
8 Derry (1952) p 115–118.
9 Correspondence and interview with Admiral A. D. Torlesse, 1977–9.
10 Marder (1974) p 167 fn.
11 Forbes, dispatch of 15 July 1940, Adm 199/393.
12 Torlesse, correspondence, op cit.
13 Forbes, dispatch, op cit.
14 Ibid.
15 French, interview, op cit.
16 Forbes, dispatch, op cit.
17 Jameson (1957) p 108.
18 Auchinleck, dispatch, 19 Jun 1940, Prem 3 328/5.

19 *Naval Review*, 1940, p 555.
20 Wykeham (1960) p 95.
21 Quoted in Garrett (1978) p 53; most of what follows is taken from survivors' reports, etc, in Adm 199/478; also correspondence with Capt S. W. Roskill, 1979.
22 Note by Cdr E. G. le Geyt, 15 May 1968, Adm 199/478.
23 Capt C. Moody (DNAD), 18 July 1940, ibid.
24 Admty signal, 1706/11 Jun 1940, Adm 199/393; operational reports, Adm 199/480; interview with Lt Cdr J. Casson, 1977.
25 DNAD, 11 Jul 1940, Adm 199/480.
26 RANAS report, 1 Dec 1941, Adm 116/4455.

Chapter 2
PERSONNEL AND POLITICS
1 Admiral Sir Henry Jackson, 22 Sep 1917, secretary's records, Vol 62, RN College Greenwich.
2 Hurren (1949) p 50–1.
3 Naval Staff Notes, 10 Nov 1921, Adm 116/3417.
4 Marwick (1965) p 295.
5 Phillimore, letters, 12 Apr 1919, Adm 116/2065 and 20 May 1919, Adm 138/555, NMM.
6 Fuller, to Balfour Cttee, 10 Apr 1923, Air 8/66.
7 Oliver, 15 Sep 1921, Adm 1/8611/155.
8 This is further discussed in Chapter 8.
9 Trenchard, 22 Mar 1922, Cab 21/269.
10 Trenchard, General Note, Summer 1922, Air 8/17.
11 Roskill (1968) pp 41 & 251.
12 Roskill (1969) pp 520–2.
13 Ibid, p 255 and Boyle (1962) pp 349–50.
14 Admty letter, 22 Dec 1919 Adm 116/3430; Secretary, minute, 4 Dec 1919, Adm 1/8573/316.
15 AM letter, 16 Jan 1920, and Domvile, 24 Jan 1920, Adm 116/3430.

16 Long, 20 May, Adm 116/3417.
17 Air Staff summary of correspondence 1919–1920, Air 8/17.
18 Wilson, memo to Cab, 16 Sep 1921, Air 9/5.
19 Beatty, 13 Sep 1921, Adm 116/3430 and also letter of 21 Sep 1921 with staff discussions, Adm 1/8611/155.
20 Quoted in Roskill (1968) p 267.
21 Cipher message to First Lord, 7 Nov 1921, War Office/Admty meetings and correspondence of 31 Oct & 8 Nov 1921, Adm 116/3430; Naval Staff Notes on meeting of 14 Nov 1921, Adm 116/3147.
22 Cmd 1581, 14 Dec 1921.
23 Roskill (1968) pp 336–341.
24 Ibid, pp 357–360 and Boyle (1962) pp 407–416; Domvile diaries, 16 Mar 1922, Dom/37, NMM.
25 Chatfield, 13 Nov 1921, Adm 116/3147.
26 Quoted in Boyle (1962) p 417.
27 Roskill (1968) pp 365–370.
28 Details in Adm 116/3147.
29 Admty letter, 26 Aug 1922, Adm 116/3431.
30 Hoare (1957) p 60.
31 Quoted Boyle (1962) p 464 et seq.
32 Beatty, letter, 6 Mar 1923, quoted in Chalmers (1951) p 393.
33 Hoare, letter to Weir, 16 Mar 1923, Weir 8/11, CCC.
34 Hankey, letters to Balfour, 27 & 19 June 1923, Cab 21/266.
35 Ibid.
36 Boyle (1962) pp 489 & 492.
37 Bell Davies (1967) pp 212–3.
38 Amery, letter to Balfour 23 July and Salisbury to Hankey 24 July, Cab 21/267.
39 Keyes, letter to Chatfield, 5 Jan 1937, Adm 116/3722; Baldwin, quoted by Cross (1977) p 94–6.
40 For an effective riposte to Boyle on these matters, see Roskill (1968) pp 377–382 & p 386. Roskill's case that "there is . . . not a shred of evidence . . ." of threatened resignation seems overdrawn, however.

41 Admty draft memo and Board meeting, 1 Nov 1923, Adm 167/67.
42 Roskill (1968) pp 473–476.
43 Trenchard to Churchill, 26 Jan 1926 and to Baldwin, 4 Feb 1926, Air 8/79.
44 Roskill (1968) p 486.
45 Bullock, 15 Jul 1926, Air 8/82.
46 Salisbury, quoted in Naval Staff Survey, 16 Apr 1937, Adm 116/3599.
47 Marder (1974) p 56.
48 Evidence of Capt J. S. M. Ritchie, CO *Furious*, to FAA Cttee, Adm 116/3009.
49 Hoare, letter to Baldwin, 12 Feb 1926, Air 8/79.
50 Bell Davies (1967) p 193, and also Adm 116/2157 and 116/2330.
51 Henderson, 30 May 1938, Adm 116/3727; Roskill (1976) p 408.
52 Capt J. G. Grace, 6 Apr 1937, Adm 116/3722.
53 Cathcart Jones (1934) p 171–9.
54 Naval Intelligence Division report, 30 Sep 1936, Adm 116/3271.
55 Chatfield at Inskip Inquiry, 13 Jul 1936, Cab 16/151.
56 Ibid, 28 Jul 1936; Capt J. G. Grace, 6 Apr 1937, Adm 116/3722.
57 FAA Cttee Report, 12 Apr 1935, Adm 116/3723.
58 Inskip Report, 3 Nov 1936, Cab 16/151; Chatfield, 24 Sep 1936, Adm 116/3271.
59 Evidence at Inskip Inquiry, 17 Jul 1936, Cab 16/151.
60 Bell Davies (1967) p 215.
61 Inskip Inquiry, 14 Jul 1936, Cab 16/151.
62 Cathcart Jones (1934) p 19; interview with J. Casson, 1977.
63 Admiral of the Fleet Sir Caspar John, First Sea Lord 1960–3.
64 Paper of Dec 1926, Keyes 8/13, CCC.
65 Admiral C. E. Kennedy-Purvis, ACNS, Inskip Inquiry, 13 July 1936, Cab 16/151.
66 Roskill (1976) pp 200–1.
67 AM/Admty correspondence, Nov 1926–May 1927, Adm 167/76.
68 Inskip Report, 3 Nov 1936, Cab 16/151.
69 FAA Cttee Report, 12 Apr 1935, Adm 116/3008.
70 Monsell, letter to Chatfield, 17 Feb 1936.
71 Marder (1974) p 75 and Roskill (1976) pp 153–4.
72 Ibid pp 209–210 and Monsell letter, 17 Feb 1936, Adm 116/4023.
73 Chatfield, meeting of 1 Oct 1935, Cab 21/423.
74 Chatfield, letter to Hankey, 25 Oct 1935, Adm 116/4023.
75 Capt L. E. H. Maund, letter to Hankey, 22 Nov 1935, Cab 21/423.
76 Hankey to PM, 6 Dec 1935, ibid.
77 Monsell, letter to Chatfield, 17 Feb 1936, Adm 116/4023.
78 Monsell, letter to Inskip, 21 Apr 1936, Cab 64/23.
79 Weir, letter to Baldwin, 20 May 1936, Weir 19/14, CCC.
80 Inskip, letter to Chamberlain, 21 Jul 1937, Cab 16/152.
81 Correspondence between Hoare and Chatfield, June 1936, Adm 116/4023.
82 Swinton, third meeting, 17 Jul 1936, Cab 16/151.
83 Kennedy-Purvis, 16 Jul 1936, Adm 116/3724; Chatfield, 21 Jul 1936, ibid.
84 Inskip, letter to Baldwin, 5 Nov 1936, Adm 116/4023.
85 Chatfield, letters to Hoare of 3 & 16 Nov 1936, Cab 64/23 and Adm 116/4024.
86 Swinton, letter to Inskip, 9 Nov 1936, Cab 64/24.
87 Keyes, letter to Chatfield, 5 Jan 1937, Adm 116/3722.
88 Chatfield, letter to Hoare, 3 Nov 1936, Adm 116/3722.
88 Chatfield, letter to Hoare, 3 Nov 1936, Adm 116/4024.
89 Hankey, letter to Vincent, 28 Nov 1936, Cab 21/423.
90 Chatfield's notes for this are in Adm 116/3725, also Roskill (1976) p 400 et seq.

tfield, letter to Hoare, 12 Mar
, Adm 116/3722.
field, letter to Duff Cooper, 7
937, ibid.
to same, 28 Jun 1937, Adm 116/

Report, 21 Jul 1937, Cab 16/

n, letter to Chamberlain, 22
, Cab 64/24.
n Cab 64/26.
9 by Hurren (1949) p 120.
n, letter to Inskip, 4 Jul
99 64/26.
letter to Duff Cooper, 28
100 Adm 116/3727.
101 L summary, ibid.
Dir Personnel, report, 21
102 Ibi dm 116/4023.
Ad Sea Lord, 4 May 1939,
103 Inte 0.
ith Lt Cdr F. C. Rice,
1977.
104 Lt Cell, letter to Admiral
Dowd Apr 1938, Adm 116/
3727.
105 Boyd, Lord, 6 Nov 1943,
Adm 20
106 FAA ret Prem 3 322/5, 6 &
Prem 3 17
107 Lennox Ke 7) p 240.
108 Churchill, 7) of 18 Apr & 23 Jul
1943, Prem 1/7. Naval Staff
reactions are m 205/18.
109 Brown (1974)
110 Cunningham, l, 27 Nov 1940,
Ellis MSS, CC

Chapter 3
THE SHIPS
1 Roskill (1968) p 72 4 and Marder
(1970) p 224, 13.
2 AM/Admty Confere, 2 Jan 1919,
Ad 167/57.
3 Air Staff report, 13 Feb 24, Air 9/2.
4 Melhorn (1974) Chap 1
5 Capt G. W. Steele US quoted in
Roskill (1968) p 244.
6 Quoted Melhorn (1974) 16.
7 Beatty, letter to de Robk, 4 Jan?
1921, Robeck 6/30, CCC; also Domvile diary, 15 Oct 1920, DOM/35,
NMM.
8 Bell Davies (1967) p 197–8.
9 Report, 31 May 1923, Air 5/1096.
10 Board meeting, 24 Mar 1919, Adm
167/58.
11 Madden, letter to Admty, 2 Dec 1919,
Adm 1/8576/341.
12 Brock, 12 Feb 1920, Adm 138/610 and
Dir of Dockyards memo, 10 Jun 1921,
Adm 138/455, NMM.
13 Chatfield, retrospective minute, 9 Jun
1927, Adm 1/9276.
14 Naval Staff memo, 9 Apr 1924, Adm
1/8672/230–24.
15 Chatfield, memo, 8 Oct 1920, Adm
1/8576/341.
16 Admiral W. W. Fisher, retrospective
minute, 5 Oct 1929, Adm 116/2550
and also Cmd 2476 of 27 Jul 1925.
17 Pound, and Plans Div, minutes of 2
June 1927 and 27 May 1928, Adm 1/
9276 and Adm 116/2550.
18 Alexander (First Lord), 19 Jun 1930,
Air 8/108.
19 Churchill, letter to Bridgeman (First
Lord) quoted in latter's letter to
former of 4 Feb 1925, Adm 116/2300.
20 Madden, 5 Nov 1928, Adm 116/2550.
21 Tennyson d'Eyncourt (DNC), 4 Dec
1923, Adm 138/455, NMM.
22 Fisher retrospective minute of 5 Oct
1929, Adm 116/2550 and Admty
memo, 19 Jun 1930, Air 8/108.
23 Admiral de Bartolome (Controller),
evidence to PWQC, Jan 1920, Adm
116/2060, and also Adm 138/604 and
Adm 138/554, NMM.
24 The Japanese and US Navies were
slow to accept the idea of the island-
carrier. See US experience with
Ranger, Melhorn (1974) p 100.
25 Tennyson d'Eyncourt (DNC), 4 Dec
1923, Adm 138/455 and discussions of
1923–4 in Adm 138/456, NMM. Also
Melhorn (1974) p 77.
26 Staff discussions, Nov 1923, Adm 1/
9247.
27 Thus the 7,500-ton *Hosho* was fol-

lowed by the 30,000-ton-plus *Akagi* and the 11,500-ton *Langley* by the 36,000-ton *Saratoga*.

28 Plans Div memo, 16 Oct 1928, Adm 116/2550.

29 Plans Div memo, 13 May 1927, Adm 1/9271.

30 Ellington (Chief of Air Staff) letter to Air Marshal Longmore, 26 Mar 1935, Air 9/2; Air Staff Memo, 12 Feb 1936, ibid.

31 Conference, 15 Apr 1931, Adm 1/9330.

32 Melhorn (1974) p 128 et seq.

33 Air Staff Memo No 33, Mar 1923, Air 5/209.

34 Chatfield, letter, 23 Dec 1931, Adm 116/2682; also conference, 29 Nov 1920, Air 5/209 and Adm 1/8602.

35 DNC, 23 Jun 1925, Adm 1/8676/43.

36 Chatfield, 22 Dec 1925, Adm 138/637, NMM.

37 Backhouse, 23 Apr 1931, Adm 1/9330.

38 Admty letter to AM, 13 Nov 1923, Adm 116/3419.

39 Air Cdre R. Brooke-Popham, letter to Trenchard, 8 Sep 1920, Air 2/201/S13511.

40 Lord Lee of Fareham (First Lord) at 14th meeting, 30 Dec 1921, Adm 1/9271.

41 Madden, report, 27 Feb 1920, Adm 138/556, NMM.

42 The official decision was taken at the 54th meeting of the JTC, 22 Jun 1927, Air 5/386.

43 Cathcart Jones (1934) pp 80–1; details in Air 5/383.

44 DNC Memos, 19 Dec 1931, Adm 1/9330 and 16 Sep 1932, Adm 138/611, NMM.

45 Wg Cdr Busteed, 19 Feb 1925, Air 5/387.

46 Cathcart Jones (1934) p 80.

47 Air Staff memo, Feb 1922, Air 5/218.

48 For example, Madden, 2 Dec 1919, Adm 1/8576/341.

49 DNAD, 7 Apr 1931, and subsequent staff comments, Adm 116/2793.

50 Staff discussions, 15 A Adm 1/9330.

51 Consultations between r) Lord), Londonderry and Simon (Foreign 1932, Air 8/136.

52 Monsell, 21 Dec 193 to

53 Sassoon (S of S fo and Monsell, 23 Jan 193 der S note by Chief of Ai 1. of S for Air, 3 Feb 1 Dec

54 Monsell, memo to 1933, ibid.

55 Appendix 2, Holl ckhouse, 20 Sep 1938, Adm 116/40 6 Oct 1938, ibid.

56 Ibid.

57 Henderson, 3 Ma m 1/9399.

58 Chapman (196 interviews with Admiral ew Slattery and Capt H. St t, 1978–9.

59 Admiral, Milf n, letter, 21 Sep 1918, Roski p 717.

60 Naval Staff me ct 1935, Adm 116/3724, and Cttee Report, 20 Sep 1938, A 4038.

61 Tennyson d' t, letter, 6 Oct 1923, TdE NMM; also Air Staff discussi ir 9/1 and Naval Staff discussi dm 1/8687/178.

62 Naval Staff 17 Dec 1924, Adm 116/2300; p use, 6 Oct 1938, Adm 116/40

63 Henderson, 1936 and associated papers, Ad 99.

64 310th CO Aug 1939, Admiralty paper and ments by Pound, Cab 53/11.

65 Appendi the Holland Report, 20 Sep 1938 n 116/4038.

66 Ellington 90th COS, 21 Dec 1936, Cab 53/ Newall at 310th COS, 2 Aug 193 ab 53/11.

67 Church 11 Mar 1940, Adm 116/3722.

68 Lenton 1972) and Brown (1977) offer c ise summaries of this.

69 Alexa er, to War Cabinet, Oct 1941, em 3 322/9.

70 Admt discussion on the *Queens*, May

1942, Adm 205/18; Sinclair, War Cabinet meeting, 6 Aug 1942, Prem 3 322/10; interview with Admiral Sir Mathew Slattery and Capt H. St J. Fancourt, 1978–9.
71 Oliver Lyttleton (Min of Production), 15 Sep 1942, Prem 3 322/3, 4.
72 Brown (1977) p 51.
73 Brown (1974) pp 146–8; Poolman (1972) p 87, 112.
74 Alexander, to Churchill, 7 Oct 1943, Prem 3 322/5, 6.
75 Churchill, to Alexander, 24 Oct 1943, Adm 116/4916.

Chapter 4
THE AIRCRAFT

1 Naval Air Division, report, Nov 1918, Adm 1/8549/13; Roskill (1968) p 244.
2 Phillimore, to Balfour Cttee, 8 May 1923, Air 8/66.
3 Sueter (1928) p 56; same to Balfour Cttee, 18 Jun 1923, Air 8/66.
4 Madden, 2 Dec 1919, Adm 1/8576/341.
5 Melhorn (1974) p 98.
6 Admty letter to AM, 13 Jun 1924, Air 5/387; Adm letter, 18 Dec 1919, Adm 116/3431; conference 23 Jul 1920, Adm 138/606, NMM; Board minute 1277 & memo, 9 Nov 1920, Adm 167/60.
7 de Robeck, C-in-C Med, letters, 20 Feb, 28 Apr, 31 May & 18 Jun 1920, Adm 116/2065.
8 Cdr J. H. Godfrey, Plans Div, 2 May 1922, Adm 116/3431; Bell Davies (1967) p 203.
9 Admty letter, 8 Aug 1918, Air 2/80/B3158; Stopford, evidence to PWQC, Oct 1919, Adm 116/2060; Lt-Col J. L. Travers, Head of Air Armaments (Torpedo) AM, 23 Jan 1919, Air 2/122/B9969.
10 Dreyer, 5 Jan 1926, Adm 116/2269.
11 Madden, 2 Dec 1919, Adm 1/8576/341; conference, 23 Jul 1920, Adm 138/606, NMM.

12 Plans Div, 15 Jul 1924, Adm 116/3117; Admiral Sir O. de B. Brock, C-in-C Med, 4 Jun 1924, Adm 138/637, NMM.
13 NAS, 30 Jul 1924, ibid; Admiral Sir F. Dreyer, Board memo, 27 Apr 1926, Adm 167/74.
14 Ibid.
15 Pound, 2 Jun 1927, Adm 1/9276; Pound, Board memo, 27 May 1928, Adm 116/2550; Board minute 2532, 15 Nov 1928, Adm 167/77; A. V. Alexander, FLA, letter, 3 Sep 1929, Adm 116/3479.
16 Pound, 2 Jun 1927, Adm 1/9276.
17 Madden, letter, 2 Dec 1919, Adm 1/8576/230; Melhorn (1974) p 98.
18 Bellairs, minute, 16 Oct 1928, Adm 116/2550.
19 Dreyer, minute, 26 June, 30 July & 22 Dec 1925, Adm 138/637 NMM.
20 Stopford, report, for 1926, Adm 116/2430; NAS, memo, 27 Mar 1926, Adm 167/78.
21 Pound, 27 May 1928, Adm 116/2550.
22 BM 2589, 3 Jun 1929, Adm 167/79; Backhouse, 9 July 1930, Fisher MSS, FHR/11, NMM.
23 Sir Oswyn Murray, Secy of Admty, Board memo, 17 June 1925, Adm 167/72.
24 Backhouse, 9 Jul 1930, op cit.
25 Snowden, letter to FLA, 18 Nov 1929, Adm 116/3469; Treasury letter, 13 Mar 1928, Adm 167/78.
26 Madden, 1 Aug 1928, Adm 116/2550.
27 Madden, 14 Feb 1928, Adm 116/3479; Ellis MSS, CCC; DNAD report 1933/4, Adm 1/9007.
28 Dreyer, letter, 10 Mar 1931, Cab 21/359.
29 Naval Staff memo, Jan 1934, Air 8/181.
30 Thomson, 13 Jan 1930, Ad 116/3479.
31 A. P. Waterfield, letter to Sir Christopher Bullock at AM, 23 Dec 1929, Air 8/106; Snowden, letter to For Secy Arthur Henderson 22 Jun 1931, Air 8/136.
32 Plans Branch (Air Staff). 1 Jul 1926,

Air 8/82; notes for CAS, July 1926, ibid.

33 DNAD minute and Staff discussions leading to Adm letter, 13 May 1931, Adm 116/2793; DNAD paper, Mar 1931, Adm 1/9330.

34 Air Staff discussions, 22 Apr 1932, Air 8/136; Air Marshal Sir John Salmond, memo, 2 Oct 1931, Adm 116/2793.

35 Monsell, FLA, letter to AM, 23 Jan 1934, Air 8/181.

36 Rear-Admiral S. R. Bailey, 30 Jan 1934, Adm 1/9007.

37 Air Staff discussions, Jul/Aug 1934, Air 9/2.

38 Hoare, Mar 1937, Adm 116/3596; Monsell, memo CP 13 (39) to CID, Mar 1936, Cab 16/152.

39 Interview and correspondence with Admiral Sir Mathew Slattery, 1978–9.

40 Ibid.

41 Holland, 6 Oct 1938, Adm 116/3726.

42 Naval Staff conference, 13 Sep 1938, Adm 116/4038; Adm paper, May 1939, Adm 116/4030.

43 5th Sea Lord, report, 4 Sep 1939, Adm 116/3722.

44 Admty memo to Inskip Inquiry, 2 Jul 1937, Cab 64/25.

45 Appendix to Holland Cttee Report, 20 Sep 1938, Adm 116/4038; Air Staff notes, May 1936, Cab 64/23.

46 Holland Cttee Report, op cit; Backhouse, 8 Oct 1938, Adm 116/3726.

47 Admiral Barry Domvile, 19 Oct 1928, Adm 116/3117.

48 Joint Staff conference, 31 Mar 1927, Air 5/411; Joint Planning S/Cttee, report, 11 Oct 1937, Cab 53/33.

49 Details in Air 5/411.

50 Calvert, 30 Mar 1925, Adm 116/3117.

51 Chatfield, C-in-C Med, 10 Sep 1931, Adm 116/2682.

52 Trenchard, letter to Madden (FSL), 19 Aug 1929, Adm 116/3117.

53 Admiral B. S. Thesiger, C-in-C East Indies, 4 Dec 1929, Adm 116/2641.

54 Air Staff memo to Balfour Cttee, March 1923, Adm 116/3418.

55 Stanhope, FLA, memo to Cab, 19 Jan 1939, Adm 116/4038.

56 Cmd 1938, 2nd recommendation.

57 Tennyson d'Encourt (DNC), memo to Balfour Cttee, Air 5/5.

58 Interview and correspondence with Admiral Sir Mathew Slattery, 1978–9.

59 Air Staff notes, July 1937, Cab 16/152.

60 Ellis MSS, CCC and minute with Staff discussions, 4 Sep 1938, Adm 116/3720.

61 Dowding, 7 May 1936, Air 8/211; Air Staff notes, May 1936, Cab 64/23.

62 Backhouse, 344th CID, 19 Jan 1939, Cab 2/8.

63 Air Staff notes, July 1937, Cab 16/152.

64 Ellis MSS, CCC.

65 FAA Cttee Report, 12 Apr 1935, Adm 116/3009.

66 Ibid.

67 Backhouse, 9 Nov 1931, Adm 116/2792.

68 Interview and correspondence with Capt H. St J. Fancourt, 1978.

69 Bellairs, 19 Mar 1923, Adm 116/3432.

70 Admiral Sir Caspar John, letter to author, 1 Aug 1978.

71 Swinton, 3 Nov 1937, Cab 21/525.

72 Air Staff notes, March 1923, Adm 116/3418; DNAD minute, 3 Oct 1938, Ellis MSS, CCC.

73 Chatfield, Board memo, 1 Mar 1922, Adm 1/8621/43.

74 Royle, letter to FLA, 25 Feb 1940, Adm 116/3722.

75 CNAS memo, 16 Oct 1942, Adm 116/5348; Churchill, 23 Jan 1941, Prem 3 171/4.

76 Lt Cdr (A) R. A. Brabner, letter, 13 Nov 1941, Prem 3 171/3.

77 Churchill, 30 Sep 1941, 6 & 9 Dec 1941, ibid.

78 Alexander to Churchill, 10 Jul 1942, Prem 3 171/5; Somerville to Admty, 17 Apr 1942, Prem 3 171/4.

79 Churchill, 5 Aug 1942, Prem 3 171/9.

80 Hoare (1976) p 169; correspondence and interview with Admiral Sir Mathew Slattery, 1978–9.

81 Churchill to Alexander, undated, Prem 3 171/5; Pound to Churchill, 30 Jan 1941, Prem 3 171/4.
82 Correspondence with Admiral D. R. F. Cambell, 1979.
83 MAP telegram A, 18 May 1940, Adm 116/5348; Sinclair, S of S for Air, 14 Aug 1942, Prem 3 171/5; Alexander, 7 Jan 1943, Prem 3 171/6.
84 R. E. Willcock (AM) to DNAD, 5 May 1940, Ellis MSS, CCC and Prem 3 171/6.
85 Churchill, 28 Aug 1942, Prem 3 171/5.
86 Churchill policy paper, quoted by Air Marshal Portal, CAS, letter, 11 Apr 1942, Prem 3 171/3.
87 Auchinleck Report, 19 Jun 1940, Prem 3 328/5.
88 Slattery, 27 Oct 1943, Adm 116/5057.
89 Thetford (1971) p 207.
90 Turnbull & Lord (1949) p 322.

Chapter 5
POLICY, DEBATE AND DECISION

1 Instructions, Sep 1912, Roskill (1969) p 60.
2 Sueter, 24 Feb 1914, ibid, p 145.
3 Admty weekly order, 5 Feb 1915, ibid, p 193.
4 Fisher to Churchill, 10 Nov 1911, quoted in Churchill (1967) p 688; Williamson memoirs, p 82, CCC.
5 Cromarty station log, 2–6 Oct 1913, Longmore MSS, NMM; Bell Davies (1967) p 85.
6 Churchill to Prince Louis of Battenburg (FSL), 7 Dec 1912, quoted in Churchill (1967) p 689.
7 Sueter (1928) p 222.
8 Admiral Jackson at meeting of 3 Aug 1915, Roskill (1969) p 217.
9 Sueter to Balfour Cttee, March 1923, Cab 21/267.
10 Weekly order, 29 Jul 1915, Roskill (1969) pp 212–3; Admty letters, 26 Oct & 1 Sep 1915, ibid, pp 247 & 224–5.

11 Raleigh & Jones (1928) p 486.
12 Williamson memoirs, p 74, CCC.
13 Samson (1930) p 291.
14 Sueter Cttee Report, 21 Nov 1916, Adm 138/554.
15 Williamson memoirs, CCC and correspondence with author Aug 1976; Richmond diary for 16 Apr 1917, quoted in Marder (1952) p 245.
16 Curzon Air Board, First Report, 23 Oct 1916, Roskill (1969) p 398.
17 Sueter, discussions of 27–8 Nov 1916, ibid, p 428.
18 Notes of 10 June 1915, plus staff comments, ibid, pp 207–9.
19 Sueter, article, 13 Oct 1915, ibid, p 81; Sueter, letter to S of S for Air, 28 July 1922, Air 5/1074.
20 Williamson memoirs, CCC, pp 102 & 88.
21 Ibid, p 105, also memo of Jan 1917, Roskill (1969) pp 455–6.
22 Beatty, letter, 22 Aug 1917, ibid, p 520.
23 Beatty, letter, 12 Aug 1917, ibid, p 497.
24 Beatty, letter, 19 Nov 1917, ibid, p 586.
25 Naval Staff memo, 19 Dec 1917 plus Staff comments, ibid, pp 603–4.
26 Geddes, draft letter, c 20 May 1918, ibid, pp 669–70.
27 Beatty, letter, 30 Jul 1918, ibid, pp 685–6.
28 Sueter, letter, 25 Apr 1918, and subsequent papers, Adm 116/1822.
29 Air Staff note, 20 May 1919, Air 2/109/A19438.
30 AM letter, 11 Mar 1921, Air 5/209.
31 Bell Davies (1967) p 191.
32 Steele, 30 Jul 1924, Air 5/384.
33 Richmond, diary, 13 Dec 1919, Ric / 15, NMM.
34 Domvile, diary, 15 Dec 1919 et seq, Dom/34, NMM.
35 Williamson memoirs, p 148, CCC and correspondence of 1976.
36 Naval Staff remarks, Jan 1921 and Capt J. Kelly, 2 Aug 1919, Kel/107, NMM.

37 Phillimore, letter, 12 Apr 1919, Adm 116/2065.
38 Beatty, 21 Sep 1921, Adm 1/8611/155.
39 Board minute, 19 June 1919, Adm 167/56.
40 PWQC Report, 14 Nov 1919, Adm 1/8573/316.
41 Roskill (1968) pp 113–4.
42 Richmond, diary, 17 Oct 1919, Ric/15 NMM.
43 Admiral de Bartolome, note, 13 Oct 1919, TdE/14 NMM.
44 Bonar Law Inquiry Report, 2 Mar 1921, Cab 16/37.
45 Lloyd George, 135th CID, 23 Dec 1920, Cab 2/3.
46 Quoted, Roskill (1974) p 207.
47 Richmond, diary, 10 Nov 1920, Ric/15 NMM.
48 Frequent references in Domvile diaries, Dom/36 NMM, and contemporary Naval Staff minutes, Adm 116/3610.
49 Scott, letter to *The Times*, 3 Jan 1921.
50 Bellairs, letter to Richmond, 3 Jan 1921, Ric 7/4 NMM.
51 Dir of Naval Intelligence, 13 Mar 1934, Adm 1/8766/66.
52 Adm letter, 12 Jun 1920, Adm 1/8589.
53 Adm Memo, 30 Apr 1926, Adm 116/3478; Dreyer, letter to Keyes, 25 Nov 1925, Keyes 8/13 CCC; office memo, 21 Dec 1928, Adm 116/2683.
54 Controller, Instructions for Departments, 16 Aug 1922, Adm 1/8663/119.
55 Such as a report circulated by Chatfield in Mar 1921, Adm 1/8602, and also Roskill (1968) p 264.
56 Bell Davies (1967) p 193.
57 Admty letter to Treasury, 17 Feb 1927, Keyes 8/3 CCC.
58 Roskill (1968) p 474.
59 James (1951) p 150–1.
60 Admty letter to Treasury, 17 Feb 1927, Keyes 8/3 CCC.
61 Melhorn (1974) p 17.
62 Capt H. Fitzherbert, 25 May 1930;

Madden, 26 May 1930, Adm 116/2771.
63 Chatfield, quoted in Cunningham (1951) p 199.
64 Admty Cttee report, Mar 1938, Adm 116/3722.
65 AM paper, July 1937, Cab 16/152.
66 Naval Staff report, 14 Dec 1936, Adm 116/3722.
67 Naval Staff notes, 16 Apr 1937, Adm 116/3599.
68 Naval Staff notes for Inskip Inquiry, July 1937, Adm 116/4033.
69 Admty Cttee report, Mar 1938, Adm 116/3722.
70 R. H. A. Carter, 23 Dec 1937, Adm 116/4194.
71 Melhorn (1974) p 98.
72 Domvile (DNI), 19 Oct 1928, Adm 116/3117.
73 Clark (1967) p 32.
74 Turnbull & Lord (1949) pp 157, 171, 190–1; King (1952) pp 208–12, 247–51.
75 Byrd (1928) p 109.
76 Staff memo, 13 Mar 1936, and Draft Memo on FAA Tactics and Equipment, Vol 1, Adm 116/4030.
77 Henderson, 12 Aug 1936, ibid.
78 Chatfield, 3 Oct 1936, ibid.
79 DNAD Summary, 26 Apr 1939, ibid.
80 Holland Cttee Report, 20 Sep 1938, plus staff comments, Adm 116/3726.
81 Pelz (1974) p 87.
82 Cameron (1972) p 72.
83 King (1952) p 291.
84 Chatfield, to Bonar Law Inquiry, 27 Jan 1921, Cab 16/37.
85 Bell Davies (1967) p 194.
86 Quoted, Cameron (1972) p 40.
87 Dreyer, to Colwyn Cttee, 12 Nov 1925, Adm 116/2374.
88 Naval Staff memo to Geddes Cttee, 24 Oct 1921, Adm 116/3417.
89 M Branch memo, 17 Jul 1930, Adm 116/2771.
90 Capt H. C. Rawlings, 3 Oct 1932, ibid.
91 Admty letter, 31 Jul 1919, Adm

1/8563/196.
92 Marder (1974) pp 173–8 and Roskill (1977) pp 283–99.
93 Capt G. A. Rotherham, memoirs, Chap 16, CCC.
94 Ibid.
95 Ibid.
96 Capt R. M. Ellis, memoirs, CCC.
97 Interview with J. Casson, 1977.
98 Roskill (1977) pp 230–1.
99 Admiral Sir Mathew Slattery, interview and correspondence, 1978–9.
100 Interviews with Admirals Sir Richard Smeeton and E. H. Shattock, 1977.
101 Lt Cdr (A) R. A. Brabner, 13 Nov 1941, Prem 3 171/3.
102 Hoare (1976) p 168.
103 Churchill to Alexander, 2 Nov 1940, Prem 3 171/3.
104 AFO 2112/41 and staff discussions, Adm 116/5057.
105 Slattery, 28 Oct 1943, Adm 116/5348.

Chapter 6
DOCTRINES OF BATTLE
1 Examples from Exercise JK, 7 Jul 1926, Kel/32, NMM and Day Approach Exercise, 9 Mar 1938, Adm 116/3873; RA (S) comments on exercises conducted during summer cruise of the Home Fleet, June 1933, Adm 116/3872.
2 Jellicoe, 22 Jun 1916, Adm 138/554, NMM; de Robeck, letter 13 Aug 1921, Adm 116/3430; Capt Munro Kerr, report, 8 Sep 1925, Adm 116/3478.
3 Exercise JK, op cit; report by CO *Courageous*, 17 Jan 1930, Adm 116/3478.
4 AM letter and enclosure, 20 Feb 1925, Adm 116/2464.
5 Memoirs of Capt G. A. Rotherham, CCC.
6 Details in Adm 116/3872.
7 Keyes, C-in-C Med Fleet, 10 Aug 1927, Air 9/26.
8 Draft Memo on FAA Tactics and

Equipment, 13 Mar 1936, Adm 116/4030.
9 Torpedo Aircraft Attack Instructions, 1 Aug 1928, and Aircraft Carrier General Memoranda 102 & 103, 1 Dec 1936, Adm 116/3871.
10 Capt Barry Domvile, diary, 7 & 28 Jul 1924, Dom/39, NMM.
11 Chatfield, letter to Backhouse, 17 Jun 1936, CHT/4/1, NMM; Pound, 2 Jun 1927, Adm 1/9276.
12 Beatty, letter, 11 Sep 1917, Roskill (1969) pp 541–3.
13 Madden, letter, 22 Sep 1919, Air 2/3199.
14 Capt G. A. Rotherham, memoirs, CCC.
15 Backhouse, 7 May 1937, Adm 116/4030.
16 Exercise ZP Serial V, Pt II, 10 Mar 1938, Adm 116/3873.
17 Quoted in Air Cdre R. Brooke-Popham, 8 Sep 1920, Air 2/201/S13511.
18 Quoted by Wg Cdr J. A. Chamier, 30 Jan 1920, Air 2/140/16115/20.
19 Williamson memoirs, CCC and Marder (1974) pp 5–11; also King-Hall (1926) pp 268–70.
20 Beatty, letter, 10 Feb 1919, Adm 116/1836. Also Melhorn (1974) p 37.
21 Draft Memorandum on FAA Tactics and Equipment, 13 Mar 1936, Adm 116/4030.
22 Air Staff Memo of 1923, Air 5/191.
23 Adm Sir Arthur Wilson, 6 Dec 1912, Roskill (1969) p 67.
24 Thetford (1971) p 308.
25 Air Staff comments 17 Apr 1925, on report from the *Eagle*, Air 5/357.
26 Exercise ZP Serial X, 10 Apr 1938, Adm 116/3873 and FAA Cttee Report, 12 Apr 1935, Adm 116/3008.
27 Mark Kerr (1933) pp 231–2.
28 Flying Officer F. Kirk, 1 Apr 1924, Air 5/384.
29 Mark Kerr (1933) p 232.
30 Chatfield, 5 Sep 1922, Adm 138/636, NMM.; Air Staff memo, early 1931, Air 9/51.

31 Draft Memo on FAA Tactics and Equipment, 13 Mar 1936, Adm 116/4030.

32 Chatfield, 20 Apr 1937, Cab 64/25.

33 Naval Staff memo, 20 Feb 1934, Adm 116/4030.

34 Forbes, 19 Sep 1938, Ellis MSS, CCC.

35 Henderson, 1931, NHB Information (the case containing the original signal was "weeded" by the Admiralty Record Office); Chatfield, 6 Feb 1934, Adm 116/4030; Adm W. H. D. Boyle (C-in-C Home Fleet), 24 Nov 1933, ibid.

36 Exercise ZQ, 1 Mar 1939, Adm 116/3873.

37 Collard (Dir of Gunnery Div), 13 Jun 1923, TdE 14, NMM.

38 Table of Nov 1927, Adm 116/2464.

39 Exercise ZP Serial XII, 17 Mar 1938, plus comments, Adm 116/3873.

40 The ban was in March 1928. Details in Adm 116/2430.

41 Fisher, paper, 29 June 1936 to VCS, Cab 16/147.

42 Hoare, Mar 1937, Adm 116/3596.

43 Air Staff paper, 2 Jun 1937 to VCS, Cab 16/147.

44 Chatfield, 29 Mar 1931, Adm 116/2792.

45 Cdr E. B. Simeon, lecture, 11 Mar 1927, and Air Staff memo of 1933, Air 9/51; NAAGC reports of Sep 1920 & Jun 1921, Adm 186/245; Air/Naval Staff discussions of Nov-Dec 1928, Adm 1/9284.

46 Dir of Naval Ordnance, paper to ABE Cttee, 31 Dec 1937, Cab 16/178.

47 Chatfield at 227th COS, 19 Jan 1938, Cab 53/8.

48 Chatfield, 5 Sep 1922, Adm 138/636, NMM.

49 Admty letter to Treasury, 18 Jan 1928, Adm 167/78.

50 Its three reports are in Cab 16/177–9; also Ellis MSS, CCC.

51 First Interim Report, 18 Oct 1937, Cab 16/178.

52 Roskill (1976) p 421.

53 CB (Confidential Book) 3011 of 1929, Adm 186/78 and table of 1936 in Adm 116/4030.

54 Instructions for Exercise MU, 17–9 Aug 1925, Keyes 7/15, CCC.

55 Chatfield letter to Backhouse, 27 Mar 1936, CHT/4/1, NMM.

56 Dir of AM Laboratory, 16 Oct 1924, Air 5/178.

57 FAA Cttee Report, minority report, 12 Apr 1935, Adm 116/3008.

58 Air Staff memo, 2 Jun 1937, Cab 16/178.

59 Naval Staff memo, 1 Jun 1937, ibid.

60 Trenchard, 14th COS, 28 Mar 1925, Cab 53/12.

61 VCS 3rd & 4th Meetings, 6 April & 8 May 1936, Cab 16/147; Salmond, memo to VCS, 39 June 1936, ibid.

62 Chatfield to Churchill, 5 May 1936, CHT/4/3, NMM.

63 Ellington, at 9th Meeting of VCS, 9 July 1936, Cab 16/147.

64 Beatty, memo, 14 Dec 1920, Cab 16/37.

65 Beatty, memo to Bonar Law Inquiry, 26 Jan 1921, ibid.

66 Chatfield (1947) pp 100–1.

67 Acworth (1930) p 34.

68 Roskill (1968) p 532.

69 Admty letter to C-in-Cs, 2 Mar 1934, Adm 1/9007.

70 Air Staff minutes, 10 & 23 Nov 1934, Air 9/22. The DCNS at this time was the very able Vice-Admiral Charles Little. No trace of this exchange has been found in Admty records.

71 Reynolds (1974) p 484.

72 Boyle, 24 Nov 1933, Adm 1/9007.

73 Brooke-Popham, letter, 8 Sep 1920, Air 2/201/S13511.

74 Pound, at 304th COS, 20 Jun 1939, Cab 53/11.

75 Cathcart Jones (1934) p 162–3.

76 Admiral A. D. Torlesse, diary entries for March 1929.

77 Ibid.

78 Dir of Training & Staff Duties Div, 7 Jul 1930, Adm 116/2771.

79 Admiral Sir W. Howard Kelly, diary, 5 Mar 1925, Kel/31, NMM; also Dull (1978) pp 322–7.
80 Admiral A. B. Cunningham, comments on exercise on 10 Apr 1938, Adm 116/3873.
81 Admiral Toshiyuki Yokoi (1960) pp 72–4; also Fuchida Mitsuo (1955).
82 Abbazia (1975) Chap 1.
83 Quoted in Polmar (1969) pp 57–60.
84 Wilson (1950) pp 270–283. Wilson organised the tactics of this attack and his account should be compared with that in Turnbull & Lord (1949) p 272.
85 Turnbull & Lord (1949) p 320.
86 The 1923 exercise is in Adm 116/2223.
87 Report of Joint Planning S/Cttee, 12 Jun 1928, Cab 53/16.
88 Capt J. C. Leach (pro C-in-C China), 14 Aug 1937, Adm 116/4030.
89 Marder (1974) pp 101–4.
90 Waters (1957).
91 Roskill (1968) p 536.
92 Ellington, 23 Jul 1936, 504th COS, Cab 53/28.
93 Admiral Kurt Fricke, quoted in Bekker (1974) pp 29–34; also Marder (1974) pp 45–7.
94 Discussion chaired by Admiral John Cunningham (ACNS [Air]), 7 Dec 1937, Adm 116/4030.
95 Exercise AB, 25 Mar 1935, Adm 116/3872.
96 COS 344 JP, 30 Jul 1934, Cab 53/24.
97 Melhorn (1974) p 88.
98 Marder (1974) p 48; Roskill (1968) p 536 et seq.
99 Holland, 6 Oct 1938, Adm 116/3726.
100 Backhouse, 30 Nov 1937, Adm 116/4030. Also comments of Capt J. C. Leach (pro C-in-C China), 14 Aug 1937 & Admiral B. H. Ramsay (C-in-C East Indies), 2 May 1937, ibid.

Chapter 7
EXPERIENCES OF WAR
1 Auchinleck Report, 19 Jun 1940,

Prem 3 328/5.
2 Admiral Landriau, Vichy Flag Officer at Dakar, quoted in Popham (1969) p 134.
3 Churchill (1951) p 212.
4 Nimitz, report to President, December 1947, *Brassey's Annual* 1949.
5 Winton (1976) p 180.
6 Waddington (1973) p 222.
7 Forbes, dispatch, 15 Jul 1940, Adm 199/393.
8 Cunningham (1951) p 349.
9 Quoted in Kennedy (1974) p 119.
10 Cunningham (1951) p 286.
11 Breyer (1973) p 87.
12 Lenton (1972) p 66 and correspondence with Capt C. N. Lentaigne, 1979.
13 Cunningham (1951) p 260.
14 Dull (1978) p 340–1.
15 Quoted in Forrester (1966) p 136.
16 Churchill, 8 Oct 1939, Adm 205/2.
17 Alexander, 19 Sep 1940, Prem 3 322/8.
18 Churchill, 5 Jan 1940, ibid.
19 Churchill, 26 Dec 1942, and general correspondence Nov-Dec 1942, Prem 3 322/3–4.
20 Cunningham (1951) p 577.
21 Full details of this and NCP 1943 are in Prem 3 322/5.
22 Alexander, 31 Jan 1944, and full details in Prem 3 322/6; Cunningham, 4 May 1944, ibid.
23 Churchill at Cab meeting, 18 May 1944, ibid.
24 Alexander, 31 Jan 1944, ibid.
25 Cherwell, 5 July 1944, ibid; this paper is discussed in Adm 205/53.
26 Pound, 20 Apr 1940, to Forbes, NHB Information.
27 S/Lt J. L. Field RNVR to Admiral Sir James Somerville, 7 Jun 1940, Adm 116/4504.
28 Quoted by Smith (1977) p 113.
29 Chatfield (1947) p 101.
30 Morison (1958) p 241.
31 Kennedy-Purvis, 7 Sep 1942, Adm 205/18.

32 Layton, C-in-C Far Eastern Fleet, quoted in Tomlinson (1976) p 103.

33 Rear-Admiral A. W. La T. Bissett, Rear-Admiral Escort Carriers, report on Operation Tungsten, 3 Apr 1944, NHB Information.

Chapter 8
ULTIMATE CAUSES

1 Churchill, 11 Mar 1940, Adm 116/3722.

2 Monsell, letter to Inskip, 21 Apr 1936, Cab 64/23.

3 Liddell Hart, quoted in Marder (1974) pp 86–7.

4 Details of the near-miss controversy are in Air 5/178; also Barnaby (1960).

5 Admiral Sir Caspar John, letter to author, 27 Feb 1979.

6 Roskill (1972).

7 Report of Cttee of National Expenditure, 1922, Cmd 1581, p 88.

8 Salmond, letter to Trenchard, 4 May 1931, quoted in Hyde (1976) pp 264–5.

9 Peden (1979) pp 30–2, 114. The influence of the Treasury in helping define Britain's defence priorities is a major theme of this study.

10 Air Chief Marshal Sir Charles Portal (Chief of the Air Staff), 5 Mar 1942, Prem 3 11/3.

11 Pound, 19 Apr 1942, Prem 3 171/3.

12 Richmond, letter to Air Marshal Sir Wilfred Freeman, 14 Oct 1942, Ric 7/4, NMM.

13 Quoted in Powers (1976) p 114.

14 Churchill, 24 Oct 1921, Air 9/5.

15 Air Staff memo, 12 Feb 1936, Air 9/2.

16 Quoted in Powers (1976) p 148.

17 Capt J. C. Little (Director of Trade Division), 22 Mar 1922, Adm 116/3430; MacDonald, Speech, 11 Oct 1929, quoted in Air 9/108.

18 Admiral Sir Osmond de B. Brock, 10 Apr 1921, Adm 116/3147.

19 Chatfield, to COS, 9 Apr 1937, Cab 53/7.

20 Madden, papers on London Naval Conference Jan–Feb 1930, Air 8/106.

21 Details of this are in Air 9/2.

22 Trenchard, letter to Beatty, 22 Nov 1919, Air 8/17.

23 Chatfield, 1st Meeting of Inskip Inquiry, 13 Jul 1936, Cab 16/151.

24 Details in Adm 116/3722 and Adm 116/3724.

25 47th Meeting of War Cabinet Defence Cttee (Ops), 4 Dec 1940, Adm 116/4869.

26 The arguments which follow owe much to Barnett (1972) and Kennedy (1976).

27 Macmillan (1966) p 510.

28 Barnett (1972) pp 13–5.

29 Quoted in Roskill (1972) p 111.

30 This is a major theme in Peden (1979).

31 Beatty, letter to Richmond, 26 Feb 1921, Ric 7/4, NMM.

32 Barnett (1972) p 476.

33 Jones (1954) p 414.

34 Barnett (1972) pp 479–481, 584; Swinton (1948) p 104.

35 Joint Planning S/Cttee of COS, report, 19 Mar 1938, Cab 53/37.

36 Chamberlain, 25 Oct 1936, quoted Howard (1972) p 135.

37 Air Staff memo, May 1936, Cab 64/23.

38 Backhouse, 14 Nov 1938, Adm 205/3, quoted in Peden (1979) p 152.

39 Duff Cooper, memo on NCP 1938, April 1938, Prem 1/346.

40 See, for example, Chatfield at 362nd CID, 26 Jun 1939, Cab 2/9.

41 Swinton, letter to Inskip, 25 Oct 1937 and Inskip to Swinton, 4 Nov 1937, Cab 64/30.

42 Chamberlain, quoted Barnett (1972) p 500.

43 Salisbury Cttee Report, Nov 1923, Cab 16/47.

44 Chatfield (1947) p 83; Barnett (1972) pp 410–415.

45 For the figures see Peden (1979) Appendix III.

46 COS Report, 26 May 1940, quoted Barnett (1972) p 8.

47 Churchill, 9 Apr 1945, Prem 3 322/7.

SELECT BIBLIOGRAPHY

For reasons of space, this bibliography has been largely restricted to those works actually cited in the text or references and no attempt has been made to compile a comprehensive list of books relating to the Royal Navy and air power.

Abbazia, P., *Mr Roosevelt's Navy*. Annapolis, Maryland: Naval Institute Press, 1975.

Acworth, Capt B., *The Navies of Today and Tomorrow*. London: Eyre & Spottiswoode, 1930.

Barnaby, K. C., *The Institute of Naval Architects 1950–60*. London: INA, 1960.

Barnett, C., *The Collapse of British Power*. London : Eyre Methuen, 1972.

Bekker, C., *Hitler's Naval War*. London : Macdonald, 1974.

Bell Davies, Vice-Admiral R., *Sailor in the Air*. London : Peter Davies, 1967.

Boyle, A., *Trenchard*. London : Collins, 1962.

Breyer, S., *Battleships and Battlecruisers, 1905–70*. London : Macdonald, 1973.

Brown, D., *Carrier Operations in World War II, Volume I The Royal Navy, Volume II The Pacific Navies*. London: Ian Allan, 1974.

Brown, D., *World War II Fact File : Aircraft Carriers*. London : Macdonald and Jane's, 1977.

Byrd, Cdr R. E., *Skyward*. New York : Putnams, 1928.

Cameron, I., *Wings of the Morning*. London : Hodder & Stoughton, 1962.

Cathcart Jones, O., *Aviation Memoirs*. London : Hutchinson, 1934.

Chalmers, Rear-Admiral W. S., *The Life and Letters of David Beatty*. London : Hodder & Stoughton, 1951.

Chapman, H. H. B., *The Development of the Aircraft Carrier*. London: Proceedings of the Institute of Naval Architects, 1960.

Chatfield, Admiral of the Fleet Lord, *The Navy and Defence*. London: Heinemann, 1942.

Chatfield, Admiral of the Fleet Lord, *It Might Happen Again*. London: Heinemann, 1947.

Churchill, W. S., *The Second World War*. 12 vols. London : Cassell. Particularly Vol IV *The Hinge of Fate*, 1951.

Churchill, R., *Winston Churchill*. Particularly Vol 2 : *The Young Statesman*. London : Heinemann, 1967.

Clark J. J., *Carrier Admiral*. New York: David McKay, 1967.

Corbett, Sir Julian, *History of the Great War : Naval Operations*. 5 vols, last 2 by Sir Henry Newbold. London : Longmans Green, 1920–31.

Cross, J. A., *Sir Samuel Hoare*. London: Jonathan Cape, 1977.

Cunningham, Admiral of the Fleet Viscount, *A Sailor's Odyssey*. London : Hutchinson, 1951.

Davis, V., *The Admirals' Lobby*. Chapel Hill : N Carolina Press, 1967.

Derry, T. K., *The Campaign in Norway*. London: HMSO, 1952.

Dickens, P., *Narvik : Battles in the Fjords*. London : Ian Allan, 1974.

Dull, P., *The Imperial Japanese Navy*. Cambridge: Patrick Stevens, 1978.

Forrester, Vice-Admiral E. P., *Admiral Raymond A Spruance*. Washington: Director of Naval History, Department of the Navy, 1966.

Fuchida, Mitsuo, *Midway, The Battle that Doomed Japan*. Annapolis, Maryland : Naval Institute Press, 1955.

Gamble, C. F. Snowden, *The Story of a North Sea Air Station*. London: Neville Spearman, 1967.

Garrett, R., *Scharnhorst and Gneisenau*. Newton Abbot: David and Charles, 1978.

Hezlet, Vice-Admiral Sir Arthur, *Aircraft and Seapower*. London : Peter Davies, 1969.

Hoare, J., *Tumult in the Clouds*. London : Michael Joseph, 1976.

Hough, R., *The Hunting of Force Z*. London : New English Library, 1963.

Howard, M., *The Continental Commitment*. London : Temple Smith, 1972.

Hurren, B. J., *Perchance*. London : Nicholson and Watson, 1949.

Hyde, H. Montgomery, *British Air Policy between the Wars*. London: Heinemann, 1976.

Jameson, W., *Ark Royal 1939–41*. London : Hart Davies, 1957.

Jones, T., *A Diary with Letters 1931–1950*. London : Oxford University Press, 1954.

Kemp, Lt Cdr P. K., *Fleet Air Arm*. London : Herbert Jenkins, 1954.

Kennedy, P. M., *The Rise and Fall of British Naval Mastery*. London : Allen Lane, 1976.

Kerr, Admiral Mark, *The Navy in My Time*. London : Rich and Cowan, 1933.

King, E. J., and Whitehill, W., *Fleet Admiral King : A Naval Record*. New York : Norton, 1952.

King-Hall, Admiral Sir Herbert, *Naval Memories and Traditions*. London: Hutchinson, 1926.

Laffin, J., *Swifter than Eagles*. London : Blackwood's, 1964.

Lennox Kerr, J., *The RNVR*. London : Harrap, 1957.

Lenton, H. T., *British Battleships and Aircraft Carriers*. London : Macdonald, 1972.

Macintyre, Capt D., *The Wings of Neptune*. London : Peter Davies, 1963.

Macmillan, Sir Harold, *Winds of Change*. London : Macmillans, 1966.

Marder, A. J., *Portrait of an Admiral*. London : Jonathan Cape, 1952.

Marder, A. J., *From the Dreadnought to Scapa Flow*. 5 vols. London: Oxford University Press, 1961–70.

Marder. A. J., *From the Dardanelles to Oran*. London : University of Oxford Press, 1974.

Marwick, A., *The Deluge*. London : Penguin Books, 1965.

Melhorn, C. M., *Two-Block Fox: The Rise of the Aircraft Carrier 1911–29*. Annapolis, Maryland : Naval Institute Press, 1974.

Morison, S. E., *History of United States Naval Operations in World War II*. 15 vols. Boston: Little, Brown and Co, 1947–62. Particularly Vol XII, 1958.

Moulton, J. L., *The Norwegian Campaign of 1940*. London : Eyre & Spottiswoode, 1966.

Nimitz, Admiral Chester W., and Potter, E. B., *The Great Sea War*. London : Harrap, 1960.

Peden, G. C., *British Rearmament and the Treasury 1932–9*. Edinburgh : Scottish Academic Press, 1979.

Pelz, S. E., *Race to Pearl Harbour*. Cambridge, Mass: Harvard University Press, 1974.

Polmar, N., *Aircraft Carriers*. London : Macdonald, 1969.

Popham, H., *Into Wind*. London : Hamish Hamilton, 1969.

Powers, B. D., *Strategy without Sliderule*. London : Croom Helm, 1976.

Raleigh, Sir Walter, and Jones, H. A., *The War in the Air*. 6 vols. Oxford : The Clarendon Press, 1922–37. Particularly Vol I.

Ranft, B., *Technical Change and British Naval Policy, 1860–1939*. London : Hodder & Stoughton, 1977.

Reynolds, C. G., *Command of the Sea*. New York : William Morrow, 1974.

Roskill, Capt S. W., *The War At Sea*. 3 vols. London : HMSO, 1954–61.

Roskill, Capt S. W., *Naval Policy Between the Wars*. 2 vols. London : Collins, 1968 and 1976.

Roskill, Capt S. W., *Documents Relating to the Naval Air Service, 1908–18*. Naval Records Society, 1969.

Roskill, Capt S. W., *Hankey : Man of Secrets*. 3 vols. London : Collins, 1970–4. Particularly Vol 2, 1972.

Roskill, Capt S. W., *The Ten Years Rule – the Historical Facts*. London : Journal of the RUSI, March 1972.

Samson, Air Cdre C. R., *Fights and Flights*. London : Ernest Benn, 1930.

Smith, P. C., *The Great Ships Pass*. London : Kimber, 1977.

Sueter, Rear-Admiral Murray F., *Airmen or Noahs*. London : Pitman, 1928.

Swinton, Lord, *I Remember*. London: Hutchinson, 1948.

Templewood, Viscount, *Empire of the Air*. London : Collins, 1957.

Thetford, O., *British Naval Aircraft Since 1912*. London : Putnam, 1971.

Tomlinson, M., *The Most Dangerous Moment*. London : William Kimber, 1976.

Turnbull, A. D., and Lord, C. L., *History of United States Naval Aviation*. Newhaven : Yale University Press, 1949.

Vian, Admiral Sir Philip, *Action This Day*. London : Muller, 1960.

Waddington, C. H., *O.R. in World War 2*. London : Elek Science, 1973.

Waters, Lt Cdr D. W., *A Study of the Philosophy and Conduct of Maritime War, 1815–1945*. London : Naval Historical Section, Admiralty, 1957.

Wilson, E. E., *The Navy's First Carrier Task Force*. Proceedings of the US Naval Institute, Feb 1950.

Winton, J., *The Forgotten Fleet*. London : Michael Joseph, 1969.

Winton, J., *Airpower at Sea*. London: Sidgwick & Jackson, 1976.

Wykeham, P., *Fighter Command*. London : Putnam, 1960.

Yokoi, Admiral Toshiyuki, *Thoughts on Japan's Naval Defeat*. Proceedings of the US Naval Institute, Oct 1960.

INDEX

Abel Smith, Lt Conolly, 44
Acasta, HMS, 25, 27
Activity, HMS, 176
Admiralty, 17, 30, 31, 33, 34, 46, 74
  abandons One Power Standard, 91, 187
  aircraft procurement and, 100–1, 102–3, 125
  attacks idea of Air Ministry, 34–5
  decentralises responsibilities for FAA, 123, 126
  denies ship command to aviators, 45
  discounts Japan as enemy, 91–2
  faces Japanese threat, 199
  links with RAF Coastal Area, 118
  loses chance of own NAS, 35–6
  Naval Staff Division, 122, 123
  opposed to help for Japanese naval flying, 63–4
  plans for post-Second World War fleet, 181–2
  post-First World War carrier "Flying Squadron," 60, 64
  post-1940 construction policy, 80–1
  quarrels with Air Ministry, 40–1
  recruitment schemes, inter-war, 48
  support for battleship, 121, 180–2, 188
  underrates American advances, 90–1
  view of RN role, 193
  wins campaign for control of FAA, 48–55, 125, 129, 130–1, 194
Afridi, HMS, 22, 23
Air Ministry and Air Staff, 33, 36, 46, 52, 87, 103, 119, 131, 198
  and the Air Division, 117, 119
  and indivisibility of air power, 31, 193, 194
  dealing with maritime targets, 140–1
  deep-sea bomb tests, 156, 188
  keen to help Japanese naval flying, 64
  lack of interest in naval aircraft, 100
  lend RN aircraft personnel, 55

object to transfer of FAA to Admiralty, 54
  on trade protection, 174
  opposed to FAA inter-war expansion, 93–5, 190–1
  prefer high-level ship bombing, 157
  refuse to train rating pilots, 48, 49
  scepticism about carriers, 68
  stress strategic bombing, 192–3
  views on air defence of Britain, 148
Air power and attack, 185
  effect on fleet dispositions, 183–4
  in amphibious operations, 168–9
  increase in lethality, 182–3
Aircraft carriers,
  Armoured, 81, 82, 83, 197
  armoured carriers and reduction in aircraft, 76
  arrester wires, 71–2
  as targets in battle, 141
  early seaplane carriers, 60–1
  economic restraints on, 189–90
  effect of Washington Naval Treaty, 65
  Escort, 81, 82, 83, 176
  first experiments with landplanes, 61–2
  for trade protection, 77–9, 82–3
  Light Fleet, 81, 82, 83
  naval doubts on, 68–9, 70–1
  questions of design, 67
  RN view of reconnaissance use, 137, 139
Ajax, HMS, 178
Alexander, A.V., 108, 136, 180, 181, 182
Anson, HMS, 181
Archer, HMS, 176
Ardent, HMS, 25
Argus, HMS, 38, 41, 57, 60, 62, 64, 65, 66, 68, 71, 75, 77, 79, 80, 162, 164
Ark Royal, HMS, 13, 21–5 passim, 27, 56, 57, 68, 75, 76, 132, 133, 149, 176, 177, 179, 183, 184
  Ark Royal class, 80, 81, 82